Approaches to Language

LANGUAGE & COMMUNICATION LIBRARY

Volume 4—*Series Editor:* Roy Harris, *University of Oxford*

Vol. 1. MORRIS—Saying and Meaning in Puerto Rico

Vol. 2. TAYLOR—Linguistic Theory and Structural Stylistics

Vol. 3. GAGNEPAIN—Du Vouloir Dire

A Related Pergamon Journal

LANGUAGE & COMMUNICATION*

An Interdisciplinary Journal

Editor: Roy Harris, *University of Oxford*

The primary aim of the journal is to fill the need for a publicational forum devoted to the discussion of topics and issues in communication which are of interdisciplinary significance. It will publish contributions from researchers in all fields relevant to the study of verbal and non-verbal communication.
Emphasis will be placed on the implications of current research for establishing common theoretical frameworks within which findings from different areas of study may be accommodated and interrelated.
By focusing attention on the many ways in which language is integrated with other forms of communicational activity and interactional behaviour it is intended to explore ways of developing a science of communication which is not restricted by existing disciplinary boundaries.

*Free specimen copy available on request.

NOTICE TO READERS

Dear Reader

An Invitation to Publish in and Recommend the Placing of a Standing Order to Volumes Published in this Valuable Series

If your library is not already a standing/continuation order customer to this series, may we recommend that you place a standing/continuation order to receive immediately upon publication all new volumes. Should you find that these volumes no longer serve your needs, your order can be cancelled at any time without notice.
The Editors and the Publisher will be glad to receive suggestions of outlines of suitable titles, reviews or symposia for editorial consideration: if found acceptable, rapid publication is guaranteed.

ROBERT MAXWELL
Publisher at Pergamon Press

Approaches to Language

Edited by

ROY HARRIS
University of Oxford

PERGAMON PRESS
OXFORD · NEW YORK · TORONTO · SYDNEY · PARIS · FRANKFURT

U.K.	Pergamon Press Ltd., Headington Hill Hall, Oxford OX3 0BW, England
U.S.A.	Pergamon Press Inc., Maxwell House, Fairview Park, Elmsford, New York 10523, U.S.A.
CANADA	Pergamon Press Canada Ltd., Suite 104, 150 Consumers Road, Willowdale, Ontario M2J 1P9, Canada
AUSTRALIA	Pergamon Press (Aust.) Pty. Ltd., P.O. Box 544, Potts Point, N.S.W. 2011, Australia
FRANCE	Pergamon Press SARL, 24 rue des Ecoles, 75240 Paris, Cedex 05, France
FEDERAL REPUBLIC OF GERMANY	Pergamon Press GmbH, Hammerweg 6, D-6242 Kronberg-Taunus, Federal Republic of Germany

Copyright © 1983 Pergamon Press Ltd.

All Rights Reserved. No part of this publication may be reproduced, stored in a retrieval system or transmitted in any form or by any means: electronic, electrostatic, magnetic tape, mechanical, photocopying, recording or otherwise, without permission in writing from the publishers.

First edition 1983

Library of Congress Cataloging in Publication Data
Main entry under title:
Approaches to language.
(Language and communication library; 4)
1. Language and languages—Addresses, essays, lectures.
I. Harris, Roy, 1931–   II. Series
P106.A64 1983   400   82-12390

British Library Cataloguing in Publication Data
Approaches to language.—(Language & communication library; v. 4)
1. Language and languages
I. Harris, Roy   II. Series
400   P121

ISBN 0-08-028910-X

Printed in Great Britain by A. Wheaton & Co. Ltd., Exeter

Editorial Foreword

The terminology of language studies nowadays suggests a disciplinary fragmentation of bewildering extent and complexity. Linguistics, psycholinguistics, sociolinguistics, biolinguistics, philosophy of language, anthropological linguistics, phonetics, language pathology and computational linguistics are all ready to stake an academic claim to some part—and sometimes overlapping parts—of what has become a very broad territory indeed. Its divisions and subdemarcations are carried to a point where it is possible to lose sight of the fact that all these forms of inquiry centre ultimately upon questions which arise out of man's use of words, and hence have some contribution to make to our understanding of an activity which is uniquely characteristic of *Homo sapiens*.

The papers collected in this volume are by no means representative of the whole gamut of the language sciences. But they do illustrate how that common focus of attention on man's use of words is still an important underlying link between a number of disciplines. The link is not explicitly discussed in the pages that follow but, more importantly, it is exhibited in the papers themselves.

The contributors to the volume were originally brought together by being invited to take part in a series of general lectures on linguistic topics to a multidisciplinary audience at Oxford. Two of the papers have previously been published in *Language & Communication*. The other six appear here in print for the first time.

ROY HARRIS.

Contents

1
Language and Speech   1
ROY HARRIS

2
Language and Linguistics   17
FRANCIS P. DINNEEN

3
The Social Context of Language Acquisition   31
JEROME S. BRUNER

4
Language and Cognition   61
D. ALAN ALLPORT

5
Language and Truth   95
MICHAEL DUMMETT

6
Language and Social Action   127
ROM HARRÉ

7
Social Anthropology, Language and Reality   143
EDWIN ARDENER

8
Language and Communicational Efficiency: the Case of Tok Pisin   157
PETER MÜHLHÄUSLER

Subject Index   179

Chapter 1

Language and Speech

ROY HARRIS

The distinction between language and speech, like much else in the Western view of man's linguistic activities, is derived from a conceptual framework which has its origins in Graeco-Roman antiquity. George Kennedy, in his well known study of the Greek rhetorical tradition,[1†] quotes a famous passage from Isocrates which will serve as a convenient starting-point for tracing its history.

> In most of our abilities we differ not at all from the animals: we are in fact behind many in swiftness and strength and other resources. But because there is born in us the power to persuade each other and to show ourselves whatever we wish, we not only have escaped from living as brutes, but also by coming together have founded cities and set up laws and invented arts, and speech has helped us attain practically all of the things we have devised. For it is speech that has made laws about justice and injustice and honour and disgrace, without which provisions we should not be able to live together. By speech we refute the wicked and praise the good. By speech we educate the ignorant and inform the wise. We regard the ability to speak properly as the best sign of intelligence, and truthful, legal and just speech is the reflection of a good and trustworthy soul. With speech we contest about disputes and investigate what is unknown. We use the same arguments in public councils as we use in persuading private individuals. We call orators those who are able to discourse before a crowd and sages those who discourse best among themselves. If I must sum up on this subject, we shall find that nothing done with intelligence is done without speech, but speech is the marshal of all actions and of thoughts and those most use it who have the greatest wisdom.[2]

This still stands as one of the classic statements of a view which has dominated ways of thinking about language for more than two thousand years in the Western tradition. There are two important features to note. One is the insistence that speech is a specifically human accomplishment, distinguishing *Homo sapiens* from other species. The other is the implicit equation of—or failure to distinguish between—speech, language and reason. Or at least, that is how it might seem to the naive twentieth-century reader of an English translation of Isocrates.

The fact is that in English translations, the word *speech* is often pressed into service to render the Greek term *logos*: and what the Greeks meant by

† Superscript numbers refer to Notes at end of chapter.

Approaches to Language

logos is something not explained in a few words without risking incoherence. Kennedy describes it as:

> an ambiguous and sometimes mystical concept which may refer concretely to a word, words, or an entire oration, or may be used abstractly to indicate the meaning behind a word or expression, or the power of thought and organization, or the rational principle of the universe, or the will of God. On the human level it involves man's thought and his function in society, and it further includes artistic creativity and the power of personality.[3]

With the benefit of historical hindsight it is very easy to look back and dismiss *logos* as a concept so woolly as to be worthless. But before doing that, it may be as well to remind oneself that a whole family of concepts which we nowadays distinguish when we are talking about human capacities are nonetheless related to one another in part by being ultimately descended from this ancestral concept of *logos*, and the family relationship still often makes itself felt in unexpected and perhaps confusing ways. This is true of the distinction between language and speech, which has come to be a very crucial distinction in modern linguistics. But certain aspects of it will remain somewhat puzzling unless we remember that both halves of the distinction are, historically speaking, related as different facets of *logos*.

It is a rather typical process in the development of intellectual inquiry to split up a subject of study into gradually more specialized divisions. The study of *logos* had already been split up into three main divisions in antiquity, and one of these has continued to bear the name etymologically associated with *logos* down to the present day: that is the branch of study we call "logic". The other two branches that became separated in antiquity were grammar and rhetoric. This tripartite division of *logos* studies is probably one of the most important things that ever happened in the intellectual history of Western civilization, but it needs to be mentioned here simply in order to provide one vital piece of background information which is essential to an appreciation of the language–speech distinction. We have all inherited an educational tradition which sees man essentially as a "logoid" animal, distinct from all other animals which are not logoid, as Isocrates says. But furthermore the logoid nature of the human being is seen as manifesting itself in three distinct ways.

One is the capacity of the human mind to think rationally. Another is the capacity to master a set of arbitrary verbal signs. The third is the capacity to interact verbally with others, to influence and be influenced by words.

The distinction between language and speech is a distinction which relates essentially to the second of these logoid capacities of the human being: the capacity to master a set of verbal signs.

Having identified which of man's logoid capacities we are dealing with, it serves no further purpose to delay conceding that to speak simply of "the distinction between language and speech" is quite misleading. For there are at least four different, yet similarly important, distinctions relating to this particular logoid capacity which are sometimes referred to in that way. It is worth while trying to keep them separate, by calling one of them the "physiological" distinction, one the "semiotic" distinction, one the "executive" distinction, and one the "sociological" distinction. There are significant links between these four distinctions. In order to appreciate what those links might be, it is first of all important not to confuse the distinctions themselves. Confusion is unfortunately rife, however, not only because the terms *language* and *speech* are unhelpfully used to draw sometimes one and sometimes another of these distinctions, but also because they are all too frequently used by theorists who have simply not thought out which of the distinctions they are trying to draw.

Of the four distinctions, it is the physiological one which is most easily separated from the other three. The techniques developed by modern experimental phonetics can now show us exactly what the vocal apparatus does when we speak. Films can be taken which capture in detail the movements of the vocal cords in the process of phonation. And it is worth reflecting that Isocrates, who speaks so eloquently on the subject of speech, never understood what speech was in the way that such a film reveals it. As a result of failure to understand the articulatory mechanisms of the human voice, phonetics remained at a very primitive stage in Greek and Roman times, and for a long time afterwards. Not until as late as the nineteenth century did European phonetics begin to make any serious progress beyond the crude classification of speech sounds which had served as the basis of traditional statements about pronunciation.

The action of the vocal cords, as revealed to us by the modern high-speed camera, plays only a limited part in speech. It is a role analogous to that of the vibration of the reed in an organ or other wind instrument. Far more important contributions to the resultant sound are the modifications undergone as the egressive air passes through the cavities on the way from the glottis to the outside world. But without the vocal cords to produce the right kind of vibration to start with, those modifications would be ineffective. We have to learn to tense our vocal cords in the right way to do this, and that is an important stage in the speech acquisition of very young children.

Biologically, man is a species adapted for speech rather than designed for speech. There is general agreement that his so-called "vocal apparatus" does not have the articulation of speech sounds as its primary function. Speaking is a secondary activity undertaken by organs which fulfil more essential purposes such as breathing, biting, licking, chewing, tasting and swallowing. But although speech is a secondary function of organs developed for other purposes, it is in no sense an automatic or an accidental function. This is clear from the fact that animals with a roughly comparable vocal apparatus to man's do not just "happen" to speak. Nor can they be taught. The long story of attempts to teach apes to talk, from Furness in the late nineteenth century

Laidler[4] in the 1970s, is a record of more or less complete failure. Speech articulation evidently involves highly complex programmes of muscular coordination, for which man has evolved specialized mechanisms which his evolutionary neighbours lack.

Acquiring this equipment must have taken a long time in evolutionary terms. According to one estimate by Darlington, development of the requisite structural adaptations of the larynx, palate, tongue, teeth and lips, together with the muscular controls and corresponding neural organization in the brain, must on any plausible reckoning have taken "much more than a thousand generations".[5]

Linguistic evolution, on the other hand, can proceed much more quickly. For example, although French did not exist in the year A.D. 400, by A.D. 1200 it was a flourishing language with a well developed literature of its own. It follows that the great diversity of the world's languages at the present day tells us very little about how long man has been a language-using animal. As Darlington puts it, "while the evolution of speech is ancient and slow the evolution of language is recent and rapid". This underlines the contrast between speech as a primarily biological phenomenon, and language as a primarily cultural phenomenon.

Thus, how long *Homo sapiens* has been able to perform the kind of activity that a film of the vocal cords reveals we do not know. According to some theorists, speech first became possible as a result of adopting the upright posture, perhaps 10 million years ago. This may have so changed the position of the upper part of the respiratory tract that it became possible for vocal cord vibration to be modified by altering the shape of the supraglottal cavities, so as to produce the range of speech sounds which we recognize as characteristic of the languages of the world. The main differences in the vocal apparatus between man and the chimpanzee are the length of the pharynx and the more posterior position of the tongue. It has been claimed that surviving skulls of both Australopithecus and Neanderthal man indicate a pharynx and a palate more like those of ape than man. However, the claim is disputed. In the view of many people, it is highly improbable that Neanderthal man, living only 50,000 years ago and equipped with a brain comparable to our own, could not speak.

It has been suggested, however, that a crucial evolutionary development separating man from the lower hominids was the development of the "bent two-tube" supralaryngeal tract from an earlier "single-tube" version; because this increased the possible number of vowels and in particular the maximal differentiation of the vowels [i], [u] and [a], approximately as in the English words *feed, food* and *fad*. According to this theory, the relative positions of these extreme vowels allow the hearer to assess the size of the speaker's vocal tract, and this information is essential for the extremely rapid decoding of oral signals which is characteristic of speech exchange. It may be that although Neanderthal man could have produced some human speech sounds, he would have been incapable of engaging in the very fluent and controlled vocal activity which is required for speaking any human language. On the other hand, it has also been claimed that fossil skulls of *Homo habilis* and *Homo erectus* show the early development in the hominid brain of an area corresponding to Broca's area in the brain of modern man, which co-ordinates the muscles of mouth, tongue and throat when we speak. If this is significant, it might indicate that creatures capable of speech have been living on earth for 2 million years or more. But, at present, these are matters about which one can do no more than speculate.

The questions briefly touched on above are very relevant to the "physiological" distinction between language and speech. Suppose, for medical reasons, it becomes necessary for someone to have a surgical operation which removes his larynx entirely. From that moment onwards, he becomes incapable of speech—in one sense of that term—for he no longer has the physical apparatus essential to produce what we call speech sounds. But his own physiological incapacity for speech does not *ipso facto* deprive him of language. Not only will he still be able to hear and understand what other people say, but he will also be able to express himself linguistically by means other than vocalization, for instance in writing, or by means of gestural sign systems such as the deaf use. In this sense, speech can be regarded merely as a means of implementing language, but not essential to it. Even without a larynx, *Homo sapiens* could still be a logoid animal. And *a fortiori* Neanderthal man could still have been a logoid animal, even if his speech repertory was so restricted that he could not have managed to pronounce any language spoken today.

What I am calling the "semiotic" distinction between language and speech involves a different aspect of implementation of this logoid capacity. It has nothing essential to do with vocalization, nor even with the use of words. Consider, for example, the visual image presented in a well known abstract painting—Joseph Albers's *Departing in Yellow* in the Tate Gallery. In this painting, four squares of different colours are arranged one inside another, with sides parallel. The four colours range from the bright canary yellow of the innermost square, through different shades of orange to the ochre of the outermost square. Compare this visual image with that presented by the standard "No Entry" sign on European roads, comprising a long thin white rectangle positioned horizontally along the diameter of a plain red circle. These two visual patterns are different in an important respect which has nothing to do with the constituent shapes and colours as such. One of them has a certain meaning for road-users, whereas the other has not. But the visual patterns in themselves do not determine that difference. It is determined by their having or not having a role to play in a certain set of signalling conventions.

Analogously, patterns of vocal sound are not intrinsically manifestations of man's logoid capacity, even when they are systematically organized to a high degree. What makes a pattern of vocal sound a word, or a sentence, or part of a word or sentence is its membership of a set of comparable patterns functioning as signs. Humming the first few bars of Beethoven's Fifth Symphony is a highly organized piece of vocal activity, but it has nothing to do with speaking English (or French, or German . . .) any more than Joseph Albers's painting has anything to do with the Highway Code.

When the words *language* and *speech* are contrasted with this semiotic distinction in mind, we often find that *speech* is used to designate the total activity, whilst *language* is reserved to designate the patterning within that activity which identifies it as an instance of verbal signalling. In other words, only certain parts or features of a speech act are relevant to its linguistic identity. The rest is speech, but not language.

The third distinction, which I am calling the "executive" distinction, has to do with the use of a given set of signs for purposes of communication. This is very often confused with the "physiological" distinction, but the two are logically and theoretically quite separate. The executive distinction contrasts the sending of a message with the message itself. We can distinguish this from the physiological distinction by bearing in mind that the message need not be conveyed in spoken form at all. For example, if Smith wants to let a colleague at the office know that he will be back at 4 o'clock, it does not matter whether that message eventually gets to the recipient in the form of a note on his desk, or by a secretary coming into the room and telling him. The message "Smith will be back at 4 o'clock" can be executed in either written or spoken form. Now when the term *speech* is equated with execution, it can cover both vocal and non-vocal activity. It is standardly used in this way in so-called "speech act theory", where a speech act does not necessarily involve speaking at all. For instance, the speech act of "agreement" with someone can be executed in appropriate circumstances simply by nodding the head.

Finally, the fourth distinction, which I am calling the "sociological" distinction, concerns the difference between an individual's verbal practices and the accepted verbal practices of the community to which he belongs. Insofar as John Brown's English is not quite the same as Bill Green's English, neither the Brown variety nor the Green variety can be held up to the exclusion of the other as solely and sufficiently representative of English. Linguistic theorists commonly seek to ignore this distinction by the fiction of pretending that communities are linguistically homogeneous. (They openly acknowledge this to be a fiction,[6] but often fail to ask themselves whether the fiction is really necessary, or even useful.) When the distinction is acknowledged, however, the term *language* is often applied to the collective institutionalization of verbal practices assigned to the community, while *speech* is reserved for what is said by individuals, regardless of whether it conforms to the hypothesized collective practice. This provides another basis on which not everything that occurs in speech (even if it occurs with some frequency) need be treated as having linguistic status. A dictionary, however comprehensive, does not necessarily aim to include every word ever used by any monoglot member of the linguistic community in question. It need hardly be added that when this distinction is interpreted pedagogically and prescriptively, the approved collective practice is often identified with the features characteristic of some elite subsection of the community. Departures from this in speech are castigated as "incorrect".

So we have in English, unfortunately, only two terms in common use, *language* and *speech*, to cover four importantly different distinctions which relate to one facet of the logoid activities of *Homo sapiens*. This would be bad enough as a source of potential confusion, but it is made worse by the fact that modern theorists have themselves often failed to recognize the importance of these distinctions, and consequently have introduced terminology of their own which cuts across them.

One example of this is the classic distinction drawn by pathologists between "speech disorders" and "language disorders". Of this distinction, Crystal writes that it "is still in widespread use, though with the development of recent work in linguistics its applicability is increasingly being questioned". He continues:

> The origins of the distinction lie in the difference between "symbolic" and "nonsymbolic" aspects of communication . . . Grammar and vocabulary were considered to be the main symbolic factors in communication; and when speech was the medium of communication involved, it was the phonetic characteristics of speech which were considered to be nonsymbolic.[7]

Hence under the heading of "speech disorders" were grouped any disturbances arising out of damage to the motor functions of the vocal organs, including disorders of voice production, fluency and articulation. Under the heading of "language disorders" were grouped any disturbances affecting the expression and comprehension of meanings.

It is obvious that the distinction criticized by Crystal results from the crude superimposition upon pathological symptoms of an *a priori* division between what are sometimes called the "first" and "second" articulations of language. The first articulation involves units such as words and morphemes, which are envisaged as capable of having a specific meaning of their own. The second articulation involves units such as phonemes, which have no specific meaning of their own. (For example, it makes sense to ask what the meaning of the prefix *im-* is in *impossible*: but it makes no sense to ask what the meaning of *m* is in the same word.) Manifestly, this is a categorization which conflates the physiological, semiotic and executive senses of the term *speech*, and simply opposes *language* to all of these indifferently.

8 Approaches to Language

Perhaps the worst of such confusions is the muddle engendered by the misleading terms *competence* and *performance*, which are envisaged by linguists of the generative school as distinguishing two quite different types of linguistic investigation. Sometimes generativists accuse other linguists of failing to understand, or of distorting, what their terms *competence* and *performance* mean. But the fact is that this terminological distinction has been a muddle right from the moment it was introduced. As others have pointed out, these terms are not used in a clear and consistent way even by generativists themselves.[8] But generativists were not the first theorists to get into a tangle over the language–speech distinctions. The attempt to contrast competence with performance is itself an imitation of the earlier attempt by European structuralists to contrast *langue* with *parole*. So generativists cannot even claim to have made an original mistake.

One of the paradoxes of modern synchronic linguistics is that its founder, Ferdinand de Saussure, began by ignoring precisely those distinctions which it is essential to recognize if there is to be any hope at all of establishing linguistics as a form of empirical science. The confusion has been compounded by his English translators, who seem to have been quite baffled by Saussure's three key terms: *langage, langue* and *parole*. This is all the more remarkable in that the intended role of these terms in Saussure's theory is very explicitly set out in his *Cours de linguistique générale*. Of the three, the key term is *langue*, and there are crucial passages in the *Cours* which explain how Saussure envisages *la langue*. It is informative to cite two of these passages leaving the key terms untranslated, so as to make clear how what Saussure is saying is open to distortion by translation.

The passages read as follows:

(i) But what is *la langue*? It is not to be confused, in our view, with *le langage*, of which it is only a particular, although essential, part. It is both a social product of the faculty of *langage* and a set of necessary conventions adopted by the community to facilitate the exercise of that faculty by individuals. Taken as a whole, *le langage* is many-sided and heterogeneous; astride the boundaries between physics, physiology and psychology, it belongs both to the individual and to the community: it cannot be put into any category of human facts, because it has no unity we can identify.

La langue, on the contrary, is a self-contained whole and a principle of classification. The moment we give it pride of place among the facts of *langage*, we introduce a natural order into a mass which lends itself to no other classification.[9]

(ii) If we could collect the total of verbal images stored in each and every individual, we should be able to put our finger on the social bond which constitutes *la langue*. It is a thesaurus deposited by the practice of *la parole* in speakers belonging to a given community, a grammatical system existing potentially in every brain, or more precisely in the brains of a group of individuals; for *la langue* is not complete in any one, but exists perfectly only in the mass.

By separating *la langue* from *la parole* one separates simultaneously: (a) what belongs to the community from what belongs to the individual, (b) what is essential from what is subsidiary and more or less accidental.

La langue is not a function of the speaker, but the product which the individual registers passively . . .

La parole is, by contrast, an act of the will and the intelligence of the individual. In it one must distinguish: (a) the combinations by which the speaker utilizes the code of *la langue* in order to express his own thoughts: (b) the psycho-physical mechanism which enables him to make those combinations externally manifest.[10]

Now one English translator of the *Cours* makes the last sentence of the first paragraph and the second paragraph of (i) read as follows:

> Taken as a whole, speech is many-sided and heterogeneous: straddling several areas simultaneously—physical, physiological, and psychological—it belongs both to the individual and to society; we cannot put it in any category of human facts, for we cannot discover its unity. Language, on the contrary, is a self-contained whole and a principle of classification. As soon as we give language first place among the facts of speech, we introduce a natural order into a mass that lends itself to no other classification.

This translation makes the English term *speech* the equivalent of *langage* and *language* the equivalent of *langue*. It is interesting to compare this with the view of another commentator on Saussure's terminology, who produces *speech* as the English term for *parole*, *language* as the English for *langue*, and then adds "*langage* has no exact equivalent in English". But this is simply not the case. There is a perfectly good English equivalent for *langage* in Saussure's sense: it is the word *language*.

Both the translators just quoted make the same fundamental mistake, which is to start from the assumption that *language* is the equivalent of Saussure's *langue*. Both fail to recognize that the distinction Saussure makes by opposing *langage* to *langue* is normally made in English simply by the inclusion or omission of the article. We speak of *language* (without the article) when we wish to refer either to the human faculty of language or to a certain characteristic type of patterning of activity carried on in all social groups. On the other hand, we speak of *the language* or *a language* when we wish to refer to any particular code employed by the members of a particular social group. Only by failing to respect this distinction can we force Saussure to say what English translators have made him say, namely: "Language is a self-contained whole and a principle of classification". Nothing could more flagrantly contradict the logic of Saussure's thought. Having been at pains to point out that language as such is too diverse to offer any inherent basis for classification, the very last conclusion that Saussure is likely to reach is that language actually constitutes a principle of classification. What does, in Saussure's view, qualify both as a self-contained whole and as a principle of classification is what in English we call *a language*, e.g. English, French, German, Greek.

Now what is disastrous about the Saussurean *langue–parole* distinction, even when properly understood, is that it conflates precisely the four important distinctions—physiological, semiotic, executive and sociological—which are to be drawn as regards speech and language. (Needless to say, when Saussure is mistranslated, the results breed even greater confusion.) As Jean Gagnepain observes,[11] Saussure both founded modern linguistics and at the same time doomed it in advance, by confusing linguistic systems with their social institutionalization.

Although much of this may sound like terminological hair-splitting, the theoretical ramifications are very considerable, as may be appreciated if we turn to consider another type of evidence about speech which has been made available by modern experimental phonetics.

The kind of picture reproduced in Fig. 1.1 is known as a "sound spectrogram". It is made by a machine which takes as input the acoustic disturbance caused when a human being says something, analyses the vibrations present at various frequencies, or bands of frequencies, and represents the results in terms of varying degrees of black-versus-white intensity on a piece of paper. The vertical dimension corresponds to the wave bands, from 0 at the bottom to about 30,000 cycles per second at the top, which is just about the maximum frequency range of the human voice. The horizontal dimension of the paper, reading from left to right, corresponds to sequence in time. The greater the density of the black the higher the concentration of energy at that particular point in the spectrum. We are looking, in effect, at a sample of visible speech, which comes out as a pattern of energy with relative intensity varying through time.

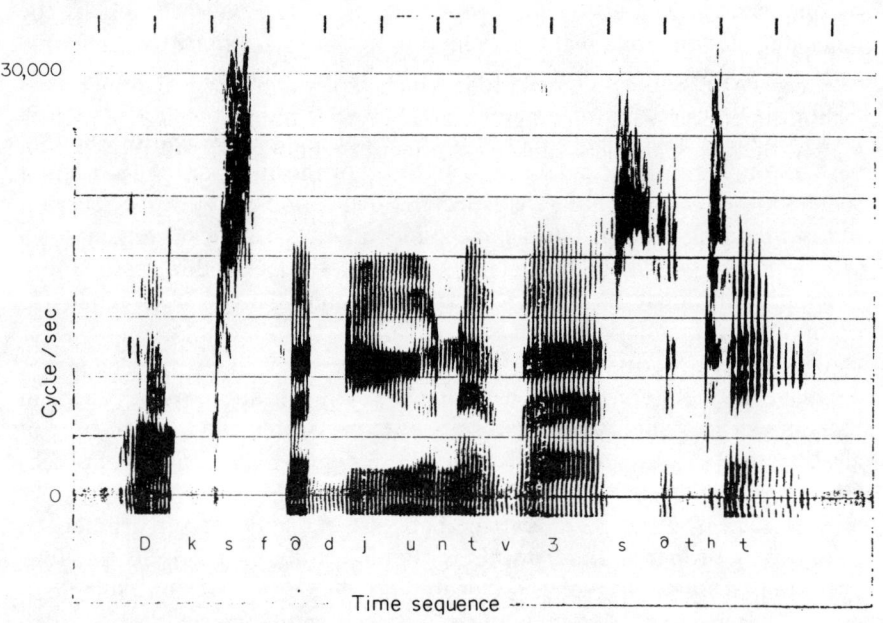

FIG. 1.1. A sound spectrogram of the words "Oxford University".

It is often possible, just by looking at a sound spectrogram, to tell what it says, provided one has worked long enough in a phonetics laboratory to become familiar with the characteristic black-and-white patterns that are produced by the various vowels and consonants. The sound spectrogram in Fig. 1.1 says "Oxford University". So it would be possible, or at least we can imagine it would be possible in a technologically advanced society, to dispense with writing altogether and use sound spectrograms instead, if we wanted for some reason to preserve a visual record of what someone said. Instead of leaving a note on Mr. Smith's desk, the secretary could leave a spectrogram, and Mr. Smith could pick it up and read it and discover that he had an appointment with Mr. Jones tomorrow morning. That particular technological development is very unlikely to take place, because we do not need it. We are already at the stage where we can transmit the vocal message itself by means of a tape recorder. But had the history of technology been different in certain respects, we might have passed through a stage in which it would have been useful for everybody to learn to read spectrograms.

I put the matter in this way because I want to draw attention to a fundamental similarity and a fundamental difference between spectrograms and writing (which are both, in a way, forms of "visible speech"). The similarity is that both involve a technique which makes it possible to translate systematically what you can hear into what you can see. The difference is that the spectrogram involves a technique which is entirely dependent on the natural laws of the universe, including those governing human physiology; whereas writing involves a technique which depends at a crucial point on the establishment of voluntary agreement between human beings. In other words, there is a physical cause-and-effect link between the utterance and sound spectrograms. But between the utterance and the sequence of written symbols O-X-F-O-R-D U-N-I-V-E-R-S-I-T-Y there is no such link. That link requires something else; and it is that something else which has a first claim on our use of the term *language*.

There are two points to emphasize in this connection. The first is that if you use the term *language* in the way I am suggesting (and one may be enough of a nominalist not to want to say that that is the sole correct use, but enough of a pedagogue to put it forward as a recommended use), then you should realize that this amounts to adopting an analysis of the linguistic process which is in certain respects quite the opposite of Saussure's, and indeed quite different from that assumed in the mainstream of modern linguistic orthodoxy. For Saussure, the voluntary act is the act of *parole*: that is the province of the individual. Whereas the use here recommended makes the intervention of voluntary decision the criterion of language. It is a use which allows voluntary intervention on both sides of the line between what belongs to the individual and what belongs to the community.

The second point is that adopting this criterion has very significant consequences. For example, it follows that language is forever beyond the reach of computers. For however ingeniously computers may be programmed to process linguistic input and simulate linguistic responses, what computers can never do is come to a voluntary agreement about how to signal. Whereas there is no contradiction in attributing linguistic competence, in the generativist's sense of that term, to a machine. On the contrary, generativists often refer to a grammar as a device or programme which generates certain sequences of symbols: and in that sense it is perfectly plain not only that a machine can master a grammar, but that in certain respects it is likely to master it rather better than a human being.

The criterion I am advocating also has a bearing on a number of other controversial issues related to the language–speech distinction. First, it has a relevance to the controversy concerning the status of phonetics as an academic study. Some linguists, as is well known, take the view that while phonology is a part of linguistics, phonetics is not. One book which surveys the whole modern development of the subject begins with the blunt although cautious assertion: "Phonology is a branch of linguistics: phonetics is often considered not to be."[12] To this one might add that the view that phonetics does not belong to linguistics is often, understandably, the view of theorists who conflate what I earlier called the "physiological" with the "executive" distinction. I say "understandably", because anyone who is guilty of that confusion automatically lumps together under the heading of *speech* the processes of phonation together with their product, the utterance. And since the utterance as such is not part of any language, but only the result of using a language, it is assumed that the study of the phonatory and auditory processes on which the production and reception of the utterance depend lie outside linguistics too.

Why that is nonsense can be clearly illustrated by a simple experiment with a tape recorder. Suppose we take a passage of speech which has been recorded at a tape speed of 2.4 cm per second. We start playing it back at the machine setting of 2.4 cm per second. But then we move the switch up to the next highest setting. Simply increasing the tape speed reduces intelligible speech to incomprehensible gabble. Now there is a quite simple relationship between the acoustic signals in the two cases. Furthermore, phonologically it is the same signal; in the sense that the phonemic distinctions registered do not alter, regardless of which of the two speeds you play the tape at. So anyone who really believes that phonetics is not part of linguistics ought to believe that to the linguist it makes no difference at all which speed the tape is played at, but only to the phonetician. Now any linguist who wants to put himself in that position is welcome to: but it is a pretty silly position to be in. For it overlooks one crucial range of factors which distinguish incomprehensible squawking from comprehensible speech. And the reason why some linguists are in that position is that their theory of language fails to acknowledge the difference between speech as phonation and speech as execution.

On the view I am advocating, phonetics is indeed an integral part of the study of human logoid capacities and activities (which is perhaps how one might most satisfactorily define linguistics), since the articulatory processes are under the voluntary control of the speaker and are manipulated by him to achieve specific acoustic effects. The division between phonetics and phonology is in certain respects an artificial and unrealistic division, based primarily upon the importance attached by some linguists to their own theoretical constructs, and in particular to that elusive and sacrosanct unit the "phoneme". How twentieth-century linguists managed to persuade themselves that they were analysing the spoken word by imposing the structure of the written word upon it is an intriguing topic, but one which cannot be pursued here.[13]

A word must be said, however, about why it is that linguistic theorists commonly appear to take it for granted that little need be said about writing as far as they are concerned. Why is it that they regard the primary concern of linguistics as being to correlate meanings with pronunciations? The answer to this lies in the doctrine of the "primacy of speech", which has come to be one of the sacred cows of modern linguistics. For this Saussure is again in part responsible. Acknowledging the "primacy of speech" was essentially a reaction against an older view, which regarded speech as an inferior form of communication to writing. But the time has come for a reappraisal of this doctrine.

It is clear that those who uphold the primacy of speech regard writing as a form of communication that is in some sense parasitic upon speech. Writing comes to be treated merely as a "transfer" of speech into a different medium. Indeed, some theorists go further and claim, as Sapir once put it, that:

> all voluntary communication of ideas . . . is either a transfer, direct or indirect, from the symbolism of language as spoken and heard or, at the least, involves the intermediacy of truly linguistic symbolism.

Sapir continues:

> Auditory imagery and the correlated motor imagery leading to articulation are, by whatever devious ways we follow the process, the historic fountain-head of all speech and of all thinking.[14]

If we try to spell out Sapir's fountain-head metaphor in somewhat more specific terms, a variety of possibilities come to mind. Writing might perhaps be regarded as secondary to speech as an historical phenomenon, in the sense that in all literate civilizations writing appears to have been preceded by communication based solely upon speech. Or writing might be regarded as secondary to speech in the quite different sense that teaching a child to write is normally a process presupposing that the child can already speak, and merely needs to master a set of graphic symbols which will correlate with the speech distinctions he has already mastered. Or again, writing might be regarded as secondary to speech in that without the support of speech, what is accomplished by writing alone would be manifestly inadequate to serve the wide range of communicational functions society recognizes and needs. Or, in yet a different sense, writing might be regarded as secondary inasmuch as writing seems to have originated as a means of recording speech, and not speech as a means of making the written word audible.

Now speech may indeed claim priority over writing in all of these respects. But that is something of a red herring when it comes to analysing the relationship between speech and writing in societies where both forms of communication coexist. Insistence on the primacy of speech is liable only to distort our understanding of the working relationship. It is in fact simply a mistake to treat writing merely as an adventitious substitute for, or extension of, speech. Historical linguistics shows us quite incontrovertibly that even within the same community a spoken system and a written system, once established, can develop independently of each other. The distinctions made in the two systems do not necessarily keep in step. Distinctions lost in speech may be kept in writing, and vice versa.

From the moment a society becomes literate, a division of labour tends to establish itself between the spoken and the written word. This division is based upon (a) the relative permanence of writing as opposed to speech (at least in the era before the development of sound recording), and (b) the relatively slower process involved in the physiological activity of writing, and its dependence on the availability of suitable materials. Furthermore, it would be an even graver mistake to suppose that speech is psychologically the same activity in a literate and a pre-literate community. Speakers who are also writers cannot escape that fact. For them, most speech is in principle capable of being put into writing, just as most written texts can in principle be read aloud. At the same time, a literate community is usually well aware that the customary expressions and distinctions of speech are by no means mirrored exactly by the customary expressions and distinctions of writing. These simple facts inevitably have a profound effect upon one's view of speech. (For exactly parallel reasons, it would be idle to pretend that the advent of the motor car made no difference to horse transport. Transportation itself becomes a different enterprise, both for society and for the individual, once there is a choice between two possible ways of making most journeys.)

In short, the view of man's logoid capacities which has been handed down in the Western tradition is unmistakably the view of a literate society. The role of writing has made an important contribution to each of the four distinctions discussed above. The contrast between oral and written messages sharpens people's awareness of the physiological distinction. At the same time, it throws the semiotic distinction into bolder relief by enabling people to compare spoken and written formulations of a given message. Thirdly, it emphasizes the executive distinction by bringing home the realization that the mechanisms of execution are not the same in the two cases. Finally, it affects the sociological distinction by tending to promote written language as ideally representative of the communal standard.

To put the point epigrammatically, in human history it was the invention of writing that made speech speech and language language. For any literate society, there can be no going back to that primal innocence in which *logos* has a single manifestation, and rationality, language and speech are one. By the same token, there can be no future for a falsely naive linguistics which tries to pretend that somehow or other that fall from pre-literate grace had never occurred.

Notes

1. G. KENNEDY (1963), *The Art of Persuasion in Greece*, Princeton.
2. G. KENNEDY, *op. cit.*, pp. 8–9.
3. *Ibid.*, p. 8.
4. K. LAIDLER (1980), *The Talking Ape*, London.
5. C.D. DARLINGTON (1968) *The Evolution of Man and Society*, New York, vol. 1, p. 26.
6. See, for example, the section on "The fiction of homogeneity", in J. LYONS (1981), *Language and Linguistics*, Cambridge.
7. D. CRYSTAL (1980), *Introduction to Language Pathology*, London, p. 124.
8. G. LAKOFF (1973), "Fuzzy grammar and the performance–competence terminology game", *Papers from the Ninth Regional Meeting, Chicago Linguistic Society*, pp. 271–291.
9. F. DE SAUSSURE (1922) *Cours de linguistique générale* (2nd edn), Paris, p. 25.
10. F. DE SAUSSURE, *op. cit.*, pp. 30–31.
11. J. GAGNEPAIN (1981), "On language and communication", *Language & Communication*, Vol. 1, No. 2/3, pp. 149–154.
12. A.H. SOMMERSTEIN (1977), *Modern Phonology*, London, p. 1.
13. Cf. R. HARRIS (1980), *The Language-Makers*, London, pp. 9–11.
14. E. SAPIR (1921), *Language*, New York, p. 21.

Chapter 2
Language and Linguistics

FRANCIS P. DINNEEN

Language has been studied since Antiquity for a variety of purposes and with different methods. The approaches found in linguistics are comparatively recent, but it is interesting to see that perspectives from older studies can still shed some light on current problems.

Over 120 years ago, in 1861, Max Müller was lecturing at Oxford on the new study of language. Because it was so new, there was no unanimity about what to call it. If the term had not been appropriated by another discipline, Müller would have preferred *mythology*, the "study of the word". The term *comparative philology* was already common in England. The French term *linguistique*, and an English neologism, *logology*, had also been proposed, but Müller suspected others would find both of these barbarous (Müller, 1899).

More interesting than this dispute about names was Müller's conception of the field. He remarked that all sciences pass through three stages, the "empirical", the "classificatory" and the "theoretical" or "metaphysical".[1†] The first stage is that of common experience; the second, of discovery and classification of hierarchic ordering in the data; and the third, an attempt to explain the causes and purposes of that order. For Müller, sciences are either physical or historical: physical sciences deal with the works of God, historical with man's works. He takes it for granted that the science of language is a physical science, concerned with language as an object; while historical philology studies language as a means to master a culture. And since the study of language is to be a physical science, it should use the methods of botany, geology or anatomy.

Today, Müller's rejected term *logology* is associated with the work of Kenneth Burke (1961). The other barbarism, *linguistics*—especially "structural linguistics"—is importantly linked to the work of Ferdinand de Saussure, who was 4 years old when Müller was giving his 1861 lectures. It was de Saussure (1922) who presented a persuasive image of how human

† Superscript numbers refer to Notes at end of chapter.

language could be studied: as a system of signs which is a self-defining structure through a small set of dependency relations. Despite later qualifications, most linguists would still agree with de Saussure's two main insights about language: (a) that linguistic signs have two main aspects, phonic and semantic; and (b) that a sign's function is importantly conditioned through contrast with other signs that might have been chosen instead of it and further determined by the signs that actually precede and follow it in an utterance.

One consequence of de Saussure's work was the development of more formal methods for describing language and a lessening of dependence on semantic intuition. We also learned from him that it is often as important to know what a form is *not* as what it *is*, since distributional relations are so important. English *you* and German *Du* might sometimes be said to have identical reference, but they do not have the same number of opposing forms. Both languages have a respect system, but English pronouns are not involved in it in the same way that the choice of *Du, Ihr* or *Sie* is in German.

In recent years, the most interesting work on language has derived from, or has been in opposition to, the insights found in the work of Noam Chomsky. Before his 1957 *Syntactic Structures* linguistics concerned itself with information within the sentence. By his suggestion that we could consider all sentences of a language as being transformationally derived from a limited number of kernel sentences (simple, declarative, in the present tense) Chomsky showed how the question, command and passive forms of the same sentence could be related in principled ways through transformations. Linguistics now dealt with intersentential, not just intrasentential, relationships (Chomsky, 1957).

Work in current transformational analysis has advanced and has been modified considerably since *Syntactic Structures*, and what transformations apply to is considerably more abstract than the structure of kernel sentences. Like Müller, Chomsky requires of linguistics not only description (Müller's classificatory stage) but explanation (Müller's theoretical or metaphysical level).[2] It has also been proposed that "explanation" will require a search for linguistic universals, both substantive (e.g. consonants and vowels) and formal (e.g. the need for transformations).

Müller's dated formulation of the goal and subject matter of Linguistics would be faulted today, but his insights are not useless. Similarly, even older discussions which might seem arcane because of the technical terminology might illuminate some current problems in linguistics. What I have in mind is the work of the *Modistae*, speculative grammarians who flourished in the 13th and 14th centuries (Bursill-Hall, 1971, 1972) and certain areas of "Case Grammar" (Fillmore, 1968; Cook, 1979).

The Modistae were given that name from a common title of their works, *De Modis Significandi*. The English "On the modes of signification" is just as ambiguous as the Latin, since it could mean "on the ways of signifying" or "on the ways of being signified," and so they were forced to distinguish active and passive modes.

John Carroll's book on Benjamin Lee Whorf (1956) was entitled *Language, Thought and Reality*. The Modistae had a similar concern for the modes of "being" (ontology, the way things are), the modes of "understanding" (epistemology, the way we know things) and the modes of "signification" (grammar). Contemporary acceptance of Aristotelian notions provided them with a good part of their descriptive vocabulary, so that they could speak of the modes of understanding and signifying as active and passive, but of the modes of being as substantial or accidental.

They also had fundamental categories such as substance and accident, substantial and accidental forms. Forms determine matter, either substantially (giving it its basic identity) or accidentally (properties which can be gained or lost without loss of identity, such as a dog's colour, height, weight, etc.). They also used the terminology of act and potency, which distinguishes things as actually realized (act) or as capable of realization (potency). The notion of potency as a metaphysical reality was Aristotle's resolution of the ancient dispute about whether the "really real" was only some kind of changeless, other-worldly platonic form, or only the concrete, always changing things of our ordinary experience. While potency as a metaphysical reality does not recommend itself to all, we mostly share the common sense notion in a serious way when considering what horse to bet on, or whether our penal system is likely to reform the criminal.

The Modistae took it to be their task to clarify ambiguities in language, to reconcile differences between the way things actually are and the way we are required to think about them and speak of them. In Latin, *scopae* is plural, while it signifies only a single *broom*. *Pulchritudo* means "beauty" and everyone accepted that this is an accidental property. But the word is a noun, and therefore signifies in the nominal or substantial mode.

The structure of Latin obviously inspired this kind of modistic speculation, since identical lexical meanings, contained in roots like *am-*, allow the same thing to be communicated in different ways or modes: the nominal *amor* (love), the verbal *amo* (I love), the infinitive *amare* (to love), the adjectival *amatus* (loved, masculine), the gerundive *amandus* (to be loved), the adverbial *amabiliter* (lovingly) and many other forms.[3] The Modistae could say of such forms that they were "substantially" identical but "accidentally" different, just as they said that the passive modes of signifying and understanding were materially identical and only formally different.

This expression may sound obscure, but behind it lies the same point of view that distinguishes levels in linguistic analysis. In English, the sound [m], for instance, can be considered "the same thing" being studied from different points of view: phonetically, it is a voiced bilabial nasal; phonologically, it is one of three contrasting nasals which differs from the velar in *sing* and the alveolar in *no*; since it can be meaningful, it qualifies as a morpheme, with no notable allomorphs, and when pronounced with a falling intonation, it qualifies as a one-word sentence meaning something like "Yes" or "I'm listening."

The Modistae provided an elaborate study of the Latin language, classifying each part of speech through its essential mode of signification and then subcategorized them through subaltern and special modes. They held, for instance, that both the noun and pronoun signified in the substantial mode, but that a word like *soldier* signified a substance determinately, while a pronoun like *he* did so indeterminately.

The Modistae were grammarians who developed the theory, but it was the theologians who applied it. Since their subject was a study of the divine, it was inevitable that language developed for ordinary considerations would do less than justice to it.

Among their concepts of God was that of infinite, changeless simplicity, so that a simple statement like *Deus creavit mundum*, "God created the world," posed problems. The expression *Deus* is suggesting, by the affix *-us* and the root *De-*, that it is complex, not simple, and also that it need not be unique. The perfect tense of *creavit* brings in the linguistically necessary concept of time which, in their view, begins with creation, but is not involved in the "act" of creation.

To deal with such considerations, the theologians used the vocabulary of the Modistae and then invoked two methods to correct possible misunderstandings, the way of negation or removal, and the way of eminent predication. The *via negationis vel remotionis* simply points out what is contained in the mode of signification (e.g. complexity, limitation in time) and denies or removes these meanings when referring to God. Eminent predication was based on the idea that all human perfections are limited participations in the infinite perfection of God as the ontological source of all good, so that human goodness, mercy and justice are weak reflections of the eminent, divine goodness, mercy and justice. Such terms, when applied to men, were considered analogical, or systematically ambiguous. Similarly, we have to systematically change the norms for predicating something like, for example, the "goodness" of a man, a book, a liar or a tool.

One of the interesting aspects of the work of the Modistae is the example they give of how we can be aware of a lack of fit between the modes of signification, understanding and being. This is counter evidence to the suggestion of Whorf that our conceptual world is determined by the structure of our language. That there is an intimate interdependence is, of course, not to be denied, and even the Modistae held that "the modes of signification follow the modes of understanding", an axiom susceptible of several interpretations.

One interpretation is that we cannot communicate more than we know. We are often understood to have said more than we intended, of course, and clever teachers exploit this. Another interpretation stresses that human information comes from the human experience, and our acquisition of knowledge is partial, analogical, imperfect and discursive, while God's knowledge does not suffer from these imperfections. Another conclusion was that there was a real interdependence between our ability to observe, our skill in conceptualizing and our ingenuity in selecting the proper modes of signification. It is sometimes possible to communicate clearly *despite* the imperfections of language.

Any analysis of language seeks to replace complexity with insightful simplicity. De Saussure studied *la langue*, an idealized form or structure which all uses of language share. In doing so, he deliberately abstracted from the actual use of language by an individual (*la parole*) because he wanted a more general, social perspective. He also considered it legitimate to ignore the well-known fact that language changes, because he thought it changed slowly enough for this not to be relevant to *la langue*, a deliberate construct of the linguist. In a similar way, Chomsky prefers to study linguistic competence, not the concrete performance of a speaker.

Much of the information we receive from language is not overtly expressed, since language is essentially a system of contrasts, and we understand an utterance, not merely because of what is said, but also because of what is not said, what is presupposed, and what the utterance contrasts with. So language can abbreviate: when we know the name of a friend, that name can summon up all we know about him, what he looks like, what he does, what he thinks. If we forget the name, we can tell other friends the kind of person we are concerned with and they can supply the name.

Similarly, the lexical decomposition of verbs shows us that there are a limited number of verb types. The disputed analysis of "kill" into "cause/become/not/alive" (McCawley, 1976) suggests that we can derive action–process verbs (transitive ones) from a state: here, the state verb would be "alive," and "kill" can be seen to be derived from it by an inchoative derivational unit, which makes it a process (become alive) and a causative derivational unit which makes it an action–process; "cause/become/alive"—"enliven". Depending on the scope of the negative, different meanings result, for which we may or may not have lexical realizations: "not/cause/become/alive" is different from "cause/not/become/alive" and "cause/become/not/alive".

Other surface verbs seem simple, too, until we take this point of view. "Import", for instance, involves buying something in one place and shipping it, or having it shipped to another. It also involves people who benefit from the transaction both at the source and goal of the shipment.

Perhaps it is useful to insert here another reading of the Modistic maxim,

22 Approaches to Language

"the modes of signification follow the modes of understanding". It suggests that the words we use do not mean *all* the properties of the thing mentioned, but only those which (a) our language institutionalizes, (b) those we know, or (c) a selection from among those we know in the forefront of attention. De Saussure illustrates this in the example where a Frenchman asks an English speaker about the names of animals, and then asks at dinner for some *pig* and *cow*. The English speaker "knew" the difference between *pig* and *pork*, *cow* and *beef*, but the distinction was not in the forefront of his awareness when he answered the original questions.

The case grammar approach employed by Wallace Chafe (1970) in his *Meaning and the Structure of Language* can be seen to be somewhat similar to the work of the Modistae, since, it is held that all verbs are intrinsically state, process, action or action–process, and that other forms are derived from the intrinsic base form, as in the analysis of "kill", where we have an example of the "same thing" being signified in various modes.

Case grammar, as developed by Fillmore (1968), Chafe (1970) and others, is summarized in Cook (1979), who provides a useful bibliography of authors. There is no established orthodoxy in case grammar, and no agreement about how many case roles there are. But there is basic agreement that the deep structure of the model is a semantic representation of the propositional content of a clause and independent of modal case roles, such as tense, aspect, declarative, etc.[4] Propositional case roles are considered candidates for universality, and therefore to be found in all languages. Some proposed "propositional" roles are "agent", "experiencer", "benefactive", "locative", and "object". *Agent* (A) is generally the human or animate cause; *experiencer* (E), the one who undergoes some psychological or internal physical change or attitude; *benefactive* (B), the role of one gaining or losing possession; *locative* (L), states or changes of position. *Objective* (O) is a case role required by all verbs and semantically the most neutral. Its role can be seen from Table 2.1.

TABLE 2.1. *Matrix display to show the role of* Object *(O) (Cook, 1979)*

Verb types	Basic verbs	Experiencer	Benefactive	Locative
1. State	Os	E,Os	B,Os	Os,L
	be true	know	have	be at
2. Process	O	E,O	B,O	O,L
	die	amuse	acquire	move
3. Action	A,O	A,E,O	A,B,O	A,O,L
	kill	say	give	bring

Here, "action" and "action–process" are coalesced into action verbs which do or do not have a readily deletable object, as in *Harriet sang* (a song) and *Michael dried the wood*. Fillmore (1968) suggested that *subject* and *object* were surface, not deep, structure roles, so that they could not be defined by deep structure dominance relations in trees. "Subject", until Fillmore's work, had been defined as the noun phrase (NP) immediately dominated by the sentence, and "object" as the noun phrase immediately dominated by the verb phrase (VP), as in the example "John saw Bill".

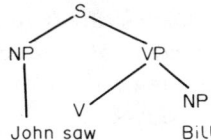

A subject selection hierarchy is illustrated in "The janitor opened the door with a key". In this sentence, the case roles are "agent":janitor, "object":door, and "instrument":key. When agent is expressed, it is the subject, as in this example. If it is not expressed, then instrument becomes the surface subject, as in "The key opened the door", and if neither agent nor instrument are expressed, then object is the surface subject, as in "The door opened".[5]

Case roles are distinguished as obligatory and optional. Object is always obligatory, and other propositional roles may be obligatory, depending on the intrinsic semantic character of the verb. In a sentence involving a process, for instance, like "He died", *he* is the object; in "John killed him", *John* is the agent and *him* is the object. In "John liked him", *John* is the experiencer, *him* is the object. In "It's here", *it* is the object. The same surface verb can function in more than one way, so that *dry* could be state, process or action, as in "The wood is dry" (state), "The wood dried" (process) or "Michael dried the wood" (action). Similarly, one could read "He acquired a fortune" as either a process or an action, depending on whether *he* merely inherited the fortune, or went out and worked for it.

The benefactive role is ambiguously named, since in "John robbed Paul" or "John gave Paul a thousand dollars" *Paul* is equally designated as benefactive. Verbs which are seen to be intrinsically locative are found in examples like "He's at home" (state), "Snow is falling" (process) and "He moved to Florida" (action).

The last example, "He moved to Florida", exemplifies a covert case role, i.e. present obligatorily in the deep or semantic structure, but absent in the surface. This sentence also exemplifies a *coreferential* agent and object, since the sentence is equivalent to "He caused himself to move . . ." vs. "The tree moves". Another reason for postulating covert roles stems from the coalescence in Cook's matrix of the action vs. action–process distinction that Chafe maintains. "Mother is cooking" could be seen as an example of Chafe's action, or as action–process with a covert object, as in "Mother is cooking (the dinner)".

Approaches to Language

Some roles are covert because they are *lexicalized* in the verb. English has numerous examples of this in verbs like *knife, whip, elbow, kiss, slap, kick*, etc., where the "instrument" has been lexicalized: "He *knifed* the intruder, *elbowed* past him into the next room and *slapped* his companion", since a knife, the elbow and open hand are intrinsic instruments in the semantic structure of these verbs. Locatives are lexicalized in expressions like "He tinned the fruit", "You jailed the Mayor" and "The Mayor pocketed the bribe", since each can be paraphrased with overt locatives, in "He put the fruit into tins", "You put the Mayor in jail" and "The Mayor put the bribe in his pocket".

With these distinctions, some of the sentences which were seen to be semantically related, but not easily explained by transformations, in *Aspects of the Theory of Syntax* (Chomsky, 1965), are dealt with in a straightforward manner such as in:

(i) John strikes me as pompous—I regard John as pompous
    O   E   O   E   O   O

(ii) I liked the play—The play pleased me
    E   O   O   E

(iii) John struck Bill—Bill received a blow at the hands of John
     A   O   O   O   A

But not in

(iv) John bought the book from Bill—Bill sold the book to John
     A   O   B   A   O   B

From a "modistic" point of view, this is interesting, since in (iv) one could conceive that we have to do with exactly the same objective situation (in the modes of being) just as we have in "The bottle is half full" and "The bottle is half empty". In each first half-sentence we conceive of first John, then Bill, taking the initiative, which makes them agents; in the second half-sentence, the identical state of affairs is understood and signified from different polar perspectives.

It is not clear that all problematic cases in case grammar are illuminated from a modistic perspective, but the viewpoint can sharpen our inquiries. If it is true that "the modes of signification follow the modes of understanding", then there is less of an anomaly in the buy–sell examples, or those involving teach–learn:

Harry taught me mathematics—I learned mathematics from Harry
 A   E   O   E   O   A

Harry taught me mathematics, but I learned it in spite of that fact
 A   E   O   A*E   O

where "I learned" means "I caused myself to learn".

A*E means agent coreferential with experiencer.

The maxim can be viewed as another way of saying that language is arbitrary, since the modes of signification are not dictated directly by the modes of being, but by the intervening modes of understanding. Semantics, in this view, is more intensional than extensional.

But there are some areas where it is not easy to decide whether we are appealing to states of affairs (the modes of being) or the way we conceptualize them (the modes of understanding). For instance, case grammar would analyse an expression like "The music was too loud" as involving an experiencer, since the subjective expression involves hearing. Even the objective statement like "The music approached 140 decibels", requires a covert experiencer (the observer of the dials) in actual states of affairs. It is questionable, however, that native speakers would feel that the second sentence does involve the experiencer semantically. Compare expressions like the following:

(i) The bus stopped.
(ii) John stopped the bus.
(iii) The bus screeched to a stop.

(i) need not involve a covert agent, if it is the case that the bus rolled down a hill, unattended, then lost momentum and stopped. Usually when we say things like "The bus stops at the corner" we presuppose a covert agent, the driver, who stops it. In (ii) the agent is overt, and in (iii) we would seem to appeal to a covert experiencer, since the unpleasant sound requires such an observer. Appeal to covert case roles appears to be a reverse of the ways of denial or removal the theologians used: in their situation, language *did* have a surface meaning which they wanted to discount; in our situation, there is no surface manifestation of what we want included. There are similar phenomena in expressions such as the following:

—The baby thumped onto the floor.
—The bullets were whistling past my ear.
—The train chugged to a halt.
—The racer screamed off down the track.

Such expressions approach onomatopoeia and pose a problem not dealt with, so far as I know, in case grammar. Should they be simply set aside as the marginal phenomenon onomatopoeia is? Or should they be handled as surface manifestations of pairs of sentences, like "The baby fell to the floor". "I heard the thump of the fall."?

Benefactive can also give problems, in verbs like *import* or *export*, since both involve an agent (the importer/exporter), an object (the goods) and location (the source and the goal). The accepted practice in case grammar allows only object case to occur more than once in a case frame. A case frame is the conventional lexical entry for a verb. For instance *sell* would be +[__A,O,B], which is to be read "the verb sell requires (+) as obligatory case roles, an agent, a benefactive and an object". But if the analysis of *import* and *export* is accurate, it would seem that the case frame for them should be at least something like +[__A*B,O,L] which only expresses that an agent, coreferential with benefactive, sends goods from a place: it does not show that there is in both verbs, a pair of places and a pair of benefactives. This latter account, of course, has more directly to do with states of affairs: it is a question for native speakers to decide whether the verbs *import* and *export* have been institutionalized on a parallel with *buy* and *sell*, and that their semantic structure is to be decided by this (social) mode of understanding, rather than the modes of being. Any verb involving human activity is susceptible of a "realistic" analysis as complex as all the sciences of medicine. What "really" happens when you obey the command, "Pick that up!" from initial neuron discharges to the final liftoff must be as complex as preparation for a space flight at Cape Canaveral, but we have institutionalized that complexity into the simplicity of the verbal form +[__A,O,L].

That an experiencer is involved in verbs like *think, talk, tell, hear, envy* and so on is clear enough, and part of the clarity may be the coincidence of our conceptualization and the way sciences tell us such process actually take place. But there are some dubious verbs, where the decision about including (or requiring) an experiencer is not so evident. Consider the following:

(1) She was lounging in the chair.
(2) The pier jutted out ten feet into the bay.
(3) He lunged at me viciously.
(4) They were going to mass troops at our border.
(5) Rich Little mimics the politicos marvellously.
(6) He asked her if she would pose for him.
(7) She was pouting for hours.
(8) I asked them to awaken me at nine.
(9) He reacted badly to the news.
(10) He vowed he would reform completely.

In (1) to (4), the verbs include an element of experiential judgement about a physical activity: the same phenomena might be judged more neutrally by other observers, as (1) sitting (2) was out (3) came toward (4) post. To describe an activity as "mimicking" requires an experiential opinion; the difference between "standing there" and "posing" is in the eye of the beholder, as is the interpretation of (7), where "pout" can either be literal protrusion of lips, or the interpretation of silence as sulking. In (8), (9) and (10) one interpretation involves a restoration to consciousness (experience) an internal experience at bad news as opposed to jumping back or the like, and an internal revision of one's experience as opposed to some visible adjustment.

Another dubious set involves the convention that only three cases are allowed per frame. If one accepts the difference between "It moved" and "John moved" as the difference between a simple process for *it*—hence only object role involvement, as opposed to a coreferential agent and object in the deliberate act of *John*—then we have to solve the difference between the inadvertent *hear* or *see* vs. the deliberate *look at* and *listen* by positing *hear* or *see* as +[__E,O,], but *look at* or *listen* would be +[__A*O*E,O] with coreferential agent, object and experiencer with respect to the object, the thing attended to.

The criteria one uses to distinguish between the verbs in sentences like "The crowd roared its approval" and "She slammed the door on leaving" also show marginal decisions: it is conceivable that one could conclude that the frame +[A,O,E]*E covert is appropriate when watching a silent film, even though there was nothing to be heard, although this would be the basis for requiring a covert experiencer. Is the proper case frame for the verb in "he itched" +[__E*O] (experiencer and object coreferential) or +[__E,O] (where experiencer and object are not coreferential)? Do we appeal to "language" (modes of signification) or "medicine" (modes of being, understanding) to decide?

The case grammar approach brings to light lexical and semantic gaps in our language. We speak naturally enough about "wintering" or "summering" in the Bahamas, but we don't "spring" or "autumn" anywhere.

There is a large number of verbs which might be called "reciprocals" or "concomitants" which also appear to call for more than the normal three-case frame. In a sentence like "He divided his wealth equally among the children" we require agent (he), object (wealth) and benefactive (children), but should the children be named, e.g. John, Mary, in which case should we have more than one benefactive? Or is benefactive indifferently singular or plural? Other examples of this type could be

—They bandied words all night.
—They married in June.
—They swapped Old School ties.
—They conversed all night.
—They discussed the project.
—They negotiated a new treaty.
—They haggled over the price for an hour.
—They coexisted peacefully for many years.
—They collaborated successfully on many plays.
—They cohabited for some time.

Other examples of such "reciprocal" verbs would include: cohere, conspire, connive, collude, counterattack, retaliate, communicate, commute, interchange, accompany, companion, concoct, concur, confer, congregate, conjoin, coordinate, correspond, cosign, costar, exchange.

It would appear that there are several types of verb which can be considered as abbreviations for more than a single proposition. There are many ways of checking our semantic intuitions about such verbs.

One way is by paraphrase. If it is accepted that the difference between

"She moved" and "The stone moved" is that "She" is a coreferential agent and object, while "stone" is only object, then the proliferation of covert roles involving verbs like "import" and "export" might be easier to accept.

Another way, for the abbreviatory type, could be to examine whether it makes sense to affirm one of the assumed members and deny the other. If the sentence "The car screeched to a halt" abbreviates "The car stopped" or "In stopping, the car made a screeching sound" it would seem strange to affirm one and deny the other, if the original had been accepted.

Raising involves similar considerations, it would seem. The sentence "Mary warmed the milk" can be displayed as:

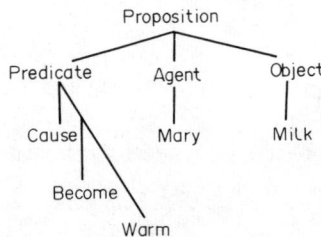

and the predicate "warm" is raised to be the main one, but understood to contain, semantically, the causative and processive predicates as well. In many languages, these would be overt; in English they are not.

The distinctions made by the Modistae might appear too mentalistic to many today, or to rely on a particular kind of psychology. Most linguists prefer to rely on more formal clues than semantic intuition. For instance, one might or might not know that the verb "bathe" is etymologically related to "bask", but comparing sentences like

—I bathed in the sun.
—I basked in the sun.
—I bathed the child in warm water.
—I basked the child in warm water.

anyone would appreciate that there is a covert reflexive contained in "bask", and, indeed, the *-sk* is an old Scandinavian reflexive.[6] No ordinary speaker of English needs to know the etymology. He has "semantic intuition" about his language and can distinguish modes of being, modes of signification and modes of understanding.

Notes

1. These are the same three stages Aristotle discusses throughout his *Rhetoric* as empeiría, techné: and episte:mé: ἐμπειρία, τεχνή, ἐπιστημή.
2. *Aspects of the Theory of Syntax*, 30–38 by Chomsky, and *passim*.
3. It is curious that there does not seem to have been any "modistic" discussion among the Arabs. The triliteral root system of semitic languages makes it easy to distinguish lexical and

grammatical aspects of the language, while the fusion of roots and affixes in Latin delayed confident morphological analysis of Latin for a considerable time past the medieval period.
4. A "case grammar" representation of a sentence such as "You have been buying horses for the Army" might look something like this:

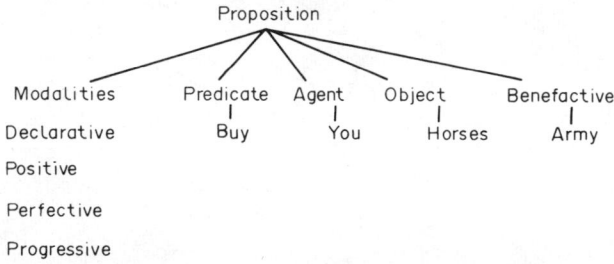

Positive

Perfective

Progressive

As in the modistic tradition, it is assumed that "the same" proposition can be manifested in many modes, so that "You have been buying horses for the Army", "Buy horses for the Army!", "Have you been buying horses for the Army?", "You have not been buying horses for the Army", "You've been buying horses for the Army!?" are substantially the same yet accidentally different.
5. The force of these examples depends on the assumption that the same situation, the same "modes of existence", are being reported. Being "open" is a *state*; the change of state from "open" to "closed" is a *process*, and case grammar legitimately ignores the question of whether change can take place without a cause, without an agent: Language is indifferent to the question. But when any event is seen to imply (responsible) activity by humans, or necessary intervention by natural forces (lightning, the wind, etc.), an overt or covert agent or instrument is looked for.
6. Cf. John Geipel (1971), *The Viking Legacy: The Scandanavian Influence on the English Language*, David and Charles, Newton Abbot, p. 182.

References

BURKE, K. (1961), *The Rhetoric of Religion: Studies in Logology*, University of California Press, Berkeley and Los Angeles.
BURSILL-HALL, G. (1971), "Speculative grammars of the middle ages, the doctrine of the *partes orationis*" in *Approaches to Semiotics* 11, Mouton, The Hague.
BURSILL-HALL, G. (1972), *Grammatica Speculativa* (an edition with translation and commentary), Longmans, London.
CHAFE, W. (1970), *Meaning and the Structure of Language*, University of Chicago Press, Chicago.
CHOMSKY, N. (1957), *Syntactic Structures*, Mouton, The Hague.
CHOMSKY, N. (1965), *Aspects of the Theory of Syntax*, MIT Press, Cambridge, p. 162.
COOK, W.S.J. (1979), *Case Grammar: Development of the Matrix Model*, Georgetown University Press, Washington, D.C.
DE SAUSSURE, F. (1922), *Cours de Linguistique Générale* (2nd edn), Paris. English translation: Baskin, W. (1959), *Course in General Linguistics*, Philosophical Library, New York.
FILLMORE, C. (1968), "The case for case", in Bach, Emmon and Harms (Eds), *Univerals in Linguistic Theory*, Holt, Rinehart and Winston, New York.
McCAWLEY, J.D. (Ed.) (1976), "Notes from the linguistic underground", *Syntax and Semantics*, Vol. VII, Academic Press, New York.
MÜLLER, M. (1899), *The Science of Language* (founded on lectures delivered to the Royal Institute in 1861 and 1863), Longmans, Green and Co., London.

Chapter 3

The Social Context of Language Acquisition[†]

JEROME BRUNER

The acquisition of language, in addition to being a psychological matter, is also a thorn in the side of linguistics, a testing ground for theories in the philosophy of mind, and a major enterprise in that part of anthropology and sociology that concerns itself with how a culture gets passed on. Entering a linguistic community, moreover, is also a question of entering fully into the life of a species, the species *Homo*, and raises many questions about the nature of Man's ecological niche in nature, a niche governed to an astonishing degree by man-made rules. To become fully a member of the species, an aspirant human being must not only learn about language as a system of well-formed, rule-bound utterances about the world, but how to get things done with words in the language in the world. In that sense, the study of language acquisition is a branch of behavioral zoology just as surely as is the adaptive signalling of great crested grebes or herring gulls.

We may distinguish three great problem spaces in language acquisition: the syntactic, the semantic, and the pragmatic. I take the first to be the problem of how we acquire our facility in managing well-formed utterances governed roughly by a grammar. The second is less easily described: let us say that semantics concerns the nature of the relation between words and possible worlds as we know such worlds. And the third has to do with the manner in which we come finally to use well-formed utterances about possible worlds to affect others. I will take the view—not a very popular one—that the last will be first and the first will be last, but more importantly, that the acquisition of language-in-use depends in a massive way upon the interdependence of well-formedness, meaning and reference, and conventions of use. I do not think that they are derivable each from the other, but rather that each serves as a scaffold for aiding in mastery of the others. And since the child masters some general aspects of communicative use before he makes much progress in either the semantic or syntactic domain, I shall try

[†] Reprinted from *Language & Communication*, Vol. 1, pp. 155–178, 1981.

to outline why I think that pragmatics provides the most general support system for mastery of the more formal aspects of language.

I shall limit myself principally to two of the great functions fulfilled through language by native speakers, even at a tender age: indicating and requesting. I shall particularly want to trace their ascent from a prelinguistic beginning to a level of linguistic proficiency where, so to speak, speakers are at the take-off point that will lead them into ordinary or conventional language use.

A Preliminary Matter

Until quite recent times—say the latter 1950s—the process of language acquisition was treated as a subspecies of learning and "explained" by general theories of learning. Most such learning theories operated with principles and with experimental paradigms that had little to do directly with the phenomena of language. The materials to be learned rarely had any internal systematicity. The learning encounters with materials to be learned were solo, between learner and task; there was no "tutor" or "model" present. Moreover, one chose one's learning tasks in such a way as to ensure that the learner had no predispositions about, or knowledge of, what was to be learned. It was assumed that language learning was much like, say, nonsense syllable learning, aided by imitation, the learner imitating the performance of the model and then being reinforced for correct performance. It was not a very serious effort at explanation. It could not be, for most usually it failed to consider the nature of the generative system that made possible the uttering of sentences never heard, failed to specify how the imitating organism figured out what to imitate and for what function, etc. It is not surprising that this approach to language acquisition grew little from its first enunciation by St. Augustine to its last in Skinner's *Verbal Behaviour* (1957).

It was to Noam Chomsky's enormous credit that he boldly proclaimed that the old scarecrow had no clothes on. It was not so much that he proposed a full *theory* of language acquisition to replace the tired old one, but that he set forth an extraordinarily counter-intuitive hypothesis that, though "wrong" in detail, had the effect of freeing psychologists and linguists from the old dogma. His proposal was that the acquisition of the structure of language depended upon a recognition device—he called it the "Language Acquisition Device" (LAD)—that was in effect programmed to accept the surface structure of any natural language as input and to recognize its deep structure by virtue of the kinship of all natural languages to a universal linguistic deep structure that humans knew innately. The output of the device LAD was, in effect, the grammatical rules of the language by which the aspirant speaker was enabled to generate well-formed utterances and none that were ill-formed. The universal grammatical categories were in the inherent structure of mind much as figure-ground formation was inherent to the processes of perception. No knowledge of the world was necessary, and no privileged communication. Syntax was independent of knowledge of the word and of meaning and of communicative function. Or more correctly, the acquisition of syntax could be conceived of as progressing with the assistance of whatever minimum world knowledge proved necessary. The only constraint on the system, what held it back, was limitation on performance: the child's limited attention and memory span, etc. The competence was there from the start, ready to express itself when performance constraints were extended by the requisite skills.

Now it is fashionable to say that the Chomskian view of LAD is dead or disproved. Certainly in its most radical form, that is surely so. But suppose we consider the possibility that performance skills are something more than the requisite attention and memory limits, that they involve a certain conceptual knowledge of the world and a certain capacity to appreciate the way language can be used. Once those requisites are present, does the child then recognize linguistic well-formedness by virtue of innate properties of mind? For certain forms of syntax to be recognized innately does not require that recognition happens on bare exposure to an input of language. It may have to be an augmented input. After all, we do not for a moment doubt that sexual behavior has a large innate component, though we know from the pioneering work of Frank Beach that a long exposure, or experience, is necessary in order for the environment to trigger the innate sexual response. In effect then, radical Chomsky (which was mostly a hyperbole of hungry psycholinguists) is undoubtedly wrong. LAD may require priming in order to operate. And it may in fact get the priming it needs, as we shall see. In any case, Chomsky succeeded in getting people to look afresh at language acquisition, and to look at it as the acquisition of *real* language rather than in the form of nonsense syllables or pigeon peckings. Never mind that his undoing was in formulating too simple a theory. This may all be an old story, but it may not be a finished one yet.

It was natural that the first step toward revision should be in the direction of noting that children, indeed, had a working knowledge of the world before they acquired language and that such knowledge of the world might and did assist them in mastering the language that in some fashion "corresponded" to their conceptual knowledge. There were many efforts to develop a generative semantics out of which grammatical hypotheses could be derived. It is difficult to put this correctly. A knowledge of the world, organized in terms of a system of concepts, might give one hints as to where distinctions could be expected to occur in the language, might even alert one to the distinctions. But the *linguistic* distinctions and their mode of being realized (whether morphologically or syntactically, for example) have to be acquired as well. The issue of whether rules of *grammar* can somehow be inferred or generalized from the structure of our knowledge of the world is a very dark one. There is a strong form of the claim that insists that syntax can be derived from semantic knowledge in some way.

Perhaps the best strong claim comes from case grammar, and surely it is an interesting claim, at least psychologically. Formally, or linguistically, it is based on the reasonable assumption that there is some sort of cognitive primacy to the concept of action and to what are called the arguments of action: who performed the action, on what, toward whom, where, by what instrument, and so on. In Fillmore's phrase, "meanings are relativized to scenes" and this involves an "assignment of perspective" (1977). Particular words used impose a perspective on the scene and sentence decisions are perspective decisions. If, for example, the agent of action is forefronted in perspective, the nominal which represents it must be the "deep subject" of the sentence. This is all very fine for adult speakers of the language, where in Fillmore's words "semantics" is the study of cognitive scenes that are created or activated by utterances (Fillmore, 1977). But how does the child get to the point of being able to put together verbal strings in a way to create utterances that assign appropriate perspectives to scenes? The evidence is interesting but in that special way in which, as in Japanese prints, landscapes are interesting by virtue of being enshrouded in mist. Brown (1973) points out, for example, that at the two-word stage and immediately after, more than three-quarters of the child's utterances are accounted for by little more than a half dozen semantic relations that are, at base, case or case-like relations. Do these relations generate the language? Case notions of this kind, Fillmore (1968) tells us, "comprise a set of universal, presumably innate, concepts which identify certain types of judgments human beings are capable of making about the events that are going on around them . . . who did it, who it happened to, and what got changed". The basic structures are these action categories, and different languages go about realizing them in different ways: by function words, by inflexional morphemes as in the case endings of Latin and by syntactic devices like passivization, and so on. These grammatical forms are the surface structures of language that depend for their acquisition on an understanding of deep semantic, indeed protosemantic, concepts about action.

Greenfield and Smith (1976) attempt to show, for example, that the earliest one-word utterances, richly interpreted as combining with context, can be accounted for as realizations of case-like concepts at the level of utterances—whatever else is required for the child to venture into the making of utterances at all. And more recently, Nelson (in press) has renewed her argument that the child approaches the task of acquiring language already equipped with concepts related to action.

The "functional core model" (FCM) essentially proposed that the child came to language with a store of familiar concepts of people and objects that were organized around the child's experience with these things. Because the child's experience was active, the dynamic aspects would be the most potent part of what the child came to know about the things experienced. It could be expected that the child would organize knowledge around what he could do with things and what they could do. In other words, knowledge of the world would be functionally organized from the child's point of view.

To this earlier view she has now added a temporal dimension—the child's mastery of "scripts for event structures", a sequential structure of "causally and temporally linked acts with the actors and objects specified in the most general way". These scripts provide the child with a set of syntagmatic formats that permit him to organize his concepts sequentially in a sentence-like form. The capacity to do this is not seen by Nelson as a developmental achievement beyond the earlier functional core set forth in her earlier paper. Rather, it is a basic form of representation that the child uses from the start and gradually elaborates. In effect, it is what guides the formation of utterances beyond the one-word stage.

I shall need to come back to these issues later, particularly in dealing with the child's acquisition of prelinguistic and linguistic means for making requests; for requests are in the deepest sense dependent upon the child's understanding of action and how to enlist another in carrying out one's own actions. But before doing so, let me turn to the third approach to language acquisition, the pragmatic. This takes us directly into the issue of the social context of language. For up to now, the child has either been portrayed as simply a consumer of linguistic input (as in the syntactic model) or as a rather lone problem solver sorting out the world around him in terms of his actions upon it and generalizing that knowledge to language.

The interest in pragmatics began not so much in linguistics or psychology as in the philosophy of language. And as one often dates the resurgence of work in syntax by the publication of Chomsky's *Syntactic Structures* in 1957, one can date the pragmatic awakening with the publication of Austin's *How To Do Things With Words* in 1962. His argument is by now so well known as to need little recounting. Utterances, he insisted, cannot be understood in terms of their propositional content. They also have a performative function based on convention. The utterance "Would you be so kind as to pass the salt?" is not designed to prove the limits of the listener's compassion, but rather is a conventionalized request for the condiment named that also takes into account certain conditions imposed on discourse—e.g. that the voluntarism of the addressee be recognized in the framing of a request. Mastering a language, then, involves not only knowing how to string together propositions, but also how to meet the conditions on the appropriate making of utterances. An utterance can be thought of as containing not only a propositional form, its locution, but also an illocutionary force whose uptake by an interlocutor guides his assignment of interpretation to the locution. Is he requesting, indicating, promising, what? The relation between the form of the locution and its force remains obscure. The accomplished speaker can use many alternative forms to achieve the same force (e.g. "I wonder where the salt is"). Philosophically, it may be well and good to draw a sharp distinction, as Grice (1968) did, between two types of meanings—timeless meaning, or the intrinsic meaning of the locution, and utterer's meaning, which includes a specification of speaker's intent. But is there any psychological reality to the timeless meaning of an utterance? Can one *ever* assign a meaning to an utterance in natural language without regard to its context of utterance?

While all this seems at first to be far from the cockpit of debate about how language is acquired, it soon raises two questions crucial to acquisition. The first is about communicative intention. Is *it* what must get decoded in speaking and understanding a language? The second has to do with the question of shared presuppositions. For on this view, using a language depends not only upon a shared grammar and a shared lexicon that makes it possible for speaker and hearer to map each other's utterance into world context if they are to extract meaningful propositions from talk. It also depends, and powerfully so, upon shared notions about intentions of and conditions on utterance. Speech acts (as the combined locutionary form and illocutionary force are now called) are described by Searle (1969) as having at least three conditions: a preparatory condition (laying appropriate ground for the utterance), an essential condition (meeting the logical conditions for performing a speech act, as for example being uninformed as a condition for asking for information related to a matter), sincerity conditions (meeting the psychological requirement that, for example, you really want the information you are asking for, and can do so while also regulating appropriately the affiliative bond between speaker and hearer, as in our first example of recognizing the voluntary status of the requestee).

Curiously enough, the learning of speech acts seems, somehow, less mysterious than the learning either of syntax or semantics. And easier. Syntactic rule-following is rarely followed by corrective feedback. And even semantic mastery often seems strikingly unassisted. Speech acts, on the contrary, work or don't work and are often corrected. What is striking about them, too, is that, as Dore (1974) first taught us, they are present in some recognizable form even before lexico-grammatical speech develops. The child learns how to realize his intentions communicatively by conventionalized gestural or vocal means before ever he learns to do so by the use of locutions. In this sense, primitive speech act patterns may be established in the child's repertory as a kind of matrix into which syntactic and semantic achievements can be set. Indeed, Jill de Villiers (in preparation) has recently proposed a few reasonable hypotheses about how the child might make the transition into lexico-grammatical realization of his speech acts that are singularly unmysterious.

Now what is very apparent in examining any early corpus of discourse (not just speech, but discourse in which the mother is included) is that the child does quite well in making his intentions clear, and that the mother (as we shall see) is very much more preoccupied with teaching the child how, when, and where to make appropriate utterances than she is with issues of syntax or meaning. In contrast, it is very rare to find any early instances of syntactic correction and there is even some suspicion (as Nelson has noted, 1973) that semantic corrections may lead to the suppression of the lexical items that produced the difficulty. It suffices to note only that there is a large investment of time and energy during acquisition in helping the child learn how to say it in a fashion appropriate to the discourse, even if syntax is ragged and semantics hazy.

This brings us directly to the heart of the problem relating to a pragmatic route into language. What is the role of the "tutor" in language acquisition? The pragmatician's greater stress on shared convention and presupposition and "intersubjectivity" requires a far more active role for the adult in the child's language acquisition than just being a "model". The pragmatic route requires that the adult be a partner. You need a partner to learn how to converse. This raises an extremely interesting set of questions. Can conversation help the child learn to master the lexicon, grammatical rules, semantic relations, and the like? If so, how?

There is an intriguing dilemma here. The research of the last several years—a great deal of it summarized in Snow and Ferguson's *Talking to Children* (1977)—does indeed indicate that parents play a far more active role in language acquisition than simply modelling the language and providing input for LAD. The best way of characterizing their role is by the current phrase: it is "fine-tuned" to the level of the children with whom the adults are interacting. Semantically, syntactically, lexically, intonationally, in terms of sentence length and complexity, parents get down to the level on which their children are operating and move ahead with them at a rate that shows remarkable sensitivity to their child's progress. In the current jargon, parents are very skillful in using the BT (Baby Talk) register and the level of their speech matches strikingly well the level of their children's speech. The dilemma, as Brown (1977) puts it, is how do you teach children how to talk by talking baby talk with them at a level which they already understand? And the answer has got to be that the important thing is to keep communicating with them for by so doing one allows them to learn how to extend the speech that they have into new contexts, how to meet the conditions on speech acts, how to maintain topics across turns, how indeed to regulate turn-taking and adjacency pairing, and so on. And above all, they are learning (to borrow the title of Ducrot's intriguing book) *Dire et ne pas dire*, what's worth talking about, when and how. They are learning what Nelson calls scripts, but they are not just scripts about the world, but about interaction with others in that world through communication. They are learning how to frame their speech in context, how to create detachable modules of speech procedures and thereby, as Shatz (1978) so strikingly demonstrates, to use their cognitive processing capacity more economically so that they can attend to wider ranges of the world and of the language.

But that still leaves us with a rather vague picture of how *using* language in interaction leads the child to learn how language is put together. Is there anything that is constitutive about the skills learned in interaction with respect to the formal structure of the language itself? Or is it simply a matter of their learning about discourse rules, about handling presupposition, about conditions on speaking, and the like? We shall have to take that up again in the more specific setting of children learning how to handle the formalisms of indicating and requesting.

To conclude this preliminary discussion of the three routes into language acquisition, a comment about how they may be related to each other. The weakest claim has to be that language itself, i.e. its formal structure, is not learned in isolation from the child's learning of concepts about the physical and social world or from his learning about how to communicate. At the very least, his conceptual and communicative achievements clue him about the kinds of linguistic distinctions to look for. The claim is that a conceptual or communicative distinction predisposes the child to notice a corresponding distinction in the lexical, intonational, or grammatical domain when he needs it to communicate. If this is the weakest claim, then the strongest is that world knowledge and/or knowledge of the requirements for dealing with communicative interaction are constitutive elements in language itself in the sense that a grasp of the nature and the arguments of action provide the core understanding of grammatical case categories. The extension of the knowledge of action and its arguments requires only that one figure out the forms required for the realization of these ideas in the language—but that is a quite big "only". For the systematicity of our conceptual representation of the world is *not* in the same coin as that governing the grammatical structure that will eventually have to be mapped on to one's conceptual structure.

I do not think that our knowledge of language acquisition is such that we can be clear about the constitutive issue. I think there is very little question that the weaker form of the relation has been demonstrated to hold many times. The most recent instance I have encountered is the acquisition of the perfective postposition *-bo* in Brazilian Portuguese by infants scarcely into the one-word stage. De Lemos (1979) and Campos (1979) report that children, intending to signal that a task is complete, use *-bo* in isolation in an utterance or add it to a babble string months before there is any evidence of mastery of the inflexion morphemes by which tense and aspect are marked in Portuguese. Is it constitutive in the sense of indicating a beginning grasp of such systematic post-postional marking or is it only an illustration of a Slobin-like sensitivity to starting and closing phoneme clusters that accompany certain regularities in the child's world? We cannot say for sure. What is abundantly clear, however, is that we should keep an eye out for all possibilities.

Intentions and Formats

Before we look more specifically at indicating and requesting, there are two matters that must occupy us briefly in order to avoid misunderstanding later on. One of them has to do with what can be meant by intentions and particularly "the intent to communicate". The other has to do with the nature of contexts in early language.

With respect to the first of these, communicative intentions, consider the so-called Gricean cycle. Grice (1968) takes it as a hallmark of mature language that there is an intention on the part of the speaker to communicate with the hearer by conventional or non-natural means which he in turn presupposes the hearer will take in just that sense. For Grice, it is the first step into the Cooperative Principle that underlies language and which, in its elaborated form, is governed loosely by such maxims as "be relevant", "tell the truth", "be concise", and so on—all of these to be violated only for fulfillment of some other intention.

Plainly, the infant at the outset cannot be said to be participating in a Gricean cycle. He cannot have that much self-consciousness about his intentions or be sensitive enough to the perspective of another. Nor can he perform the subtle speech acts, like promising, that John Searle has so subtly decomposed. Nor can he, early on, use so many locutionary (or even gestural) forms to accomplish a single illocutionary intent. I would think that the child would have first to achieve a degree of reflectiveness about his communicative acts before his entry into the Gricean cycle could be proclaimed. We shall most certainly want to examine this matter carefully. But besides, the child will have to learn a good deal about the possible vicissitudes of action carried out jointly with another if he is to meet the conditions on making his intentions clear by conventional communicative means. For the illocutionary element in a speech act and the meeting of conditions on it really involves predictions about troubles in effecting uptake by your hearer—and that means knowing something about possible scenarios or scripts. Why else do we prepare our hearer, exhibit the logic of our act, keep our relations well buttered-up?

What we shall find is that, from very early on, the mother constantly assigns intentional interpretations to the child's utterances, at first based on her reading of the context, and then gradually on her appreciation of the child's mastery of illocutionary procedures. One can either take the view that the child is naturally if incompletely intentional in his signalling (in some junior version of the Gricean cycle) or that the mother eventually teaches him to act as if he had intentions until he finally has them—which sounds absurd psychologically. I can live with the notion that the young child has goals in mind that he can foresee, that he has alternative means for achieving them, including some communicative ones, that he is able to persist and to correct his procedures and otherwise behave in a manner consistent with rigorous definitions of intentionality (e.g. Anscombe, 1957). I am one with Harré (1973) and Peters (1958) in the belief that a human being, even a very young one, is best treated "as a person that is a plan-making, self-monitoring agent, aware of goals, and deliberately considering the best way of achieving them" (p. 148). Käsermann and Foppa (1981) have shown the degree to which even 18-month-old infants repair their utterances when they are greeted with signs of incomprehension (hardly ever simply repeating them), and my own work with 6-month-old infants sucking blurred pictures into focus and desisting when sucking drives clear ones into blur tells me that the apprentice language learner probably has the requisite means–end sensitivity to cope with communicative intentions.

With respect to contexts in early communication, I think that the communicative life of the young child is circumscribed by a highly limited set of them. Another way of saying it is that young children don't do many different things. Or in Nelson's terms, the young learner of languages has a rather small library of scripts. I shall later call this limited set of basic scripts *formats*, and they are of crucial importance in the child's mastery of the arguments of action and of the "functional core" that he builds up. They provide steady frameworks in which he learns effectively and by dint of interpretable feedback how to make his communicative intentions plain. And just as strikingly, these reliable and rather monotonous formats provide the mother as well with a basis for interpreting the child's communicative acts. These formats are, so to speak, the microculture of mother and child. They often have a game-like or playful quality along with a rule structure that develops within them. Mothers say the same things over and over with only a few variations. Even linguist mothers, listening to tapes of their interactions with their own children, are struck by this.

A format is a constrained and segregated transaction between child and adult with a goal, a mode of initiation, and a means–end structure that undergoes elaboration. A format provides a familiar locus and a familiar routine in which communicative intentions can be conventionalized and interpreted. As it becomes increasingly familiar and conventionalized it comes to serve as matrix for organizing presuppositions about what is given and what is new. Above all, a format is what frames communication and locates it in a particular segment of reality where the child can cope well enough to steer his hearer. We shall meet several of them in detail in the second half of the chapter.

The existence of formatting adds to Brown's dilemma. He asked how can children learn a language when what they hear from adults is language they already understand? I want to add this dilemma to it: children talk almost exclusively about highly familiar matters that they already know about. How can they learn language when they are talking about matters that they already know about and know how to talk about?

One last point about types of intention-dominated formats. Although I know that speech act classifications have not proven very fruitful, I would like to speculate that there are probably four basic, innate communicative intentions that govern a great deal of the child's communication during the early acquisition of language. The first is to achieve and regulate joint attention with another. The management of joint attention is probably as ubiquitous and dominant a form of human species-specific behavior as any that exists. It begins with the irrestible tendency for mother and child to make eye-to-eye contact, but that soon passes into other equally irrestible elaborations. I believe it to be the impelling force behind early indicating forms of communication.

A second communicative intent is seeking help from others in carrying out one's own goal-directed acts. For the young child, caretaking adults are the chief instrument for carrying out acts beyond one's own means–end capability. Aid-seeking communicative conventions very quickly get established once the child learns to modulate natural crying, and request formats are early in evidence.

A third intentional system is affiliative. This can be best illustrated by citing the work of investigators like Stern (1977), Brazelton, Koslowski and Main (1974), and others. Stern shows the degree to which mother–infant pairs very rapidly fall into a pattern of reciprocal turn-taking under conditions of modern activation. Each becomes active as the other becomes receptive—in terms of vocalization, gesture, and expression. Under conditions of high activation, infant and mother respond simultaneously, mutually reinforcing each other's "high". Turn-taking and joint arousal represent a kind of protoformat that will become socialized as a kind of carrier wave in communication.

The fourth general communicative intent is forced on me by my own observation of children. It is the tendency in young children not only to pretend and to simulate, but to draw others into their pretense and simulation with evident delight. Miller comments in *Spontaneous Apprentices* (1977) that most of the conversations recorded in the group of nursery school children he studied were in playful situations that were more make-believe than real. And of course it starts much earlier. Ratner and Bruner have reported (1978) how pretend-playful situations become quickly organized into rules about adjacency pairings, substitution, privileges of occurrence during the first half of the second year. These rules have a generativeness well in advance of those that govern speech in such "real" activities as feeding, noise-making, etc. Could it be that language from a very early age functions as an hypothesis generator about systematic possibilities?

In the second half of this chapter I shall examine the first two communicative intents and their formatting: the management of joint attention and the organization of joint action toward goals.

Indicating and the Management of Joint Attention

I now wish to consider some observational data on what, technically, might be called the ontogenesis of reference. The philosophical and linguistic complexities of reference I will come to presently. But first I should like to describe some major steps along the way to the mastery of reference with particular regard to the transition to linguistic procedures for referring. As regards my philosophical biases, I will confess to a strong interest in the Kripke (1972) and Putnam (1975) account of the historical-causal theory of reference.

I shall limit myself principally to describing two children, Richard and Jonathan, and also lean upon evidence from a variety of experimental studies. Richard and Jonathan were two English, English-speaking children of middle-class parents whom we studied intensively from 5 to 24 months and from 3 to 18 months, respectively. We videotaped their play with their mother at home once a fortnight all during these periods, occasionally more often when things were moving too fast for that. And occasionally the parents borrowed the video equipment to take some footage of events that they thought were important that we were missing—as, for example, behavior in the crib when the children first waked or were put to bed, behavior in the bath, and so on. The parents were educated and interested and kept diaries as well.

The most striking thing about the first steps in the management of joint attention (prior, roughly, to 6 months when the child has mastered reaching and taking) is the amount of concentration that goes into its initial cultivation. As Robson (1967) and others have noted, the earliest phase of joint attention is the establishment of sustained eye-to-eye contact. This is often an important milestone for the mother in the sense that, as Robson notes, it is the point at which the mother reports that her child is a "real human being". There is a great deal of vocalization from the mother and, shortly after, from the child, and by the end of the second month this has become well established and reliable with the mother and child beginning to show turn-taking in terms of "turning on". All of this occurred before we began our observations. After it had become established, when our observations begin, the mother began introducing objects as targets for joint attention.

In the case of Jonathan at 3 months, his mother introduces objects in two ways. One is by interposing an object between her and Jonathan while they are in eye-to-eye contact. As she does so, she changes expression to "object vocalization" on a characteristic form:

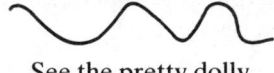

See the pretty dolly

It is a very wide band intonation with peaks and troughs of the kind reported by Garnica (1977). She characteristically moves the object to keep it in the child's line of regard as he moves. (Collis and Schaffer, 1975, note that when at play together, mothers constantly monitor the child's line of regard in this way.) The second approach is to pick up an object the child's line of regard seems to have focused upon, then move it towards him. Both of these are accompanied by a considerable amount of highlighting or forefronting of the object, the mother typically shaking the object to be regarded (one comes to appreciate the technology of the rattle!) or looming it in and out toward the child.

Once the children showed a reliable, readily evoked orienting reaction to objects presented in this way, each mother developed a characteristic, routinized way of preparing for presentation when the child was *not* in eye-to-eye contact with her. This took the form of a highly routinized attentional vocative:

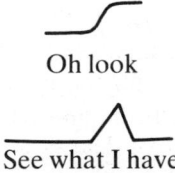

Richard

Jonathan

Which by five months is indeed responded to by the child looking toward the mother and searching for her offered attentional target. This is very soon accompanied by the usual expansion

Oh look

See what I have

and the like. Lyons (1977) in his intriguing discussion of Quasi-English as a developmental starting language speaks of such attentional vocatives as "undifferentiated deictics" that specify that there is something in the environment or context to attend to. But what is very striking is the speed with which these expressions by the mother (which are, as noted, rather routinized) take on a general property of alerting the child to the possibility of a shift in attention. Here the work of Ryan (1976) is particularly relevant. She worked with mother–baby pairs with the infants aged 12 months ± 10 days, the mothers all native speakers of Glaswegian English. She found, first, that mothers when attending to a different toy than one the children were playing with were much more likely to use a rising intonation pattern when referring to it than when attending to the toy the child was playing with. The second finding was striking: when the mother spoke with raising-intonation pattern (as in the conventional interrogative form), the "baby was likely to change the focus of her attention to the toy her mother was holding". There is currently a good deal of work in progress on the attentiveness of children to such intonational deictic cues and it would seem as if the rising intonation may not have its power only by virtue of its association with mother's shifting attention. But this is a matter that need not concern us now.

The first phase of managing joint attention, very much under the control of the mother, appears to result in the child learning that there are signals in the mother's speech envelope that indicate that there is "something to look at" that the mother is attending to. It is hard to date the end of the phase but 6 or 7 months seems a good point at which to talk about the peak of this period of mastering the attentional vocative or "undifferentiated deictics".

The second phase is more specific, and relates to the child being able to spot what it is that occupies another's attention. In its simplest form, it consists of the child's ability to follow another's line of regard to a target a distance removed from the two of them. Scaife and Bruner (1975) did the first simple experiment, involving an adult sitting opposite an infant (subjects ranging from 3 months to somewhat over a year), making eye-to-eye contact, then turning 90 degrees either to left or to right and looking intently. By 8–10 months, two-thirds of infants were following line of regard, and by a year 100% were. The experiment was done more carefully by Butterworth (1979) and he noted several additional features to this gaze-following pattern. The first and most important was that the child by a year would look out along the line of regard, search for an object, and would return to the adult's face for a second look if he found none, following which he would turn outward again. There seemed to be the expectancy that a target could be found. The second point was that the infant would not turn out a greater distance in search of the object than the point at which he still held the adult's face in the periphery of his gaze. In effect, he was looking for an object, but doing so while keeping the adult in his visual field. The concurrent search for a target and the maintaining of contact suggests that we are indeed dealing with a very concrete form of joint attention management. Unfortunately, this type of more specific deictic marking of a putative referent has not been experimentally combined with the non-specific attentional vocative discussed earlier, but Scaife and Bruner did note that the likelihood of a child following gaze direction increased when the experimenter's turned gaze was accompanied by some such expression as "Oh, look".

I must digress for a moment to comment on the seeming departure from egocentrism these infants showed. After all, they *were* able to "take another's perspective" in searching the environment. Doubtless there are many respects in which infants and young children are egocentric in the sense Piaget (1936) intends. But I think it is important to recognize that there is an important countervailing tendency operative. I think the briefest way of characterizing it is to say that infants and young children from very early on appear, like adults, to be "naive realists" who believe that there is a world of objects out there and that others are experiencing the same world as they are. And indeed, whatever philosophical position we may eventually take, however constructionalist our epistemology, I think it is everybody's working belief—a point that has been made with some force by Hilary Putnam.

By the sixth or seventh month, the child's attention becomes dominated by his efforts to reach and take objects, to exchange them, and so on. We shall speak of this later in connection with request. Here it suffices to say only that joint attention in the months after reaching is well developed becomes dominated by joint action while the child develops the kinds of "action schemas" and scripts about the world that we discussed earlier. The principal achievement during this active phase is that the child now becomes a giver of signals about objects desired and is not only involved in comprehending and decoding others' efforts to direct his attention.

A crucial next phase begins with the emergence of pointing by the child. "Pure" pointing, so-called, emerged at 9½ months in Jonathan and at 13 months in Richard. It does not appear to be an extension of reaching, even of ostensive or conventionalized reaching of that effortless kind by which the child indicates an object that he wishes to be obtained for him without quite reaching for it. It seems more likely that pointing is part of a primitive marking system for singling out the noteworthy. Obviously, the child has been exposed to pointing by adults and his ability to comprehend an adult point precedes his own production by a month or two in our records. In Jonathan's case, his own first pointing is toward near-distant (and surprising) objects seen through the garden window, the point sometimes being accompanied by a proto-demonstrative *um*. In Richard's case, his first points (sometimes accompanied by *da*) are for old objects seen in new contexts (cup which Mother has put on her head), and for familiar objects in non-action contexts (pictures in book as Mother turns the pages). It also occurs in "hypothetical" contexts. I must say a word about a concurrent development before I can explain what that means.

That concurrent development is the appearance of the PCF, the "phonologically constant form" by which the child comes to "indicate" objects. These take the place of the demonstratives *da* and *um* in pointing and indeed come to be used alone. It is difficult to state with assurance that these PCFs represent the emergence of the Semanticity Hypothesis—that particular sound patterns indicate particular classes of objects. I think that hypothesis may go through different stages itself—first that any sound, including babble-strings, indicate objects in a vague way, and then that (at least in Richard) an object indicated gesturally takes an accompanying privileged sound—in his case *da*, later to be replaced by the sound cluster *ghee* at 17 months. *Ghee* persisted until 24 months, even after Richard had begun to produce PCFs modelled loosely on adult speech, e.g. *apoo* for apple, *boe* for bird, etc. It was in connection with *boe* that we observed pointing in what I called a hypothetical setting. He had been observing birds, rooks and some magpies, flying about in the field by the family's summer cottage in the afternoon. In the evening when he was indoors, seated on the floor, fortunately being observed, he sat quietly for some moments, pointed upwards and uttered rather absently, *boe*.

Once pointing and PCFs appear, they immediately become embedded in ritualized dialogue of the familiar "Where" and "What" games. Long before, both our mothers had established a "slot" for points and PCFs, Jonathan's mother beginning with questions like "Where's the X?" "Where did it go?" even as early as 4 months and Richard's mother with "What's this?" as she presented objects at 9 months—neither case with any possibility of appropriate response (i.e. point to the object or give label). Once pointing appears, "Where's the X?" becomes a real demand for a point to a specific object (well established for Jonathan by 12 months and for Richard by 13–14 months). At 15 months, this query is embodied for both children in the formatted game procedure of pointing to body parts. At about the same time, "What's that?" becomes a demand for a PCF and, later, for a specific name.

We can see more clearly what is involved in the establishing of constraining formats if we look closely at one of them. Ninio and Bruner (1978) have done a close analysis of "book reading", a labelling game that has a lively and long history that extends from the beginning to the end of Richard's second year.

The first crucial point about the mother's role is that she drastically tailors her output at the start to the nature of the task and to the child's apparent competence. She changes with a steady regularity from the eleventh to the eighteenth month as she observes her child's changing competence. There are four constituents that make up her side of the dialogue, four key utterance types that appear in a strikingly fixed order: an **Attentional Vocative**, *Look*: a **Query** with a distinctive rising contour, *What's that?*; a **Label**, *It's an X*. Finally, there is a **Feedback Utterance**, *Yes*. For each of the types, a single token accounts for from nearly 50% to more than 90% of the instances. The mother's utterances, moreover, are organized almost exclusively in the order stated and far in excess of what might have been predicted by chance, and the successive deployment of its four constituents is highly linked to what the child says or does. Mothers interacting with infants in communicative exchanges are very steady, and when they vary it is with good reason. If the child responds, the mother responds to him, and if he initiates a cycle by pointing or vocalizing, she responds even more often. Her "fine tuning" is fine indeed—for example, if the child succeeds in labelling after her **Query**, she will virtually always skip the label and jump to feedback.

To assure that two minds are indeed focused on a common topic, the mother develops a technique for bypassing the Wittgensteinian dilemma of how to know what feature a label refers to: 90% of her labels refer to *whole objects*, and since half of the remainder are made up of proper nominals which also stand for the whole, she seems to create few difficulties of this order. They seem to be together on the referent. This supposes that the child responds to whole objects as well—a point most recently urged by Quine (1973) and by Schlesinger (1978) and referred to as "body-mindedness". It seems highly unlikely that body-mindedness solves *all* of the Wittgensteinian dilemma, but it certainly seems to help in this instance.

The mother's (often quite unconscious) approach is indeed exquisitely tuned. When the child responds to her attentional vocative by looking, she follows immediately with a query. However, the child initially responds to the query, by gesture or smile, she will then supply a label. But as soon as the child shows he can vocalize at the query juncture (no matter how) she raises the ante: she will withhold the label and repeat the query until the child vocalizes, and then give the label (often, as Garnica, 1977, has shown, with heavy stress). Later still, when the child has learned to respond with shorter, morpheme-length vocalizations to the mother's query for a label, she will no longer accept an indifferent vocalization. When the child begins producing "phonologically constant forms" (PCFs, Dore, 1975), she holds out for them. Finally, the child produces appropriate words in the correct privilege of occurrence in the dialogue. Even then, the mother remains tuned to the developing pattern, helping the child recognize and further partition the labelling task. After a certain period, for example, two forms of intonation develop for the "What's that" query: one with a falling intonation contour inquires about those words for which, in the mother's estimate, the child already knows the label; one with a rising intonation is for those that are newly introduced. So that even in the simple labelling game, mother and child are well into making the distinction between the given and the new (see

Chafe, 1970; Clark and Clark, 1977). Chafe makes the important point that the distinction between old and new information is closely akin to that between topic and comment, or subject and predicate. And it is of more than passing interest that the old or established labels are the ones around which the mother will shortly be elaborating comments and questions for new information, such as,

    M: What's that? (Falling intonation)
    C: Fishy
    M: Yes, and see him swimming?

Note too that after a label's acquisition is taken as given or shared or old, the initial attentional vocative is most usually dropped from the mother's portion of the dialogue.

I do not mean to burden the discussion with the petty particulars of acquisition, only to highlight that in the petty particulars the mother is giving the child useful cues about the structure of the language. Her provision of the cues is based not simply on her knowledge of the language (obviously), but upon her updateable knowledge of the child's capabilities for grasping particular distinctions, forms, or rules at particular times. How is she achieving her effect? Is it that she knows exactly when to imitate or echo the child's effort in order to reinforce it? Or is there something more general than this in her strategy of providing one new procedural step at a time that is both carefully prepared and presented when the child is ready? What about imitation? If we take first the child's repetition of a label after feedback from the mother, we find that there is not much difference in his rate of repeating whether his mother has imitated his label, simply said "Yes", or only laughed approvingly—in all cases the child repeats about half the time, about the same rate as he would repeat his label given "no" feedback at all from the mother. More negative evidence comes from examining the likelihood of the child producing a label in response to the question "What's that?" in contrast to producing one after the mother has just uttered the label. The chances are roughly eight-fold greater in the former case than in the latter that the child will label. So plainly the child is highly sensitized to certain constraints in the dialogue structure and does *not* seem to be directly imitating.

Consider now some general properties of the growth of indicating between 3 months and 2 years. The first has to do with the intent to indicate, and here I mean it in the Gricean sense of "conventional" rather than "natural" means for doing so. Attending jointly at the start seems to be the outcome of natural, non-intended, preadapted processes. It seems highly unlikely that gaze following or the catching of the child's attention by highlighting objects depends at the start on anything other than fairly primitive and natural processes. But as soon as attending to indicated objects occurs consistently in the child's repertory, the mother frames them in formats that permit the child to recognize what signs lead to what consequences. She steadily if unconsciously conventionalizes her way of signalling change of referent until the child shows an uptake of her conventionalized form, and then she imbeds the newly-established and reliable routines into higher order routines. It is striking that each step in the progress she is establishing a place-holder for a higher order, more symbolic routine to be substituted later. Undifferentiated deictic markers and undiscriminating attentional vocatives like *da* and *umm*, once attained, are quickly replaced by pointing and then by PCFs and genuine morphemes. Undifferentiated babbles in book reading are first replaced by morpheme-length sound patterns, then by words. Or if we go up to the end of the second year when Richard has managed *dere* and *Nana* (the name of a familiar dog) each separately, he now handles them together as *dere Nana* in the same indicating context where each sufficed on its own. (The same for *bebe ouse* or *mummys gaggas* combined for indicating.)

One has the sense in all this that when the infant has mastered the routine of the prior level there is now enough processing space for him to manage the next step. What permits the steadying to occur is the opportunity to try out the routines in mother-steadied formatted dialogue and to gain more real-world scripted knowledge about the situation in which the dialogue or action is occurring. If you should now ask what leads the child to take the step forward, why he does not stay at the level where he was, then I will speculate that you are back with LAD. That is to say, the performance condition necessary for the child to take a next step forward is not simply a natural growth of attention and memory, but a step toward steadying of use in context that allows him to recognize regularities in the mother's (or another adult's) speech. That is to say, the necessary input to the language acquisition device is *not* simply undifferentiated speech, but rather contextualized speech, contextualized in world knowledge and in discourse. It is then that the child develops appropriate recognition hypotheses about how to do it more appropriately in the language.

If what I am saying is correct, then what is necessary for LAD to operate is a "Language Assistance Support System" under the control of the mother or the adult speech community. This is the system of fine-tuned responding that brings the child's efforts into appropriate contextualization to make a suitable input into LAD. Perhaps I will be permitted an acronym for the Language Assistance Support System, LASS. In my view, the function of LASS is to assure formatting and economical development of speech forms at a lower level in such a manner that they constitute an appropriate input for LAD. My speculative hypothesis is that LAD operates in small, context-sensitive leaps rather than by taking in all of language as in input at once and attempting to extract all the rules of grammar from it in one big laundering operation.

There are several things about the acquisition of indicating that relate to issues in the philosophical analysis of reference. First of all, the issue of illocutionary force. As Wittgenstein remarks about Augustine's theory of language acquisition, how does the child know that the adult, using words, is *indicating* something in the adult world rather than warning his listener or expressing his satisfaction? I think that the answer to this dilemma comes initially from a deep biological base: the recognition of shared experience. The child looking back and forth between an interposed object and his mother and eventually grasping the object proferred by her is experiencing something that we shall never, of course, be able to penetrate. We cannot ask him for a gloss of his behavior; that is the restriction on working with children. They cannot tell you what it means. Probably the adult cannot do so very well either (cf. Snow, 1977), but they can tell you things that help your inference about what they mean or what interpretation they are assigning to the scene. But by 6 or 7 months, the child does look back to the adult's gaze in order to do what—check or confirm or share? He may indeed look back and smile or laugh if it were something unusual he has seen. And I have observed a 12-month-old baby reach up and turn his mother's head toward what he was looking at. Then child's mother, as we have noted, gives rich signals that it is the child's attention she is seeking—intonational, by arranging formats, by lexical invariance (e.g. the "Oh look, Jonathan" routine). And as Atkinson and Griffiths (1973) point out, many of these same attention-calling devices continue in adult language. Conventional devices very soon come to take the places of such natural procedures as highlighting and interposing objects.

As for the child's own performance (rather than his comprehension of his mother's) it would be hard to know how to interpret longitudinal data from studies like Brown's (1973) or Bowerman's (1973) or Greenfield and Smith's (1976). They report the first occurrence of the use of words to indicate objects, and these usually appear around 8 or 9 months. But we have no data on the child's first use of undifferentiated deictics, attentional vocatives, or demonstratives—save in the matter of first pointing, which comes long after the child has used many other devices to indicate an object that he wishes to bring to the attention of another. Jonathan pointed clearly at 9 months, Richard at 13 months. But a month before Richard pointed, he accompanied looking intently at an object with *da* as an attentional vocative, and also looked back to his mother. Before that, one gets the impression that perhaps as early as 6 months he was anticipating that his mother would be activated by the same focus of attention as the one he was looking at.

There are "weak points" in both children at 6 months, but it is hard to know how specific the child's attention-sharing signals are intended to be. It is very difficult to draw any sensible conclusion about how the child's attention-calling to objects develops. There are too few data. All we can say is that it lags far behind his sensitivity in being able to comprehend indicating signals from the mother. And in any case, it is very plain that he knows how to produce a reliable illocutionary act marking his intention of indicating before he is able to use any of the linguistic modes of realizing reference by determiners, by demonstratives, by nominals, etc. As Dore (1974) has long since pointed out, the apparatus for marking major forms of illocutionary force is well developed before the child has learned to deal with construction of locutions. There is, so to speak, a well-established place marker for indicative illocutionary procedures months before the child develops linguistic means for realizing them, judging by his skill at producing them gesturally and by his uptake of his mother's signals.

Let me turn to the question of whether early reference is "singular definite referring" to a particular object or whether, in Putnam's (1975) terms, it is governed by a "Principle of Reasonable Ignorance", How definite *is* reference? "The Principle of Reasonable Ignorance", as Putnam frames it, "is simply that a speaker may *have* a word in the sense of possessing normal ability to use it in discourse, and not know the mechanism of reference of that term, explicitly or even implicitly." To take his example, a speaker can know the meaning of the word "gold" without knowing implicitly or explicitly the criteria for establishing that something is gold. The Principle of Reasonable Ignorance "forbids us to assume that any speakers are philosophically omniscient". Reference or indicating can be, and often is, partial and halting. This follows from Putnam's view that there is a division of labor within the linguistic community as to what terms refer to, and one establishes reference by tracking back how the term was used in the historical chain whose last link is the present speaker. There is an initial dubbing ceremony when, for example, somebody tells you that the tree before you is an ash. You then are faced in discourse by somebody who challenges and says that it is a beech. But you do not know how to distinguish a beech from an ash. You will then refer your interlocutor back to the original informant who told you or, if you are literate, send him to Roger Tory Peterson's *Field Guide to the Trees*.

A great deal of early indicating and "reference teaching" is precisely of this order. The mother treats her infant with a lively sense of the Principle of Reasonable Ignorance. She does not know and early on knows that she *can* not know what it is that the infant is referring by a morpheme-like babble or even by a specific nominal. Take the following example from Book Reading at 23 months.

M: What's that?
C: Ouse.
M: Mouse, yes that's a mouse.
C: More mouse (pointing to another picture).
M: No, those are squirrels. They're like mice but with long tails. Sort of.

C: Mouse, mouse, mouse.
M: Yes, alright, they're mice.
C: Mice, mice.

On later occasions, doubtless, the negotiations will continue and Richard will eventually settle down on a reasonable handling of rodents much as, for example, the subjects in Susan Carey's experiment (Carey and Bartlett, cited in Miller, 1977) settle down to a reasonable way of handling the word *chromium* after negotiating their alternative hypotheses about what color it stands for. They depend upon the existence of corrective possibilities within the linguistic community of which they are a part. All of which suggest as well that Quine's view of referential learning starting at the specific, concrete and particular and being generalized to the categorial level must have something deeply wrong with it. If anything, reference seems to begin at some categorial level that in effect has negotiable boundaries. And that, I suspect from the work of Rosch (e.g. 1973) and her coworkers, is the way in which much of categorial learning proceeds.

Negotiable reference, as in the Carey experiments on children learning colors by launching hypotheses for later test, can be found as early as 22 months. It consists of the child trying out the limits of a new lexical item in the hope of finding where the boundary can be drawn. Consider the episode involving Richard and his mother at that age. They are examining an English penny together.

R: (Points to picture of the Queen on coin) Nanny, nanny.
M: What? That's not Granny. It's a lady, yes. Nini is a lady, isn't it?
R: (Points to coin again) Nanny, nanny.
M: You think that's Granny? Oh well, I don't think she'd mind too much.
R: Layly (with smile to mother).
M: It's the *Queen*.
R: Lili.
M: Queen.
R: Nanny, nanny.
M: It's *not*.
R: (Points and says) Nini.
M: Have they all got ladies on?
R: Nanny, nanny. (Points)
M: No it isn't.
R: Nini.

And so he is on his way to distinguishing Granny from ladies in general from the Queen! I shall not deal here with later episodes, but only assure you that the negotiation has by no means been settled forever. Note, by the way, the typical insistence on the part of the mother that the child stick to an established PCF—nini for lady in general. This is a particularly striking episode, for its background is rich. At 18 months, *nini* and *nanny* were PCFs for juice. At 20 months, *eeni* was for lemon and *nana* was for nothing there when something was expected. Now *nani* may be money, and *nini* lady and there is much sorting still to be done. By 23 months, for example, *nini* disappears. At 24 months he says *There's a lady*.

So much for indicating. It develops slowly out of the conventionalizing and formatting of what seems to be a natural function. It is managed successively by forms of increasing conventionality and complexity until, finally, the child is able to combine words grammatically—an attentional demonstrative plus a nominal. Soon after, as reported by Karmiloff-Smith (1979), he learns to contextualize the nominal anaphorically in discourse by the choice of definite and indefinite articles. The mastery of each new procedure seems to make him sensitive to a next one of greater complexity. There is no great leap to be reported. The real leap is his entry upon the step-by-step procedure. That procedure is a very decided one that depends on participation in discourse with a hearer who is fine-tuned to the child's level of development.

The Nature and Development of Request

When we request something, we must specify two things: *that* we want, and *what* we want. What we want may be as various as the range of reference that we can manage. The form of requesting usually falls under a relatively small number of generic headings: principally, assistance in our own ongoing goal-directed activity, joint participation in some more or less ritualized atelic activity, and information. Request for assistance puts "the other" into the role of instrument; when we invite we request another to act as a coagent or coexperiencer as in a game or ritual; asking for information involves using the other as a resource to fill a gap in our knowledge or representation. Each goes along a somewhat different course of development and, for the sake of concision, I shall concentrate on requests for goods and/or services, requests proper.

As with indicating, the growth of requesting begins non-specifically—with the child making signs that are interpretable merely as indicating a state of want. In Grice's sense, there is nothing non-natural about them: fretting, crying, etc. There is some evidence from Ricks (1971) and others that the mother is able when the child is 4 or 5 months old to distinguish different kinds of cries—hunger, pain, etc. But in the main it is the case that the mother interprets *what* the child "needs". Context is all. There is an interesting point here about the form of inference involved. Pratt (1978) in his Oxford thesis on the socialization of crying reports that up to about 26 weeks of age, an infant's cry is interpreted "causally" by the mother—the result of a physical condition like hunger, fatigue, wind or pain. After that age, crying is increasingly interpreted psychologically as indicating frustration, a desire for an object, a wish to be picked up, etc. The mother is probably showing early fine-tuning, for Pratt also finds that before 26 weeks the child is more likely to stop crying as a result of physical intervention by them other (feeding, resettling, etc.), whereas after 26 weeks he is increasingly likely to respond to "psychological" interventions such as giving him an object, distracting him with "conversation" and the like. The crucial factor in the change is discernible a few weeks later, at 8 months, when the child begins to show the first interpretable indication of *what* he is requesting that goes along with his by now quite socialized "demand" crying—a form of crying that is much more ritualized, much narrower in sound spectrum in the manner of voicing, much less persistent, much more accompanied by pause patterns during which the child scans to check on uptake by the mother. In a word, the conventionalization of the illocutionary force of the request is far in advance of the indicating element that signals target.

Space does not permit a detailed analysis of the details of the early phases of requesting, but an outline of some of the major steps in the progress tells the tale well enough. To begin with, let me note in passing that the child's first interpretable (i.e. reliably codable) requests for objects (and these are the first to appear) are almost invariably for objects that are being held by the mother. This is true for both Richard and Jonathan. The child reaches for them, the reach often accompanied by a fret or effort sound and with no glance at the mother at all. It is much as Sugarman-Bell (1978) describes it: the object-reaching schema of the child seems independent of the mother schema. And it is only by 9 months or so that glancing at the mother occurs concurrently with reaching for the object. Two things happen next. The first is that the child's reach for the object becomes converted into what I referred to earlier as a stylized or ostensive reach, without signs of effort or fretting, these having been replaced by stylized request calls: *huhmmm* for Jonathan and *heaah* for Richard. The child is still deficient in acknowledging receipt of the object from the mother (*ca.* 16 months), glancing toward her on receipt occurring only a fifth of the time. But by this age, the child is now beginning quite steadily to look toward the mother when he makes his ostensive reach plus conventionalized vocalization—so long as his activation is not too high. If it is, he regresses back to fret plus effortful reaching. But the formatted request, stylized directional reach plus standardized vocalization, is well established by 18 months. And then it begins to serve as a carrier for more speech-like forms.

At 16 months, for example, Richard replaces the *heaah* vocalization with his extraordinarily well-articulated *ghee*. Then that is replaced by sentence-like babble strings in the same privileged position, accompanying the ostensive, effortless "reach toward", e.g. *n-gah-gho-ah-di*. Shortly after 18 months, these delightful, rather interrogatively contoured strings drop out to be replaced in the same position by PCFs: *bauble* accompanying his reach toward a book on the shelf that contains a favorite picture of an apple. And indeed, by 20 months the ostensive reach is beginning to disappear and a new intonation pattern occurs. *Heaah* or *ghi* occurs as the head word in the utterance (but without its falling pitch) but the PCF that accompanies it is given a new stress—as in *Heaah moo-louse* with the first syllable of the PCF (indicating "mouse") being stressed. And not long after, the same format begins to carry more advanced forms as at 22 months when *heaah* is dropped altogether and two-word combinations signifying recurrence (like *more mouse*) and possession (*Richard cake*) make their appearance in the request format.

Now it is very interesting to note that there seems *not* to be any deliberate modelling by the mother of the forms that are finding their way into the child's speech. Rather, they are given by her inadvertently as *interpretations* of the child's request: "Do you want more X?" "Is that what you want?" These are genuine, non-pedagogical efforts on the part of the mother to assign an interpretation to the child's utterance. The pedagogy, rather, is reserved for making the child mindful of the preparatory, essential, sincerity, and other conditions on making a request. Richard's mother is first particularly eager to establish sincerity of his requests: "Do you really want it?" being one of her consistent utterances. She is then rather obsessed with one of the essential conditions on requesting: whether Richard can carry out the act on his own: "Come on, you can do it, come on", and on one occasion, "Come on, you make the ultimate effort". But there is also a quite generalized pressure from the mother for her son to use the advanced forms he has already shown himself able to use in discourse. She withholds and says things like: "No, banging won't produce it", or "What's that all about. It's not very informative, you know". Indeed, half of Richard's mother's utterances in request formats up to 14 months include an effort to make him carry out the act on his own or to specify more clearly the target he is seeking.

The request format becomes elaborated in a major way about the middle of the second year with the emergency of two new features of requesting: displaced requesting for absent objects, and requests for assistance in carrying out an ongoing activity. The first of these forces a new degree of specification on the child's requesting—one manifestation being through the use of nominals which surge ahead concurrently with the new development as if the child, finding a new and indispensable function for nominals in displaced reference, latches on to them as a new and powerful device. But obviously, it is impossible to be sure whether form follows function—do nominals enter to meet the need for displaced reference?—or function follows accessible form. I sometimes wonder, I confess, whether that is a distinction that makes as much sense in the small detail of acquisition as in general theory. Both seem to operate. The second way of managing remote reference is through the use of deictic and nominal specifiers of canonical locus—pointing to or naming the icebox when an otherwise unspecifiable food delicacy is desired. Both of these procedures increase the child's range of requesting enormously and extend the request format well beyond the visual range in which it previously operated.

The emergence of requests for assistance in *action* is a qualitatively different kind of achievement. Now the child must combine his knowledge of action scripts with his procedures of request (see Bruner, Roy and Ratner, in press, for details). Very characteristically, his knowledge of action scripts is well in advance of his knowledge of how to communicate what kind of assistance he needs. His first requests for assistance, consequently, take the form of bringing the incomplete task to the mother or the mother to the task and is a variant of using the conventional request procedure of that stage of development—as when Richard brings a music box to be rewound to his mother, marking it with an undulating intonation on the sound pattern *mmmmmm* rather than by *heaah*. This is then elaborated further by indicating, either through pointing or by a lexical item, the element that needs tending to: as when he takes his mother a saucepan top with the handle off, points to the missing element and says *scooo* with a demand contour. In the final phase, he attempts a new procedure: steering the mother's *actions* into the line of assistance needed. In the case of Richard, this took the form of running through a script successively, illustrated in the following:

Mummy, Mummy; Mummy come.
up, up
cupboard
up cupboard, up cupboard; up cupboard
get up, get up
cupboard, cupboard
cupboard-up; cupboard-up; cupboard-up
telephone
Mummy
Mummy get out telephone

His mother objects and asks him what he wants after each of the first two requests. She is trying to get him to set forth his request in some "readable" order *in advance* of her starting to respond—to give a *reason* in terms of the *goal* of the action. He, meanwhile, achieves something approaching a sentence request by organizing his successive utterances in a fashion that seems to be guided by his conception of the needed steps in the action. The initial grammar of the long string of task-related requests is, then, a kind of temporal grammar based on an understanding not only of the constituent actions required, but of the order in which these must be executed. This is an interpersonal script based on knowledge of what is needed in the real world.

And of course the procedure is shot through with the child's sense of the action required and of the arguments of the action through which the task is to be completed.

The further development of requesting depends very heavily upon the child's management not only of action scripts but of their appropriate placement in speech act formats. He very soon becomes linguistically skilled in being able to indicate as Martens (1979) and Farwell (1977) put it, the goal, the gap, the skill required, the agency, the instrument, etc. These forms and the requisite rules for dealing with them syntactically in order to represent the action are surprisingly well established by the third year. I do not know how so much progress gets made on the syntagmatic side in the short period from the second to the third birthday. All that I can suggest is what I have already intimated. Firstly, that the child's own "language research" in that year is, to begin with, highly targeted research. His communicative formats provide a matrix that permits substitution of higher order forms for lower order ones. And his knowledge of the action patterns and scripts to which the formats relate also grows apace. There is, as we have seen, a powerful shaping of both of these by adult interaction—what I have called the "Language Assistance Support System". For the rest, I can only offer the speculation again that such input into a "Language Acquisition Device" probably cues certain preadapted, innate ideas about the structure of language. I cannot believe that such rapid linguistic progress could occur without there being present a grammatical hypothesis generator like LAD whose input must be language by the adult already somewhat constrained by world knowledge and discourse requirements.

As for how the child acquires the quirky, maxim-like illocutionary aspect of requesting, I am greatly taken by the point made by deVilliers (in preparation) and by Reeder (1979). Children seem to be highly sensitive to social context; they know what it is that is intended almost without attending to the locution. Even at 2 years, they are able to recognize correctly from layout when a request and when an invitation is intended, as in Reeder's experiment. Yet, a study of Garvey's (1975) indicates that 4-year olds' requests for action from another child are already quite elaborate and contain preparatory locutions, reason-bearing adjuncts, clarifications, and acknowledgements as well as the request itself—yielding successful outcomes from a half to three-quarters of the time they are used. They may at the start be using mainly context to infer the intent of speakers, but it is quite plain that by age 4 they have picked up enough about the discourse rules to be able to utter well-formed speech acts that are sensitive to appropriacy conditions and to grammatical rules. Another perhaps better way of saying this is that as soon as their language acquisition progresses they incorporate their new-found competence into the formulating of speech acts.

Conclusions

The first conclusion I would wish to draw reiterates the starting point of my introduction. Language acquisition occurs in the social context of discourse, in the miniaturized culture that governs the communicative interaction of children and adults. Discourse occurs in highly framed or formatted contexts that provide a manageable setting in which children can convert communicative intentions into communicative conventions and in which adults and children alike can more easily figure out correct interpretations of each other's conventionally expressed intentions. We have tried to show that formats like those used in indicating and requesting—designed to achieve joint attention and joint action—serve several crucial linguistic functions. They structure the problem space in which semantic and syntactic development must occur by specifying the communicative targets that must be met and the conditions of appropriacy that must be fulfilled in hitting these targets. More concretely, they relate the action scripts that the child is learning to communicative requirements, as for example in requesting aid from another in achieving one's own goals. But above all, because discourse involves a transaction between an aspirant novice with a high readiness to learn the rules of the system and an expert adult extraordinarily well-tuned to the needs of the novice, the result is a strikingly swift achievement of the syntactic, semantic, and pragmatic features of language.

Part of the speed in language acquisition surely has to do with the successive substitution of higher forms of linguistic realization for communicative conventions already established. But part of it must surely stem from the operation of a Language Acquisition Device that recognizes linguistic regularities of a form that are shaped by a matching Language Assistance Support System. For reasons I have already suggested, I am willing to take the view that both of these—the early human capacity to recognize the constitutive rules of the language and the matching adult capacity to frame input to make it acceptable as input to this system—operate in unison as preadapted species-specific systems. The task that remains for psychology and linguistics is to explore more fully the nature, the conditions, and the course of the transaction between these two systems—the Language Acquisition Device and the Language Assistance Support System.

References

ANSCOMBE, G. (1963), *Intention*, Cornell University Press, Ithaca, N.Y.
ATKINSON, M. and GRIFFITHS, P.D. (1973), "Here's here's, there's, here and there", *Edinburgh Working Papers in Linguistics* 3, 29–73.
AUSTIN, J. (1962), *How To Do Things With Works*, Oxford University Press, Oxford.
BOWERMAN, M. (1973), *Early Syntactic Development*, Cambridge University Press, Cambridge.

BRAZELTON, T.B., KOSLOWSKI, B. and MAIN, M. (1974), "The origins of reciprocity: the early mother–infant interaction", in M. Lewis and L. Rosenblum (Eds), *The Effect of the Infant on its Caregiver*, Wiley, New York.
BROWN, R. (1973), *A First Language: the Early Stages*, Harvard University Press, Cambridge, M.A.
BROWN, R. (1977), "Introduction" to C.E. Snow and C.A. Ferguson (Eds), *Talking to Children: Language Input and Acquisition*, Cambridge University Press, Cambridge.
BRUNER, J.S., ROY, C. and RATNER, N. (In press), "The beginnings of request", in K. Nelson (Ed.), *Children's Language*, Vol. IV, Gardner Press, New York.
BUTTERWORTH, G. (1979), "What minds have in common space: a perceptual mechanism for joint reference in infancy", Paper presented to the Developmental Psychology Section, British Psychological Society, Southampton, September 1979.
CAMPOS, F. (1979), "The emergency of causal relations and the linguistic development of Brazilian children", Ph.D. dissertation, University of Campinas, Brazil.
CHAFE, W.L. (1970), *Meaning and the Structure of Language*, University of Chicago Press, Chicago.
CHOMSKY, N. (1957), *Syntactic Structures*, Mouton, The Hague.
CLARK, H.H. and CLARK, E.V. (1977), *Psychology and Language: An Introduction to Psycholinguistics*, Harcourt Brace Jovanovich, New York.
COLLIS, G.M. and SCHAFFER, H.R. (1975), "Synchronization of visual attention in mother–infant pairs", *Journal of Child Psychology and Psychiatry* **16**, 315–320.
DE LEMOS, C. (1979), "Prelinguistic games and the development of proto-aspectual words", Paper presented at the Child Language Seminar, Netherlands Institute for Advanced Study, Wassenaar, Holland, May 1979.
DE VILLIERS, J. (in preparation), "Form and force interactions: the development of negatives and questions", in R.L. Schiefelbusch (Ed.), *Communicative Competence*, University Park Press, University Park, M.D.
DORE, J. (1974), "Communicative intentions and the pragmatics of language development", Unpublished manuscript, City University of New York.
DORE, J. (1975), "Holophrases, speech acts, and language universals", *Journal of Child Language* **2**, 21–40.
DORE, J. (1978), "Conditions for the acquisition of speech acts", in I. Marková (Ed.), *The Social Context of Language*, Wiley, New York.
FARWELL, C.B. (1977), "The primacy of *goal* in the child's description of motion and location", *Papers and Reports on Child Language Development*, Department of Linguistics, Stanford University.
FILLMORE, C.J. (1968), "The case for case", in E. Bach and R. Harms (Eds), *Universals in Linguistic Theory*, Holt, Rinehard & Winston, New York.
FILLMORE, C.J. (1977), "The case for case reopened", in P. Cole and J.M. Sadock (Eds), *Syntax and Semantics*, Vol. 8: *Grammatical Relations*, Academic, New York.
GARNICA, O.K. (1977), "Some prosodic and paralinguistic features of speech to young children", in C.E. Snow and C.A. Ferguson (Eds), *Talking to Children: Language Input and Acquisition*, Cambridge University Press, Cambridge.
GARVEY, C. (1975), "Requests and responses in the speech of preschool children", *Journal of Child Language* **2**, 41–63.
GREENFIELD, P.M. and SMITH, J.H. (1976), *The Structure of Communication in Early Language Development*, Academic Press, New York.
GRICE, H.P. (1968), "Utterer's meaning, sentence-meaning, and word-meaning", *Foundations of Language* **4**, 225–242.
HARRÉ, R. (1973), "Rules in the explanation of social behavior", Paper presented at Oxford University.
KALNINS, I. and BRUNER, J.S. (1973), "The coordination of visual observation and instrumental behavior in early infancy", *Perception* **2**, 307–314.
KARMILOFF-SMITH, A. (1979), *A Functional Approach to Child Language*, Cambridge University Press, Cambridge.

KÄSERMANN, M.L. and FOPPA, L. (1978), "Evidence for linguistic awareness in the young child's repairs", in W. Deutsch (Ed.), *The Child's Construction of Language*, Academic Press, London.
KRIPKE, S. (1972), "Naming and necessity", in D. Davidson and G. Harman (Eds), *The Semantics of Natural Language*, D. Reidel, Dordrecht.
LYONS, J. (1977), "Deixis as the source of reference", discussed in Chapter 15, Vol. 2 of *Semantics*. C.U.P., Cambridge.
MARTENS, K. (1979), "Communicative patterns in support formats between child and caretaker", paper presented at the Max-Planck-Gesellschaft Projektgruppe für Psycholinguistik, Nijmegen, The Netherlands.
MILLER, G.A. (1977), *Spontaneous Apprentices*, Seabury Press, New York.
NELSON, K. (1973), "Structure and strategy in learning to talk", in *Monographs of the Society for Research in Child Development* **38**, Serial No. 149.
NELSON, K. (in press), "The syntagmatics and paradigmatics of conceptual development", in S. Kuczaj (Ed.), *Language, Cognition and Culture*, Lawrence Erlbaum, Hillsdale, N.Y.
NINIO, A. and BRUNER, J.S. (1978), "The achievement and antecedents of labelling", *Journal of Child Language* **5**, 1-15.
PETERS, R.S. (1958), *The Concept of Motivation*, Routledge and Kegan Paul, London.
PIAGET, J. (1952), *The Origins of Intelligence in Children* (first published 1936), International Universities Press, New York.
PRATT, C. (1978), "The socialization of crying", unpublished doctoral dissertation, University of Oxford.
PUTNAM, H. (1975), *Mind, Language and Reality*, Cambridge University Press, Cambridge.
QUINE, W.V. (1973), *The Roots of Reference*, Open Court, La Salle, Ill.
RATNER, N.K. and BRUNER, J.S. (1978), "Games, social exchange and the acquisition of language", *Journal of Child Language* **5**, 391–401.
REEDER, K. (1979), "The early recognition of offers and requests", unpublished manuscript, School of Education, University of Birmingham.
RICKS, D.M. (1971), "The beginnings of vocal communication in infants and autistic children", unpublished, M.D. thesis, University of London.
ROBSON, K.S. (1967), "The role of eye-to-eye contact in maternal–infant attachment", *Journal of Child Psychology & Psychiatry* **8**, 13–25.
ROSCH, E.H. (1973), "Natural categories", *Cognitive Psychology* **4**, 328–350.
RYAN, M.L. (1976), "Contour in context", paper presented at the Psychology Language Conference, Stirling, Scotland.
SCAIFE, M. and BRUNER, J.S. (1975), "The capacity for joint visual attention in the infant", *Nature* **253** (No. 5489), 263–266.
SCHLESINGER, I.M. (1978), "The acquisition of words and concepts", unpublished manuscript, The Hebrew University, Jerusalem.
SEARLE, J.R. (1969), *Speech Acts: An Essay in the Philosophy of Language*, Cambridge University Press, Cambridge.
SHATZ, M. (1978), "The relationship between cognitive processes and the development of cognitive skills", in B. Keasy (Ed.), *Nebraska Symposium on Motivation 1977*, University of Nebraska Press, Lincoln.
SKINNER, B.F. (1957), *Verbal Behavior*, Prentice Hall, Englewood, N.J.
SNOW, C.E. (1977), "The development of conversation between mothers and babies", *Journal of Child Language* **4**, 1–22.
SNOW, C.E. and FERGUSON, C.A. (Eds) (1977), *Talking to Children: Language Input and Acquisition*, Cambridge University Press, Cambridge.
STERN, D. (1977), *The First Relationship: Infant and Mother*, Fontana/Open Books, London.
SUGARMAN-BELL, S. (1978), "Some organizational aspects of pre-verbal communication", in I. Marková (Ed.), *The Social Context of Language*, Wiley, New York.

Chapter 4

Language and Cognition

D. ALAN ALLPORT

Intelligence and Natural Language

For hundreds of years men have speculated about our peculiar human capacity for language, and its relation to other aspects of human intelligence. In this chapter I want to approach these questions from the standpoint of a biologist, using the methods of *cognitive neuropsychology*. Briefly, this is the application of information-processing analyses to the behaviour of brain-damaged patients, with the aim of identifying separable information-processing subsystems. That is a very bare definition. What it means will become clearer as we go along.

I shall take as our starting point the following question: "In what way (if at all) do human intellectual abilities depend on the continued possession of natural language?" To put the question slightly differently: "Is it possible to lose the faculty of language yet to retain other intellectual functions?" As our enquiry develops we shall of course need to make this question more precise. Indeed, one of the aims of this chapter is to clarify what is meant, in information-processing terms, by "the possession of natural language".

Clearly there are many other questions about the interrelation of language and cognition that are outside the scope of this discussion. For example, neuropsychological evidence has little to tell us about the part played by language in the evolution and transmission of culture in society. Neither shall I be concerned here with the role of language in the intellectual development of the child, although both issues are undoubtedly of great interest and importance. My questions are about the psychological mechanisms that operate on natural language in the adult individual, that enable the individual both to generate language and to understand it, and the relation between the possession of these capacities and other cognitive abilities that may or may not also be specific to language.

Man Without Language

In contrasting *speech* and *language*, Roy Harris (chapter 1) invited us to consider the case of someone who has suffered surgical removal of the glottis (or of some other essential part of the vocal apparatus). The person is thereby deprived of speech; but he is manifestly not robbed of language. He understands what is said to him as before; if literate he still reads and writes; his ability to formulate messages is essentially unaffected.

But now consider the complementary case. Suppose instead someone sustains an injury to the cerebral cortex: specifically to a region centred around the base of the superior temporal gyrus, the so-called Wernicke's area. What then? In some cases he may still be able to produce the sounds of speech. Indeed, his vocalization may be fluent, sounding rather like phrases in an unfamiliar dialect; the rise and fall of his voice may still apparently signal questions, assertions, emphases and a variety of emotional nuance as in the prosody of normal speech. Yet it is speech without intelligible words: speech, in effect, *without language*.

This is the condition known as *jargon aphasia*, in its severest and most complete form (Brown, 1981). One patient of this sort whom I have studied, a man (HK) who suffered a stroke in his early 60s, had lost not only the ability to speak or to write intelligible words but also to understand them. He was unable to understand or respond in an appropriate and consistent way to even the simplest words or phrases, either written or spoken to him (Funnell, in preparation). Extensive testing over many weeks, in the period following his stroke, was able to uncover only one communicative symbol system that he could reliably understand, namely written Arabic numerals. He could match numerals appropriately to numbers of objects or to arrays of dots, and he could even carry out some elementary, single-digit addition and multiplication. On the other hand he could not reliably operate in these ways on spoken or alphabetically-written number names, though his performance on some subtests was just better than chance guessing. All other areas of language that we could assess were even more severely compromised. We tested his comprehension of spoken or written words and phrases, by asking him to pick out and point to the object or event thus named, from among a small array of unrelated alternatives. In these tests his performance was generally no better than would be predicted by chance. Occasionally, with the names of a few of the most common, everyday objects he scored just better than chance level. Yet on a subsequent occasion, with the identical test, his performance would once more be no better than guesswork. Nevertheless it was apparent that he understood the nature of the task required of him, and in equivalent versions of these matching tasks with written numerals he could perform quite competently.

HK's speech was a fluent but uninterpretable babble, devoid of all recognizable lexical content. His writing, too, was a corresponding kind of graphemic jargon, a small sample of which is shown in Fig. 4.1. For all practical purposes, then, HK was a man without either receptive or expressive language.

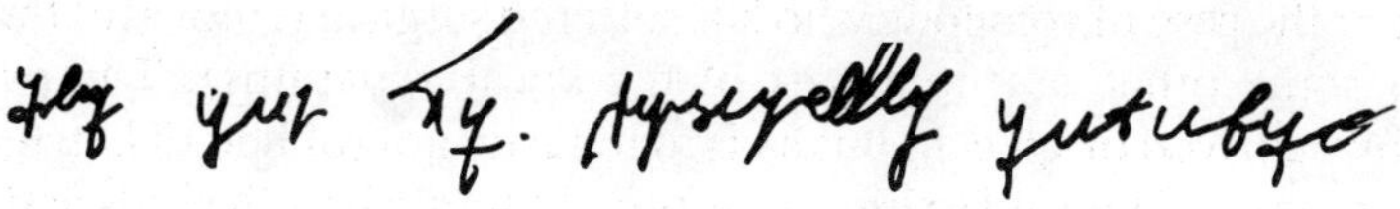

FIG. 4.1. Sample of HK's spontaneous writing—"graphemic jargon".

Naturally we were anxious to discover what mental abilities might remain in a man thus "without language". It is of course no easy matter to assess cognitive or intellectual capacities in someone so profoundly and comprehensively deprived of linguistic communication. I shall not describe here our (unsuccessful) attempts to teach HK a substitute, visual symbol system. But even without embarking on formal testing it was clear that an impressive range of cognitive skills was still available to him. For example, HK, who lived in London, had an excellent mental map of the metropolis. Without language, he could still make his way safely, by himself, across central London. From the passenger seat of a car he was able to direct the driver on a variety of complex routes (for example, from Westminster to Richmond and back), by indicating left, right or straight ahead at each junction, without error. He could play successfully various board-games, and learn new ones with complex rules. Moreover, he was still capable of forming and maintaining vigorous and courteous social relations. HK was a distinctive, and memorable personality. Sadly, he later suffered a second stroke which left him much more extensively handicapped, and we were unable to continue further testing.

Such tragically comprehensive destruction of an individual's linguistic competence is, happily, relatively rare. A more common sequel of stroke, or of other kinds of local brain pathology, is the loss or impoverishment of one or more components of language, while other linguistic abilities are relatively or completely spared. But, for the moment, let us concentrate on those cases (like HK) of the most severe or global aphasia, in which the comprehension as well as the expression of language, both written and spoken, is profoundly compromised or is indeed abolished altogether.

As might be expected, the more extensive the neurological injury the more likely it is that many different functions will be impaired. Occasionally, however, a lesion will be restricted quite sharply to some particular subsystems, producing selective and often dramatic dissociations between the breakdown of any tasks that depend on the damaged subsystems and the execution of other skills, which can remain unaffected. Luria, Tsvetkova and Futer (1956), for example, described the case of a quite distinguished Soviet composer who suffered a severe, predominantly sensory aphasia as the result of multiple left-hemisphere stroke. Yet even during the months immediately following the stroke when he was totally unable to understand speech or to speak himself, as well as during the subsequent years when very limited fragments of language had returned, he continued to compose notable sonatas, quartets, even a full symphony, at a creative standard that his contemporary critics, such as Shostakovitch, held to be the equal of his output before his illness.

Incidentally, it is not unusual to observe something like the complementary dissociation: selective loss of musical abilities with intact language (e.g. Shapiro *et al.*, 1981). Parallels to this kind of functional dissociation between linguistic and musical skills can also be seen, in a limited way, in the performance of intact, normal individuals. Musicians of ordinary ability, for example, are able to play unfamiliar keyboard music from a score while *at the same time* continuing vocally to shadow (i.e. to repeat back, and also to understand) a passage of prose that they hear. With minimal practice both these tasks can be maintained at the standard of speed and accuracy attained when either task is performed alone, and unaffected by variations in the level of difficulty (and hence the proficiency of execution) of the other concurrent task (Allport *et al.*, 1972). A variety of similar examples, of independent concurrent performance between functionally diverse tasks, further encourages the view that mental processes are arranged, generally, in the form of a collection of highly specialized and remarkably independent but cooperating subsystems (Neisser, 1976; Allport, 1980a, b), a view that is increasingly compellingly corroborated by neuropsychology (Shallice, 1981).

Group Studies of Intelligence in Aphasia

There are numerous studies in which the performance of severely aphasic patients has been assessed in terms of non-verbal reasoning ability (Lebrun and Hoops, 1974; Kertesz, 1979). One of the tests widely used for this purpose is Raven's Progressive Matrices (RPM; Raven, 1958), a test requiring various kinds of reasoning by analogy, symbolic manipulation and spatial extrapolation (Hunt, 1974), and, formerly at least, highly regarded as a measure of so-called "general intelligence" or g (Vernon, 1960; Humphreys, 1979). Jensen (1972), for example, refers to the test as the best single measure of the g factor available. An illustration of a typical item from the RPM test is shown in Fig. 4.2. Another non-verbal test requiring a particular kind of analytical ability is the Embedded Figures Test (EFT) illustrated in Fig. 4.3.

In some studies of this kind *no* overall differences have been found between the performance of aphasic and non-aphasic control groups at these (and other) non-verbal tasks, and, more importantly, little or zero correlation between the severity of aphasia and proficiency at non-verbal reasoning (e.g. Basso *et al.*, 1973; Corkin, 1979). In other studies, on the contrary, the authors conclude that their aphasic patients (or particular subgroups of them, especially those with the severest comprehension deficits) are gener-

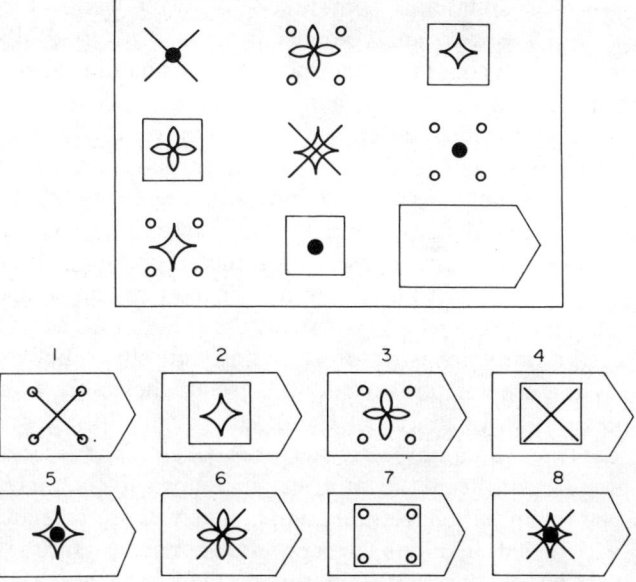

FIG. 4.2. Matrix test: example. Above is a 3 × 3 pattern with one of the pieces missing. The task is to select from the eight alternatives below the piece which appropriately completes the pattern. The complete test contains a series of items of increasing, or "progressive", difficulty (Raven, 1958).

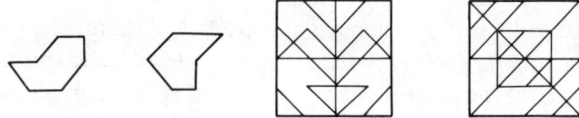

FIG. 4.3. Embedded Figures test: example. The task is to find the small shapes on the left concealed in one or other of the larger figures on the right.

ally less competent at some of these non-verbal intelligence tests than their non-aphasic controls (e.g. Bay, 1962; Colonna and Faglioni, 1966; De Renzi et al., 1966, 1968; Orgass et al., 1972; Kertesz and McCabe, 1975).

Unfortunately, in the majority of such investigations the relative performance of aphasic and non-aphasic subjects has been evaluated and presented *as a group* (or by subgroups), rather than in terms of individual cases. However, if we are interested in a *causal*, rather than merely statistical, dependency between language and other cognitive abilities, it is frankly irrelevant whether aphasia is sometimes—or even frequently—accompanied by non-linguistic, cognitive deficits. Even if this kind of statistical overlap were found, it could result simply from the anatomical proximity of functionally quite independent mechanisms. There is also obvious room for disagreement about which other group(s), if any, it is appropriate to compare as "controls" against the performance of the aphasic patients. If a population of normal subjects without brain injury is selected, how are we to identify which relative deficits in the aphasic group, if any, are due to the brain injuries specifically responsible for their aphasia, and which are consequences of other, additional features of their brain-damaged condition? The problem is in no way dissolved by taking as controls other brain-damaged but not aphasic groups. In any clinically available group of patients, resulting from natural accident, there are inevitably differences in the size and location of lesions. Patients with really "pure" or clear-cut functional deficits are, in any case, necessarily rare. The larger, or more heterogeneous, or diffuse, the injuries, the more likely therefore that deficits in one realm of behavioural competence will be correlated, across the group, with deficits in others, even though there may in fact be no causal or functional dependence between the psychological mechanisms that underly them.

The crucial question is therefore whether major impairment of language competence is *invariably* accompanied by loss or reduction of other intellectual functions. Even a single contrary instance could, in principle, upset the hypothesis that intact intellectual function is dependent on intact linguistic function. In this respect, the neuropsychological single-case method is radically at odds with the so-called "psychometric" approach (Guilford, 1967) to the mapping of human abilities.

The critical evidence for which we must seek will therefore be in the form of data concerning individual patients: in particular in the form of contrary instances—cases of the clear-cut preservation of specific intellectual abilities in the presence of severe aphasia.

Despite this essential point, the research literature continues to be occupied by group studies, in which the only data reported are simply averaged scores for the whole group, often without even including an index of the disperson of scores within the group (e.g. Wapner and Gardner, 1981). Nevertheless, fragmentary accounts of some theoretically critical dissociations can be found scattered throughout this literature, although the amount of detail available generally leaves something to be desired. I shall confine discussion here to investigations which have used versions of Raven's Progressive Matrices test (RPM) of non-verbal reasoning, though similar examples could be given for a variety of other standard tests.

A notable exception to the tradition of reporting only group data is a paper by Zangwill (1964), in which he itemized the RPM scores for ten individual aphasic patients. Several of these patients obtained relatively high RPM scores, in three cases near or even above the 90th percentile level for the general population. These included one patient, a former medical consultant, described as a case of "total aphasia", and two cases of jargonaphasia. A more detailed account of the latter (Kinsbourne and Warrington, 1963) makes clear that these two patients, though profoundly impaired, had not suffered nearly as complete extinction of linguistic abilities as KH, the patient whom I described at the beginning of this paper. Zangwill refers to the "total" aphasic as being "speechless, or virtually so"; but, unfortunately, little or no detail is given about the nature of his comprehension loss, nor how it was assessed, except that it was "appreciable". Regrettably, we have no direct information either about the level of performance which these patients might have achieved in the RPM test, prior to the onset of their aphasia.

Lebrun and Hoops (1974) have compiled a number of similar examples. Relevant to the question of pre-morbid test level, Van Harskamp (1974) described the case of a 21-year-old patient who underwent a variety of psychometric tests both before and after a neurosurgical operation that, in the event, left him deeply aphasic. There was a massive drop in his linguistic comprehension as assessed by the Token Test. Yet, in terms of RPM, his non-verbal reasoning ability was substantially unaffected.

Van Harskamp also cites averaged RPM scores for a group of three patients with severe receptive aphasia but, exceptionally, without clinical indications of "constructional apraxia" as assessed by a simple drawing test. This group, in marked contrast to a group of similarly aphasic patients who did exhibit constructional apraxia, scored above the normal average on the RPM test. Welman and Lanser (1974) report some rather similar results.

In a typical group survey described by Kertesz (1979), the ten patients classified as having the most severe ("global") aphasia with profound loss of language comprehension also obtained, *as a group*, the very lowest scores on a simplified version of RPM (averaging no more than 10%). However, the author mentions that *one* patient in this group in fact obtained an RPM score "within the normal range". No further details are given. To cite one more example, Kreindler, Mihaelescu and Alexandru (1974) compiled an assortment of other tests of logical and problem-solving ability, which they administered to six aphasic patients and to six normal subjects matched to them in age and educational background. Four of their aphasic patients gained overall performance scores on these tests in the same range as their normal controls. One, indeed, equalled the highest score obtained by any of the normal subjects, though at a slight cost in speed of performance.

As in all these reports, quantitative—or even qualitative—data regarding the patients' residual language capabilities, if any, are for the most part seriously deficient, and the range of intelligent non-verbal abilities tested is generally small: frequently confined to a single performance measure. Nonetheless, these admittedly crude and inadequately documented reports are perhaps sufficient to establish a limited conclusion—*that at least some forms of human reasoning can survive, and at a level of competence that evinces (within the conventions of IQ testing), a high level of relative intelligence, even when the cerebral machinery necessary for the generation and the comprehension of natural language has been substantially destroyed.*

This somewhat circumspect conclusion will discountenance only the extreme view[1†] to the effect that *all* thought (or even all human intelligence) is dependent on language; the view, naively formulated, that all thinking is necessarily done "in words". But our conclusion seems unlikely, in itself, to open up any major new insights into the nature of thought, or intelligence! Manifestly, human intelligence includes a great range of abilities which are scarcely to be satisfactorily captured by the RPM test alone, nor for that matter by any subset of the standardized tests commonly used to assess non-verbal intelligence in a normal population.

The notion of "non-verbal intelligence" implies its contrast term, "*verbal* intelligence". Within the terms in which the research I have just been reviewing is conceived, might we not go on to ask some more subtle, more revealing question about the relation of aphasia to this hypothetical "verbal intelligence"?

At this point it is worth reminding ourselves that the notion of "intelligence" invoked by this contrast refers, in practice, to nothing more theoretically substantial than *relative* differences in achievement at particular tests. And the "verbal"/"non-verbal" contrast is itself based on a quite informal separation of those subtests which, respectively, do or do not require the use of language for their administration or execution, plus the empirical observation that test-scores tend to intercorrelate, in the general population, slightly more highly within than between these two very loosely defined groups of tests (e.g. Wechsler, 1955). But that is all. The conceptual armoury that has accumulated from pragmatic attempts to quantify *relative* intelligence (intelligent quotients, or IQ) will not enable us even to formulate the question about the relation of aphasia and "verbal" intelligence coherently, let alone to answer it. The temptation even to try was just an example of trying to do science *in words*. It is high time, therefore, to turn round on the terms in which the question, whose pursuit has led us to this rather unenlightening position, was initially formulated: that is, the terms of "ordinary" language.

† Superscript numbers refer to Notes at end of chapter.

Have We Been Asking the Wrong Questions?

Ordinary Language

Major advances in our understanding of the relations between "cognition" and "language", I believe, must have fundamental implications not only for linguistics and psychology but for our whole philosophical conception of man. For this reason it seemed natural, and perhaps appropriate, to try to formulate the scientific questions involved, in a way that would appear to bring out most directly their *philosophical* relevance. Natural, but mistaken. "Philosophical" questions—perhaps it is better to say the puzzles that typically exercise philosophers—are generally expressed in terms of culturally conventional, i.e., "ordinary" language. Perhaps in the hope of engaging these great issues of philosophy, investigators have recurrently attempted to translate questions such as "Does thought depend on language?", or "Does human intelligence depend on the possession of some undifferentiated faculty of language, or language competence?", quite directly into a research design, as though these were empirically decidable questions. The research I have just reviewed was, often quite explicitly though with more or less variations in sophistication, dictated by questions of this "ordinary language" form. This was also, and transparently, the reason why the results were so generally uninformative.

Fortunately, we are no longer confined—except by this misdirected pursuit of the philosophical broad sweep—to the unsystematic taxonomy of mental faculties implicit in the categories of ordinary language. Until relatively recently, it is true, there was little serious alternative. The cognitive psychology that flourished before about 1918 (including its masterpiece: James, 1890) was formulated almost entirely in the hybrid phenomenological categories of ordinary language. After that period, and until the 1950s or 1960s, psychology, now in the grip of Radical Behaviourism, struggled on with a meagre, pseudo-technical vocabulary drawn, in fact, from the same source but supposedly (and completely unsuccessfully) pruned of reference to subjective experience. The principal exceptions to the Behaviourist rule were, first, the Gestalt psychologists, who continued to use, unexpurgated, the ordinary vocabulary of phenomenal experience; and second, curiously enough, the neurologists, who remained even more catholic in their use of the psychological vernacular.

Beginning in the 1950s, however, an alternative conceptual vocabulary to that of ordinary language, for the analysis of mental processes, began at last to take shape. This development was the product of an entirely new scientific paradigm: the design and study of intelligent artefacts, the discipline known, rather unfelicitously, as "artificial intelligence" (AI). The concepts of information-processing and of physical symbol systems (Newell, 1981), developed and explored in AI, became, as is well known, the essential basis of the new cognitive psychology from the early 1960s. There has taken place, since then, an accelerating convergence of interests and approach between cognitive psychologists and those, within AI, whose explicit aim is the creation and testing of theories of *human* cognition (Norman, 1981). This "convergence", it is fair to add, has involved considerably greater change, in fundamental conception of their discipline, on the part of cognitive psychologists than it has among those already engaged in AI! And there are many other areas of psychology, for example, the study of cognitive development, on which the information-processing paradigm has scarcely begun to impinge. Nonetheless, it seems no exaggeration to suppose that the conceptual vocabulary that is in course of development through the study of AI will come to play a role, *vis-à-vis* the future of psychology, comparable, at least, to the place of mathematics in the classical sciences.

This is not the place to review these developments. I have attempted, elsewhere, to assess some of their implications for cognitive psychology (Allport, 1978, 1980a). Relevant to the present chapter, however, are a number of very general reflections derived from cognitive science about what are, and are not, scientifically fruitful ways of asking questions about mind.

Cognitive Science and Natural Language Understanding

In work on natural language understanding, the first generation of AI projects to achieve some operational success still focused largely on the analysis of isolated sentences (e.g. Winograd, 1972; Schank, 1975). The operational criteria of "understanding" adopted in projects of this kind were much the same as the ones people use, informally, to assess whether another person has understood: the ability to paraphrase, or to answer questions about what one has been told, or otherwise to act on it as an instruction or request. (For a discussion of these criteria, see Searle, 1980). These machine systems depended for their successful performance on translating sentences into a *language-independent*, conceptual (or "semantic") representation, which could then be related to other conceptual information possessed by the system. Only in this form could the new information be interpreted or acted upon, or further inferences be made.

Cognitive psychologists have also provided numerous empirical demonstrations that the way in which *human* subjects encode and remember linguistic episodes (stories, instructions, even isolated sentences) includes a representation that is wholly independent of the original linguistic construction and wording, and in which inferences made by the subject are not subsequently distinguished from propositions contained in the original text (Bransford and Johnson, 1973; Sanford and Garrod, 1981). Surface linguistic detail is generally found to be explicitly available to human listeners (or readers) *only* in respect of the current, or most recent, phrase or sentence (e.g. Jarvella and Hermann, 1972; Sachs, 1974), though in some individuals with acquired defects of verbal "short-term" memory even this may be unavailable (e.g. Saffran and Marin, 1975). (Interestingly, despite this deficit, such patients can demonstrate adequate comprehension of most kinds of ordinary language.)

This is not to deny that many surface-specific details of experience (not only linguistic detail) are encoded, and can affect subsequent behaviour over much greater time intervals (e.g. Kolers, 1978). The important point to be made here, however, is that in many cases human subjects are unable to identify retrospectively even the medium in which they experienced some happening—for example, whether in pictures or in words—although the underlying event itself is remembered (e.g. Davis and Sinha, 1950; Rosenberg and Simon, 1977). This kind of result appears to demand a common mode of representation, regardless of the medium, language or non-language, by which the information was acquired.

Manifestly, much of our (culturally transmitted) knowledge about the world is acquired through the medium of natural language. But this does not, in itself, carry any implications about the code(s) in which the results of that learning come to be represented.

Returning now to work on natural language understanding in AI, the focus has shifted almost entirely to the comprehension of extended discourse (stories, dialogue, etc.) although the operational criteria of comprehension—summarizing, question-answering, etc.—remain much the same. In this work it is a commonplace that the greater part of the "understanding" process needed to achieve these criteria consists of inference and expansion, a kind of *problem-solving* activity resulting in the "filling in" of contextual, referential and causal continuity, preconditions, motives, etc., on the basis of knowledge which the speaker (or writer) normally expects to be shared by his listener (reader), and which he therefore need not make explicit (e.g. Charniak, 1976; Grosz, 1977; Schank and Abelson, 1977). Again, this contextual knowledge is not itself represented *in* natural language. Of course, how knowledge should be, or can be, represented and used—even, whether the currently fashionable notions of "representation" are appropriate at all to biological embodiments of mind—are the central issues of debate in Cognitive Science (cf. Winograd, 1981). For now, the essential point is that there can be no language understanding without the appropriate "pre-understanding", i.e., without a framework of prior knowledge about the subject of discourse, into which the new information can be integrated and from which missing information can be inferred. It follows that there can be no such thing as a *general* "language understanding device", *separate* from the rest of the cognitive system.

Of course, there can be *specialized* language understanding systems, whose knowledge is confined to some particular, partially-independent domain of reference, from Winograd's *Blocks World* to geology or chess or electronics or cooking or medical diagnosis or politics, or indeed to some subset of common human plans, goals, and their interactions. Indeed, for each of these domains there is an AI system that can claim some degree of "understanding". But language understanding (and meaningful language production) can occur *only* insofar as the system performing it also embodies knowledge, outside of natural language, that it can in some way apply to the topic of discourse, to what the language is *about*.

To conclude, these knowledge-based, intelligent (i.e. problem-solving) processes, though necessary to the understanding (and meaningful generation) of natural language, are in no sense specific to, or "part of", language itself. Neither do they depend on it.

Information-processing Components of Mind

Ordinary language provides an abundance of descriptive categories of cognitive ability or achievement, including the conventional mental *faculties* of "thought", "perception", "memory", "language", "reasoning", "imagination", "attention", as well as evaluative categories—"intelligence", "creativity", and so on. In all information-processing analyses of the phenomena (or dispositions) to which these categories loosely refer, and in all AI attempts to reproduce them, one general theme emerges again and again. This is that these phenomena, wherever they can be observed, are generated through the *interaction* of many different subprocesses or subsystems. There is not some subprocess, nor any *collection* of subprocesses, called "perception" (for example) that we could *separate off from other subprocesses* called "memory", "attention", "reasoning", still less from "intelligence"; nor vice versa. In other words, these descriptive *faculties* (or whatever they are) are not *parts* of the mind. They do not partition its structure. They do not, together, make up the constituents of mind. But on the contrary many different constituent processes interact, in overlapping combinations, to make *them*.

Nevertheless, the belief that we can usefully think of these emergent faculties as separable compartments of mind is extraordinarily hard to shake off. Traditionally, the study of psychology was divided up into supposedly distinct topics such as "perception", "learning", "memory", "skill", "attention", which were actually thought of, and taught, as quite independent subjects, sharing only, and to a limited extent, a common set of experimental methods. Indeed, some undergraduate psychology courses are still organized on these lines!

Once this essential lesson has been assimilated, it is natural to look again for the ways in which mental architecture *can* be appropriately segmented, if not in terms of these conventional faculties. The pursuit of this question has in fact been the principal goal of the whole "information-processing" approach to psychology over the past 20 years, viz. the identification of separable subprocesses (Posner, 1978; Lachman, Lachman and Butterfield, 1979). It is only recently, however, that information-processing psychologists have woken up to the extraordinarily powerful source of evidence on this issue in the study of individual brain-injured patients. We turn shortly to examples of this approach, illustrating some of the subprocesses of language. But, before doing so and at the risk of slight repetition, one or two cautionary remarks have still to be made about the logic of this approach, if we are, at last, to begin to ask the right questions.

The Neuropsychological Single-case Method

It would obviously be foolish to assume that we know in advance in what ways the specialized subsystems of the brain are segmented, nor into what, more elementary, building-blocks particular human faculties, let alone the performance of specific experimental tasks, can be broken down. The selective effects of neurological lesions on everyday skills can be, and often are, extraordinarily counter-intuitive. In the present state of knowledge, these complex patterns of selective loss and preserved ability can be charted only by detailed and extensive testing of *individual* patients, generally needing many hours or even weeks to complete. Grouping patients together *a priori* on the basis of some broad behavioural or linguistic typology, or on the basis of approximate lesion site, as is still all too frequently done, is bound, at best, to lose much of the power and precision of the individual case study. At worst it may promote fundamentally misleading conclusions about the functional interdependence of different mental abilities.

The primary goal of neuropsychology is to try to identify these functionally separable, or independent, mental "components". Its principal means of doing so is by the discovery of so-called "*double dissociations*". It is no matter how strongly two different kinds of ability may be correlated in the general population (or in some pathological subgroup). If, in some individual, ability A is intact where ability B is seriously impaired or even totally absent, then the performance of A cannot be functionally dependent on the ensemble of mechanisms, B′, responsible for B. Moreover, if another patient is found to exhibit the complementary pattern of disabilities, where A is impaired but B intact, then there is strong reason to believe that A and B reflect truly independent functional subsystems. This combined pattern of results is referred to as a double dissociation of the functions A′ and B′. Naturally, A′ and B′ may themselves subsequently be fractionated into yet more elementary components, by the discovery of further dissociations.

This inference from double dissociations assumes that psychological mechanisms A' and B' are organized essentially in the same way in both patients, prior to their injury. Furthermore, if the inference is to be generalized to the normal population, it assumes that these patients do not happen to share some quite idiosyncratic functional arrangement of information-processing systems. Our confidence in this assumption will naturally increase if we find other individual patients with similar patterns of selective preservation and loss.

An objection that is sometimes raised against the use of data from brain-damaged patients, to infer the organization of normal mental function, is that the pathological behaviour may reflect the creation of quite new, compensatory processes never observed in normal function. Indeed, this is a possibility of interest in its own right, for which we should constantly be on the alert. On the other hand, in many cases the impaired performance can be very naturally and consistently interpreted as the product simply of a diminished set of subsystems—the same subsystems as those responsible for normal, intact performance (see below). Besides, specific patterns of impaired performance often emerge too soon after brain injury for it to be plausible that they are the product of radically new functional systems. Second, specific disabilities resulting from brain injury often show tragically little change or recovery over long periods of time. Third, and most important, in a rapidly increasing number of instances to which this methodology has been applied the selective deficits observed are found to correspond with modular, information-processing subsystems and their interrelations that can also be inferred from the experimental analysis of *normal* psychological function.

The clinical case-study has a long and distinguished tradition in the neurological literature, but its systematic integration with the information-processing analyses of cognitive psychology is of quite recent origin. Some historically significant benchmarks in this development are Warrington and Shallice (1969), Marshall and Newcombe (1973), Marin, Saffran and Schwartz (1976), Coltheart, Patterson and Marshall (1980). Valuable further discussion of the methodology, its strengths and pitfalls is given by Shallice (1979, 1981).

I now turn to examples of this approach, pointing to separable components within the language system. These, in turn, raise more specific questions about the relationship of cognition and language.

The Separability of Language Functions

The question of intelligence and aphasia, with which we began, was framed in terms of some undifferentiated "language faculty", a global language competence. However, one of the most striking aspects of aphasia is the way in which particular components of language ability can be disrupted more or less independently. Insofar as language competence must have, in some form, a physical embodiment in the brain, we find ourselves compelled to think not in terms of *one competence* but of many distinct but interacting *competences*.

Lexicon

<blockquote>Adam gave names to all cattle, and to the fowl of the air, and to every beast of the field.

Genesis (2:20)</blockquote>

The function of natural language which is perhaps apparent before any other is this one of naming or, more generally, referring. In aphasia one of the most frequently made observations is that this *referential*, or *lexical* ability can be impaired apparently independently of *syntactic* and other functions of language; and vice versa. Here, for example, is a transcript from the speech of an aphasic patient (AL). He is describing a picture that I have put in front of him. The picture, a somewhat crowded kitchen scene, portrays a score of aggravated "dangers in the home". (On the cooker a saucepan is boiling over, another gas-ring flares up, while dishtowels hang inches above a third, uncovered, gas flame. The oven door is left open. A small boy reaches for an open box of matches. Also within his reach is a pill-bottle, the cap off, some pills scattered beside it. In the background a teenager is tossing paraffin onto a smouldering fire, while another child is about to insert a screwdriver into an electric power socket, etc.) AL worked his way around this catalogue of incipient disasters, starting with the cooker:

> "You never do *that* with a place there, you push it and do that (gestures to cooker controls). That is the same thing underneath; there's a little one to do that as well. *That* you don't have to do, either . . . I don't know what's happened to that, but it's taken that out. That is mm there without doing it, the things that are being done—you know the thing I mean? . . . That's the same too; that's all wrong. What else is there? . . . Oh yes, she's doing some stuff here and it's really rather bad to do things there. You don't do *that*; you take it and do it slow, . . . And not *that* anyway: it's usually somebody else (an electrician?) . . . Oh, of course, I'm sorry, I should have told you that *those* things there (pills?) were done from—mm—and put . . . (gestures) . . . Can you understand what I'm doing? This is usually made, mm (gestures closing lid) and put somewhere well out of the way . . . I expect there's even more if I can only see . . . ."

What is immediately apparent in AL's speech is the absence of the words that normally refer to *particular species* of objects and events. In their place, AL falls back on a restricted vocabulary of the most general, referentially non-specific words in the language: demonstratives; pronouns; nouns like *thing, stuff, place*; verbs such as *do, make, put, see*. In an extended sample of his spontaneous speech, no more than 1% of the words were nouns with specific, concrete reference like "car". Confronted with a specific object which he is asked to name, he is at a loss. Yet his speech is otherwise fluent, prosodically expressive and the sentence structures, apart from some fragmentation and false starts as he gropes for a specific word, apparently normal.

At first sight AL's severe expressive anomia is not paralleled by any significant defect of lexical *comprehension*; at least so it appears in conversational situations where extra-linguistic cues to specific reference are generally available. Formal testing, however, reveals a more complex picture (Allport and Funnell, 1981; Funnell, in preparation). To begin with, we can ascertain that the word-forms (specific object-names) which he cannot himself evoke either in spoken or written form must still somehow be represented in his mental lexicon. Thus, presented with a series of object-names, he can readily distinguish them, as real words, from similar looking or sounding nonsense-words. He can, without error, match a spoken object-name to the correct one of a dozen written names, though he cannot do this task with nonsense words. He can even read some common object-names aloud (65% of our sample). Yet he is *completely* unable to read aloud written nonsense words of similar length and orthography, confirming that his successful reading aloud of object-names must be *lexically* mediated.

Further, presented with a specific object (say, a carpenter's nail) and two semantically dissimilar names (e.g. Nail and Bird) to choose between, AL has no difficulty in selecting the appropriate name of the object. When this task is made a little more exacting, however, for instance by confronting him with two semantically closely related names (e.g. the words Screw and Nail, and the picture of a screw (Fig. 4.4); Brush and Comb, together with the picture of a comb; Shoe and Boot; Wall and Fence, etc.) AL's choices become hesitant and he sometimes chooses incorrectly. That is, he can assign words to a broad semantic field, but he has difficulty in making more precise *differentia* of word-meanings.

Nail   Screw

FIG. 4.4. Picture-word matching task.

It is important to stress, however, that this loss of "semantic" boundaries does not in any way imply that the underlying concepts have lost their distinctiveness. Thus, AL has no difficulty in matching, for example, pictures of either a hammer or a screwdriver appropriately to the *picture* of a screw or a nail, nor in miming their use, nor for that matter in using the real objects. (Indeed, AL cuts his own special-purpose screw-threads on his home lathe.) The same applies to the other objects (brush and comb, etc.) whose *names* he cannot reliably distinguish in meaning.

The nature of AL's lexical, or referential disability can now begin to be picked out. First, spoken (and written) word-forms themselves appear to be unimpaired. Second, and importantly, the concepts to which these specific object names properly refer are similarly intact. Consequently, it appears that his disability must be located in the processes that translate *between* the word-forms and their underlying conceptual representations.

Several recent studies have investigated the de-differentiation of semantic boundaries, and the reduced ability of object-names to evoke semantically related words, in some groups of aphasic patients (e.g. Lhermitte *et al.*, 1971; Goodglass and Baker, 1976; Caramazza and Berndt, 1978; Grossman, 1981). However, these experiments explored only the patients' understanding of the *words*; they did not separately investigate their understanding of the same contrasts and relationships extra-linguistically. In pointing to "semantic" disturbances in aphasic patients, it is important to discriminate between, on the one hand, a disorder affecting the non-linguistic mental representation of objects, actions, relations, etc.—what I have referred to as their "conceptual" representations—and, on the other hand (as in the case of AL), disturbance to the processes by which *words* are *mapped onto* these representations, either expressively or receptively. These are issues of course closely related to the central topic of this chapter, and urgently in need of further empirical and theoretical clarification.

Syntax

AL's speech was marked by an inability to evoke the names of specific species of objects or actions. Yet his prosody, and syntax, were otherwise apparently normal. Contrast this with another patient, RC, whose disability appears to be precisely the opposite. Here is a brief excerpt of her speech, describing the same picture as AL:

> "Fire . . . open . . . matches . . . light matches . . . naughty boy . . . ha, ha . . . shut the door . . . knife . . . water . . . tablets . . . shut . . . (pointing to high shelf) up . . . children . . ."

In RC's speech there is little or no sentence structure, and long pauses occur between each holophrase. Indeed, the direct *naming* of objects or actions, so conspicuously lacking in AL's speech, appears to be just about the only linguistic function that remains in RC's utterances.

This apparent "double dissociation" between syntactic and lexical functions of language, evident between different types of aphasic patient, was emphasized long ago by the linguist, Roman Jakobson (1964), and has been noted and commented on many times since (Lesser, 1978). Some evidence that this may not be quite the straightforward and unambiguous "double dissociation" that it seems, however, has been put forward by Allport and Funnell (1981).

In many cases, at least, "agrammatic" patients like RC are found to be impaired not only expressively, in the *generation* of syntactic construction but also receptively, in their *comprehension* (Caramazza and Zurif, 1976). Again, an important and interesting question arises, whether this "agrammatism"—this deficit in generating or interpreting structural relations in language—is confined strictly to linguistic comprehension, or whether it is, necessarily, reflected also in impaired understanding of the *conceptual* relations and contrasts—such as those between agent and patient, between container and contained—which such patients demonstrably fail to understand syntactically, through language. Saffran, Schwartz and Marin (1980) have recently been able to show that, in some clear-cut "agrammatic" aphasics at least, there is *no* such corresponding conceptual disability.

In the studies of intelligence-test performance in aphasic groups, reviewed earlier (e.g. Kertesz, 1979), the agrammatic patients generally obtained similar scores to their normal controls. Conversely, there is some indication that syntactic processes can be doubly-dissociated, surviving the destruction of other cognitive abilities. There are a number of detailed accounts of profoundly demented patients, apparently incapable even of minimal goal-directed action (e.g. turning a door handle to open a door) let alone of achieving a score on conventional intellectual tests, yet whose syntactic skills were impressively well preserved (e.g. Whitaker, 1976; Schwartz et al., 1979).

Modality-specific Systems

Syntax

The preceding discussion may have given the impression that syntactic competence is either lost, or preserved, as an undifferentiated whole. Of course, this too is an oversimplification. Students of aphasia have described a hierarchy of increasingly severe syntactic deficits in the spontaneous utterance of different aphasic patients (e.g. De Villiers, 1974). I am not aware that a similar classification has yet been made in respect of syntactic *comprehension*. More interestingly, there may be at least some degree of *modality-specific* specialization of syntactic mechanisms: i.e. independently for written and for spoken language. Thus, patients are occasionally seen who show selective syntactic deficits in processing the *written but not the spoken* form (e.g. Low, 1931; Allport and Funnell, 1981). There are also occasional reports of bilingual aphasic patients who suffer acquired lexical or syntactic deficits in one language, but not in another (Albert and Obler, 1978; Silverberg and Gordon, 1979).

Some further evidence that appears to point to the independence of syntactic processing in spoken and written language comes from the analysis of normal subjects. Tierney (1973) and Shaffer (1975) asked typists to transcribe two unrelated texts concurrently: one which they typed from a written copy, the other which they listened to and repeated back orally ("shadowed") at the same time. It is well known that typing, like oral shadowing, is both faster and more accurate when the text to be transcribed consists of syntactically well-formed phrases, rather than the same words in syntactically unstructured lists. In both Shaffer's and Tierney's experiments the striking feature of the results was that, after only a small amount of practice, their subjects were able to carry out *both* these tasks at the same time, without losing either speed or accuracy. Certainly there was not the reduction in *either* performance that would be seen in typing or shadowing syntactically unordered word-lists. This seems to imply that their subjects were able to take advantage, simultaneously, of the independent syntactic structure present in *both* the written and the spoken texts. In contrast, when both texts were presented auditorily, one to each ear (and in a number of other interesting conditions), concurrent performance turned out to be more or less impossible. A number of issues are involved in these results, which go beyond the present discussion (see Allport, 1980b). However, insofar as there are, in the brain, mechanisms specialized for *syntactic* processing (as the selective deficits in aphasia appear to imply), these dual-task results with normal subjects go further to encourage the view that we may have not just one, mode-independent syntactic system, but separate, mode-specific systems respectively for spoken and for written language.

If this conclusion is correct, there seems no compelling reason to suppose that the two systems work in formally equivalent ways. This possibility—that the two systems are not equivalent—prompts the following conjecture. When theoretical linguists consult their own intuitions about the syntactic acceptability of particular sentences, they do so typically in respect of the *written* expression. Could it be that the intuitions which they thus evoke, and hence the theoretical devices they invent to accommodate them, draw principally (even exclusively) on just *one* of these psychological systems, namely those specialized for the processing of written language? If so, this might have something to do with the curious discrepancies that are sometimes noted between judgments of linguistic "acceptability" made by theoretical linguists and by more ordinary, perhaps more aural, individuals.

Lexicon

In the case of lexical mechanisms there is more substantial evidence for the functional autonomy of systems representing, respectively, spoken and written language. Most immediately dramatic is the evidence provided by so-called "*deep dyslexic*" patients, attempting to read aloud, or, in some cases, to write to dictation, individual written words (Coltheart *et al.*, 1980).

Both these tasks require some kind of translation process, though in opposite directions, between the written and spoken forms of the word. For some words with completely "regular" spelling, one might perhaps expect to be able to carry out this translation without recourse to specific (i.e. *lexical*) knowledge about individual words.[2] But for many words in English—or French or, for that matter, in Chinese—the pronunciation of the word cannot be unambiguously derived from its written form without referring to some lexical knowledge of the particular word. In fact, when deep dyslexic patients are asked to read aloud even orthographically regular written nonsense-words, like *wid* and *gloob*, they are unable to comply. They also fail to read aloud many familiar real words. Not only can they not overtly *produce* the spoken form of the word (though the same patient can repeat it orally without difficulty when he *hears* it), they are also unable to judge whether different written (but not spoken) words would sound alike when pronounced, or to make any other judgments about the pronunciation of written words (Saffran and Marin, 1977; Patterson and Marcel, 1977). In other words, deep dyslexic patients are apparently unable to translate, *directly*, between written and spoken language, between spelling and sound.

In spite of this, deep dyslexic patients do succeed in reading aloud a large proportion of real words, particularly words that have concrete or "imageable" reference. (For an admirable survey, see Coltheart, 1980.) But the most striking phenomenon in deep dyslexia—Coltheart argues that it should be treated as the defining phenomenon—is the occurrence of "*semantic*" errors in reading aloud. Examples of some typical "semantic" errors made by a patient (SK), whom I have studied, are shown in Table 4.1. Approximately 25% of SK's incorrect responses are of this kind. These errors occur even when the patient is slowly and carefully reading isolated written words, with unlimited time to look at the word and to correct her responses. Their obvious property is that they preserve at least some of the meaning of the "target" word that the patient is attempting to read. Thus *balloon*, like *parachute*, is an anti-gravity device, perhaps also sharing some of its visual attributes; *catapult*, like *propellor*, is a means of rapid propulsion through the air; and so on. In the examples on the right of Table 4.1 (*anecdote → narrator*, etc.), the link between target word and response suggests association through a shared "schema".

The preservation of meaning from target word to spoken response (often with considerable accuracy: *commerce → business*; *mishap → accident*) confirms that the written word, for which the patient cannot generate the correct spoken form, nevertheless must have succeeded in evoking some representation of its meaning. Other tests, for instance in which the patient is asked to make synonymy, judgments between pairs of written words that

TABLE 4.1. *Examples of errors in reading aloud isolated words by a deep dyslexic patient (SK)*

Word presented	Reading response	Word presented	Reading response	Word presented	Reading response
parachute	→ balloon	commerce	→ business	anecdote	→ narrator
propellor	→ catapult	mishap	→ accident	ambition	→ career
binocular	→ telescope	victory	→ triumph	jest	→ clown
sandal	→ slipper	arithmetic	→ mathematics	applause	→ audience
apricot	→ peach	receipt	→ voucher	quarantine	→ injection
gnat	→ insect	earl	→ duke	saddle	→ stirrup
geranium	→ nasturtium	element	→ substance	thermometer	→ temperature

he cannot reliably read aloud, or to match the referents of written words and pictures, bear out this conclusion in a more controlled situation (Patterson, 1981). Beyond doubt, in deep dyslexic patients, written words can still gain access to referential word-meanings; and in some of these patients at least they do so with great precision.

The important point for our argument, however, is that the *written words must evoke word-meanings without being able to evoke the corresponding spoken word-form*. This combination—of inability to derive a phonological representation of a written word, while successfully evoking its meaning—is direct evidence both for the independent mental representation of written word-forms *and* for their independent access to word meanings. To make room for this combination of disabilities and preserved abilities, we shall have to recognize at least three functionally separable systems of representation in the mental lexicon, each having independent (and hence independently vulnerable) channels of communication to the other two systems, as illustrated in Fig. 4.5.

In terms of Fig. 4.5, the symptoms of deep dyslexia result from a breakdown in the direct communication (or "translation") between orthographic (**C**) and phonological (**B**) word-forms, i.e. in channel **e**. Consequently, reading aloud, for these patients, must depend on route **cAb**. In addition, the often imperfect semantic overlap between target-word and spoken response suggests some degree of malfunction within the remaining route **cAb** also. In certain patients (Marshall and Newcombe, 1980) there is evidence that channel **c** must be compromised. In others, in whom semantic judgments about written words, *without* the requirement of overt naming, appear to be error-free, there remains a deficit of spoken naming—i.e. channel **b** (Patterson, 1981).

Other, selective deficits in the lexical comprehension and production of spoken and written language can be represented, similarly, in terms of damage to one or more of the ten channels of communication shown in Fig. 4.5, or to any of the three main lexical components, **A**, **B**, or **C** themselves

82   Approaches to Language

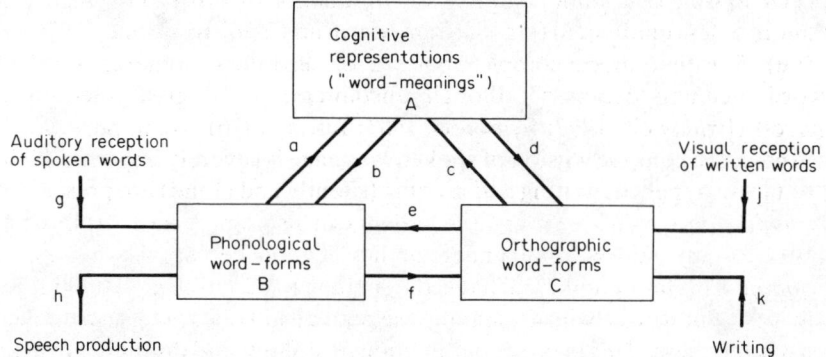

FIG. 4.5. Components of the mental lexicon. Each of the three principal codes (A, B and C) and the channels linking them (a–k) are independently vulnerable to cerebral injury (see text).

(Allport and Funnell, 1981). Here, first, are some disorders in the processing of *written* language (Ellis, 1981; Patterson, 1981; Shallice, 1981).

(i) "Semantic" errors in writing to dictation (e.g. Marshall and Newcombe, 1980; Morton, 1980) implicate a breakdown in channel **f**.

(ii) Breakdown of normal reading with preserved ability to write, both spontaneously and to dictation. This basic pattern can take more than one form, depending on the quality of reading ability, if any, which remains. In terms of the highly simplified diagram in Fig. 4.5, however, this state of affairs is represented by damage to the *pre*-lexical channel **j**.

(iii) Breakdown of reading ability (still with preserved auditory comprehension) is more commonly accompanied by a corresponding loss of written spelling, though not necessarily by a loss of the ability to form, or to copy, letters. This state of affairs can be simply represented as the result of damage to, or functional isolation of, the orthographic word-forms themselves (**C**).

(iv) Other patterns of selective reading disorder can be shown to depend on either complete (Coltheart *et al.*, 1982; Patterson, 1982) or partial (Warrington and Shallice, 1979) failure of written word-forms to evoke their appropriate word meanings, i.e. failure of channel **c**, though spoken words may still be understood normally.

Selective disorders of *spoken* language include the following:

(v) Pathology restricted to the *post*-lexical mechanisms of speech production, without other language disorder, represented by impairment of channel **h**.

(vi) Conversely, so-called "pure word-deafness" can be economically attributed to the *pre*-lexical channel **g**. The patient, without significant non-linguistic hearing loss, is profoundly impaired in the comprehension of spoken words. He is also unable to write to dictation. Yet his spontaneous speech, as well as his understanding and production of written language, can be more or less unaffected (e.g. Saffran, Marin and Yeni-Komshian, 1976).

(vii) A rather more complex pattern of disorders, sometimes called "word meaning deafness", though uncommon, is of great theoretical interest (Bramwell, 1897; Symonds, 1953; Luria, 1976). As in pure word-deafness, the comprehension of spoken language is severely impaired while spontaneous speech, writing and reading (silently and aloud) are preserved. But *unlike* pure word-deafness, the patient can also repeat back orally what is said to him (still without understanding it) and he can also *write it to dictation*. This latter ability includes the spelling to dictation of orthographically irregular words, whose meaning the patient still does not grasp until he has written them. This bizarre combination of abilities and disabilities can be quite economically accounted for, in terms of Fig. 4.5, as a selective breakdown of channel **a**, while the phonological and orthographic word-forms, and the channels between them (**e** and **f**) must be intact. On the other hand, for any model of language mechanisms that does not recognize the separability of the lexical components **A**, **B** and **C**, and the independent status of channels **a** and **c**, this pattern of language disorder must be frankly inexplicable.

The Psychological Embodiment of "Words" and "Meanings"

A Modality-independent Lexicon?

In theoretical linguistics the *lexicon* possessed by every skilled user of a language is commonly represented as being in some way *independent of the medium*—speech, writing, etc.—*in which it is manifest* (e.g. Lyons, 1981). This notion seems to imply that, besides the psychological codes representing individual *phonological* and *orthographic* word-forms—whose independent existence the evidence I have just reviewed compels us to acknowledge—the mental lexicon must include some third, *modality-independent* or *abstract* representation of each individual word or lexeme in the subject's vocabulary. Thus, in place of the direct, modality-specific communication between (respectively) phonological and orthographic word-forms and what I have referred to, so far, simply as "word-meanings", as shown in Fig. 4.5 and again in Fig. 4.6a, the postulate of an underlying, *abstract* lexicon suggests an alternative arrangement like that shown in Fig. 4.6b. (A similar argument might presumably be applied to the modality-specific *syntactic* mechanisms that I discussed earlier.) This proposal, in turn, has major implications for our whole enquiry into the relations of "language" and "cognition". For if there exists some deeper, modality-free embodiment of our lexical (and possibly syntactic) knowledge, besides the specific phonological and orthographic codes we have already identified, then the

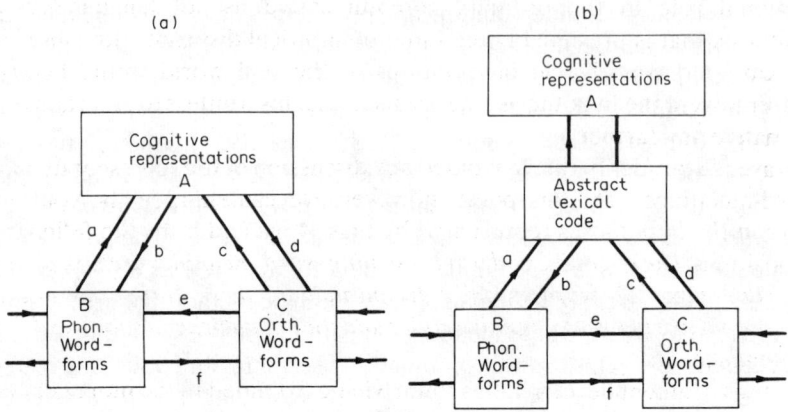

FIG. 4.6. Two alternative models of the mental lexicon (see text).

demonstration of preserved cognitive abilities in totally aphasic patients could no longer be put forward as persuasive evidence concerning the independence of "cognition" and "language". That is, even though the superficial, *modality-specific* language systems might be shown to be impaired or even abolished, there would be no guarantee that the "deep", mode-independent representation in these patients was not still perfectly intact. Indeed, some aphasiologists (e.g. Weigl and Bierwisch, 1970) have even proposed that the "central" representation of language is *never* affected in aphasia!

To suppose that underlying language competence can never be affected by neural injury is surely too strong a claim, since it implies that language competence ultimately can have no physical embodiment in the brain. However, the possibility that in at least some profoundly aphasic patients—namely in those individuals in whom other intellectual abilities are well preserved!—the postulated "central" representation of language remains intact is sufficient at least seriously to weaken any arguments from this source. Certainly it is not easy to see how the postulate of intact "central" language, despite the absence of external manifestations of language, is to be ruled out in individual aphasic patients.

For this reason it will be of crucial importance for our enquiry to establish whether the mental representation of language does in fact include this kind of modality-independent, "central" lexicon. If it does exist, its function must presumably be to mediate *between* the "peripheral" (phonological and orthographic) representations of specific word-forms and the representation of word-meanings, as illustrated in Fig. 4.6b. (The alternative, that the postulated "central" lexical representation of language *exists*, but plays no functional role in the ordinary communicative use of language, is a hypothesis that is presumably immune to empirical disproof. But since, in that case, no conceivable observations in the real world would be any different, were the hypothesis true *or* false, it seems fruitless to entertain this alternative any further.)

I have, so far, deliberately avoided any discussion of the representation of "word-meanings". At this point, however, we can sharpen the contrast between the hypotheses represented by Figs. 4.6 a and b, by the following proposition: *The cognitive codes representing word-meanings are not, in any way, language- or word-specific. In particular, there is no one-to-one correspondence between cognitive codes and individual lexemes, or words, in the language.*

As the argument develops, this claim will be extended to the more general proposition that cognitive codes, in which the so-called "deep structures *of language*" are represented, do not in fact *belong to* (or depend on) communicative natural language; but that they are common to (and indeed depend on) the mechanisms responsible for our (non-linguistic) sensory and motor interactions with our physical environment.

The hypothesis of an abstract lexical code is still not an easy hypothesis to test, even granted that the postulated lexical code plays the kind of functional role in ordinary language-processing that we have attributed to it. However, the following series of observations represent one attempt to test the hypothesis. The experiments were carried out by Elaine Funnell and have been briefly described elsewhere (Allport and Funnell, 1981). However, the hypothesis under test is sufficiently important, and is apparently sufficiently widely held, to justify going through the argument here in some detail. The results, as it turns out, appear to be incompatible with the hypothesis.

As will become clear, our experimental test of this hypothesis could not be performed on normal subjects, in whom we can assume there to be available *direct* means of translation between orthographic and phonological word-forms (channels **e** and **f**). The argument is instantiated, instead, through the cooperation of an aphasic patient, AL, whom I described earlier in this chapter.

The tests consisted of a series of five simple experiments. Between them they establish that the preconditions for testing the hypothesis were in fact satisfied by the patient, AL. The final experiment then constitutes a critical test between predictions derived from the alternative hypotheses, represented, respectively, in Figs. 4.6 a and b.

All five experiments required the comparison of spoken and written words. The standard format of each experiment was as follows. On each trial the subject was presented with two written words, each one typed individually on a plain white card. The experimenter then said one word, and the subject's task was to point to the written alternative that he believed best matched the spoken name.

(i) In the first experiment, AL was presented with the written names of the related common objects, e.g. SOCK and GLOVE, and the spoken name of one of them (e.g. "sock"). His task was simply to point to the corresponding written word (SOCK). AL performed the task without any errors, over 16 different word-triads. In terms of the hypotheses represented in Figs. 4.6 a and b, this task could be done *either* by direct translation between spoken and written word-forms (channels **e** or **f**) *or* indirectly, by mediation of a higher level code (via word-meanings, in model 4.6a, or via the common abstract lexemes of model 4.6b).

(ii) The second experiment required the subject to decide which of two written words were more nearly *related in meaning* to a spoken word (e.g. SOCK: GLOVE: "mitten"). This task can presumably be done *only* by comparing word-*meanings*; simple translation between phonological and orthographic word-forms, or into the abstract lexical code alone, would not be sufficient. Again, AL performed 16 trials of this task without error. Note that, in terms of the role attributed to the abstract lexical code in model 4.6b, in mediating access to the representation of word-meanings, it follows that this abstract lexical code, if it exists, must be operating effectively in AL!

The next, and crucial precondition for our experimental rationale was established in two steps:

(iii) First, the subject was required to compare spoken and written nonsense-words (Cobe, Doop, etc.), a task which, unlike the previous two tasks, patently cannot be solved through the comparison of word-meanings. In contrast to his error-free performance of the first two tasks, AL was now unable to pick the correct written alternative with better than chance accuracy. (He was also unable to read any of these stimuli aloud.) This inability to match spoken and written nonsense-words thus suggests a failure in the direct translation between orthographic and phonological codes. The following experiments confirm that this was not just a failure in direct translation between *non-lexical* patterns.

(iv) This group of experiments again adopted a spoken-to-written matching task, again using common, real words, but taking classes of words with minimal (context-independent) referential meaning. These word-sets included (a) quantifiers (some, all, more . . .), (b) personal and demonstrative pronouns (she, our, these . . .), (c) spatial prepositions (beside, under . . .). With these word-sets AL was generally unable to match spoken to written items consistently more accurately than he could match the nonsense-words.[3] This finding supported our contention that AL had indeed lost the ability to carry out a direct process of translation between orthographic and phonological word-forms. It also suggested that, at least for these classes of words, he was unable to evoke a common, "abstract" lexical code in terms of which he could perform the comparison.

The preceding experiments demonstrated that AL had no difficulty in making comparisons between common spoken and written object names, in terms of their referential meanings, but that he was apparently unable to carry out a direct conversion between spoken and written word-forms themselves. We now required a matching task involving simple object names, but in which the direct comparison of referential word-*meanings*, in the sense outlined above, was inadequate to control the correct matching choice.

(v) For this purpose we again asked AL, as in the first experiment, to point to one of two written words which was "the same word" as a single word spoken to him. However, in this experiment the two written alternatives were in each case as nearly as possible identical in reference (e.g. DRESS vs. FROCK, HUT vs. SHED, MAT vs. RUG, BRANCH vs. BOUGH . . .).[4] What predictions about this experiment could we make, based on the alternative hypotheses represented in Figs. 4.6 a and b? To begin with, *both* models carried the prediction that the task should present no difficulty, provided that the mechanisms of direct translation between phonological and orthographic codes are intact. The preceding experiments, however, led us to expect that AL would be unable to make use of this strategy. If this channel was ruled out, model 4.6a asserted that the *only* other means of comparison between spoken and written words was through the cognitive codes (word-*meanings*). Furthermore, if my proposal (p. 85) about the essentially *non-linguistic* character of cognitive codes was correct, the representations which these codes can embody, evoked by single words having such closely similar sensory and functional reference (DRESS/FROCK, etc.), should have been insufficient to enable their separation. In other words, unless the cognitive codes were fundamentally *linguistic* or *lexical* in character, preserving a one-to-one correspondence with individual lexemes, model 4.6a predicted that the task should have been, at the very least, much more difficult than the similar task in Experiment 1, if not substantially impossible.

In sharp contrast, if there existed a central or "abstract" lexical code into which both spoken and written word-forms had to be directly mapped if they were to be understood, as asserted by model 4.6b, then the task in Experiment 5 should have posed no difficulty, even for our subject AL. As already noted, the results of Experiment 2 confirmed AL's ability to evoke cognitive representations from spoken and written object-names. Within the structural assumptions of model 4.6b, this in turn guaranteed the integrity of the corresponding "abstract" lexical codes.

We were thus confronted with two clear-cut, and sharply conflicting, predictions. Model 4.6a predicted that Experiment 5 would be difficult, or even impossible, for AL to perform. Model 4.6b, on the contrary, predicted no greater difficulty than in Experiment 1. The result? AL's performance was no better than chance (nine out of sixteen).

This outcome, and indeed the whole pattern of results obtained in this series of simple experiments, was therefore incompatible with the hypothesis of a "central", mode-independent lexical code. It challenged the view, at least as regards *lexical mechanisms*, that the psychological representation of language could *ever* be other than mode-specific. At the same time it gave empirical support to the claim (p. 86) that the cognitive codes, in which word-meanings are represented, were not themselves properties of "language": i.e. they did not belong to *words*. Finally, the results left no comfort for the hypothesis that, even in the total aphasic dissolution of spoken and written language, a "central" representation of language might remain intact.

Cognitive Codes

Granted that the mental structures representing word-meanings do not have a simple, one-to-one correspondence with individual words, what more can be inferred about their organization from existing neuropsychological evidence? At present the answer appears to be: relatively little, certainly in contrast to the extensive work on lexical and syntactic systems. However, some observations of selective disturbances in understanding different conceptual categories of *words* may perhaps point to corresponding dissociations in the cognitive codes that underly them. For example, Warrington (1975, 1981) first documented a double dissociation in certain neurological patients' ability to understand and use what she classified as "concrete" and "abstract" words. It is not unusual for brain-injured patients to exhibit greater difficulty with "abstract" than with "concrete" words. Warrington (1975) was able to demonstrate the converse. She described an intelligent and highly educated man (AB) who, as a consequence of cerebral disease, had become unable to understand or to explain the meanings of the names of common objects like "hay", "needle", "carrot", "mosquito", yet who could give fluent and precise definitions of "abstract" words like "arbiter" or "supplication". She has provided a rich variety of other observations on this patient, indicating that his failure to understand the names of common objects was not, at root, a *linguistic* deficit, but reflected a deeper dissolution of his knowledge of objects, their physical and functional properties. Thus, shown photographs of common objects, AB could generally discriminate animals from non-living things (37/40); but, beyond that, his judgments about many other attributes of the pictured objects—e.g. their real size (11/20), weight (8/20), natural location (9/20)—were no better than chance (1/2).

More recently Warrington (1981) has documented in a different patient

(JBR) what appears to be a selective impairment in understanding the names of particular classes of material object: e.g. living things vs. man-made utensils. (See also Goodglass *et al.*, 1966.) Her method was again to ask the patient to define the meanings of individual words. Presented with a total of 80 names of man-made objects, and 80 names of living things, JBR could indicate the meaning of about 80% of the object-names but (even by a very lenient criterion) less than 25% of the set of living things. In tests with different word-sets, JBR failed to show that he understood any names of plants, fruit or foods; yet with categories like tools, clothing, and kitchen utensils he scored around 75–83%. Unfortunately, Warrington (1981) did not describe any corresponding tests in which JBR was confronted with the equivalent real objects, or pictures, so that from these data alone we cannot tell whether JBR's selective deficits are in the mapping of word-forms onto cognitive representations, or in the cognitive representations themselves.

Everyday Errors

In order to set some bounds on this discussion, I have confined myself to inferences that can be derived from the pathology of language and of cognition. Under this heading, however, it is perhaps legitimate to include the everyday pathology of language—the familiar and ubiquitous "slips of the tongue" made by normal speakers (Fromkin, 1973, 1980). These can occur at many different "levels" in the production of language, from the displacement of individual phonetic features such as voicing (e.g. clear blue sky → *glear plue sky*) or place of articulation (e.g. scatterbrain → *spatter-grain*) to transpositions of semantic components, not unlike the "semantic" errors made by deep dyslexics in reading aloud. For example, my eleven year old daughter: "Shall I put the rest of the things back in the oven—I mean, in the fridge?" Here there is an obvious conceptual overlap between the word intended and the word actually spoken; both *oven* and *refrigerator* are food containers of broadly similar size, appearance and location (large, front-opening, found in the kitchen, etc. etc.) whose primary function is to alter, and then maintain, the temperature of their contents. Where they differ is of course in the direction of temperature change—and hence in their effects on the contents. Errors of this kind are very common, in "abstract" as well as "concrete" domains ("When we went to France yesterday—er, last year . . ."; five hours → "five minutes"; the subject of the sentence → "the president of . . ."). One of the most charming is reported by Fromkin (1973) from the days of the VW beetle: the lady with the dachshund → "the lady with the Volkswagen".

Like the "semantic" errors made by deep dyslexics, these conceptually related word-substitution errors in normal speakers provide powerful motivation for the thesis that *pre-lexical* meanings, or intentions, are assembled componentially—i.e. from a set of conceptual features. It is interesting that similar if not identical categories of error can be seen in everyday slips of *action*, where no linguistic activity is involved (e.g. actually going to the oven instead of the fridge) (cf. Reason, 1979; Norman, 1981b).

Traditionally the analysis of language, in particular analysis of the systematic relations of meaning between words, has been the principal avenue to explore these underlying conceptual (or "semantic") components. The approach has undoubtedly been a fruitful one (e.g. Lyons, 1977). However, this should not lead us to suppose that the conceptual ("semantic") components are themselves a property of, or dependent on natural language, nor even that they are specially adapted to language, but rather the other way about.

Concluding Remarks

The theory put forward in this chapter can be very simply stated. It is that *human cognitive abilities do not depend on—and can be functionally dissociated from—the possession of communicative language within the individual.* The qualification implied by this last phrase, however, deserves notice. My argument has, throughout, taken the adult individual as the fundamental unit. *In terms of the adult individual*, the neuropsychological evidence that I have reviewed points unequivocally and, I believe, inescapably to this position. In closing, however, it seems desirable to make clear the boundary conditions on this theory—what it does not imply—by reference to a broader perspective.

To consider human cognition wholly in terms of the individual cognitive agent is to ignore its profoundly *social* character and origin. Individual human minds grow and are constantly nourished through communication with others. Indeed, it is possible to think of all that is distinctive of human cognition, its achievements, its very existence, as in an obscure but profound sense the product of a *collective* entity, arising through the communicative interactions between innumerable individuals across time and space. *Within* each individual the fundamental cognitive processes are computed in a medium other than natural language. But *between* individuals natural language is manifestly the principal medium of communication. Without that medium of communication, the collective potential and achievements of human cognition would be diminished beyond recognition. From this perspective, human cognition, seen as a collective, social process, is indeed functionally dependent on natural language.

Notes

1. Although it is still sometimes proposed.

2. Although this is a logical possibility, there is recent evidence that normal readers in fact may not have any strictly *non-lexical* means of translating from spelling to sound, even for nonsense-spellings (Glushko, 1980; Kay and Marcel, 1981).
3. The exception to this was found with a mixed set of syntactic functors: conjunctions, articles, etc. (the, and, with, for, to . . .) which included most of the words having the very highest frequency of occurrence in the language. With these words AL scored reliably better than chance though nowhere near as accurately as with object-names (Experiment 1).
4. No doubt members of these word-pairs can be shown to have some distinct privileges of occurrence in different linguistic contexts, idioms, etc. However, *qua* isolated words they were evidently sufficiently close in terms of simple referential meaning to satisfy the demands of our experiment in that, as it turned out, AL was unable to discriminate them!

References

ALBERT, M.L. and OBLER, L.K. (1978), *The Bilingual Brain*, Academic Press, New York.
ALLPORT, D.A. (1978), "Conscious and unconscious cognition: a computational metaphor for the mechanism of attention and integration", in L.-G. Nilsson (Ed.), *Perspectives on Memory Research*, Lawrence Erlbaum Associates, Hillsdale, N.J.
ALLPORT, D.A. (1980a), "Patterns and actions: cognitive mechanisms are content-specific", in G. Claxton (Ed.), *Cognitive Psychology: New Directions*, Routledge and Kegan Paul, London.
ALLPORT, D.A. (1980b), "Attention and performance", in G. Claxton (Ed.), *Cognitive Psychology: New Directions*, Routledge and Kegan Paul, London.
ALLPORT, D.A., ANTONIS, B. and REYNOLDS, P. (1972), "On the division of attention: a disproof of the single-channel hypothesis", *Quarterly Journal of Experimental Psychology*, **24**, 225–235.
ALLPORT, D.A. and FUNNELL, E. (1981), "Components of the mental lexicon", *Philosophical Transactions of the Royal Society* (London), **B295**, 397–410.
BASSO, A., DE RENZI, E., FAGLIONI, P., SCOTTI, G. and SPINNLER, H. (1973), "Neuropsychological evidence for the existence of cerebral areas critical to the performance of intelligence tests", *Brain*, **96**, 715–728.
BAY, E. (1962), "Aphasia and non-verbal disorders of language", *Brain*, **85**, 411–426.
BRAMWELL, B. (1897), "Illustrative cases of aphasia", *Lancet*, **1**, 1256–1259.
BRANSFORD, J.D. and JOHNSON, M.K. (1973), "Considerations of some problems of comprehension", in W.G. Chase (Ed.), *Visual Information Processing*, Academic Press, New York.
BROWN, J.W. (Ed.) (1981), *Jargonaphasia*, Academic Press, New York.
CARAMAZZA, A. and BERNDT, R.S. (1978), "Semantic and syntactic processes in aphasia: a review of the literature", *Psychological Bulletin*, **85**, 898–918.
CARAMAZZA, A. and ZURIF, E.B. (1976), "Dissociation of algorithmic and heuristic processes in language comprehension", *Brain and Language*, **3**, 572–578.
CHARNIAK, E. (1976), "Inference and knowledge II", in E. Charniak and Y. Wilks (Eds), *Computational Semantics*, North-Holland Press, Amsterdam.
COLONNA, A. and FAGLIONI, P. (1966). "The performance of hemisphere-damaged patients on spatial intelligence tests", *Cortex*, **2**, 293–307.
COLTHEART, M. (1980), "Deep dyslexia: a review of the syndrome", in M. Coltheart, K. Patterson and J.C. Marshall (Eds), *Deep Dyslexia*, Routledge and Kegan Paul, London.
COLTHEART, M., MASTERSON, J., BYNG, S., PRIOR, M. and CRITCHLOW, J. (1982), "Surface dyslexia" (unpublished manuscript).
COLTHEART, M., PATTERSON, K.E. and MARSHALL, J.C. (Eds) (1980), *Deep Dyslexia*, Routledge and Kegan Paul, London.
CORKIN, S. (1979), "Hidden-figures test performance: lasting effects of unilateral penetrating head injury and transient effects of bilateral cingulotomy", *Neuropsychologia*, **17**, 585–605.
DAVIS, D.R. and SINHA, D. (1950), "The influence of an interpolated experience upon recognition", *Quarterly Journal of Experimental Psychology*, **2**, 132–137.

DE RENZI, H., FAGLIONI, P., SAVOIARDO, M. and VIGNOLO, L. (1966), "The influence of aphasia and of the hemispheric side of the cerebral lesion on abstract thinking", *Cortex*, **2**, 399–420.
DE RENZI, H., PIECZURO, A. and VIGNOLO, L. (1968), "Ideational apraxia: a quantitative study", *Neuropsychologia*, **6**, 41–52.
DE VILLIERS, J. (1974), "Quantitative aspects of agrammatism in aphasia", *Cortex*, **10**, 36–54.
ELLIS, A.W. (1981), "Spelling", in A.W. Ellis (Ed.), *Normality and Pathology in Cognitive Function*, Academic Press, London.
FROMKIN, V.A. (Ed.) (1973), *Speech Errors as Linguistic Evidence*, Mouton, The Hague.
FROMKIN, V.A. (Ed.) (1980), *Errors in Linguistic Performance: Slips of the Tongue, Ear, Pen and Hand*, Academic Press, New York.
FUNNELL, E. (in preparation), Ph.D. Thesis, University of Reading.
GLUSHKO, R.J. (1980), "Principles for pronouncing print: the psychology of phonography", in A. Lesgold and C. Perfetti (Eds), *Interactive Processes in Reading*, Lawrence Erlbaum Associates, Hillsdale, N.J.
GOODGLASS, H. and BAKER, E. (1976), "Semantic field, naming and auditory comprehension in aphasia", *Brain and Language*, **3**, 359–374.
GROSSMAN, M. (1981), "A bird is a bird is a bird: making reference within and without superordinate categories", *Brain and Language*, **72**, 313–331.
GROSZ, B. (1977), "The representation and use of focus in dialogue understanding", Stanford Research Institute, Technical Report No. 151. Menlo Park, C.A.
GUILDFORD, J.P. (1967), *The Nature of Human Intelligence*, McGraw-Hill, New York.
HUMPHREYS, L.G. (1979), "The construct of general intelligence", *Intelligence*, **3**, 105–120.
HUNT, E. (1974), "Quote the Raven? Nevermore!" in L.W. Gregg (Ed.), *Knowledge and Cognition*, Lawrence Erlbaum Associates, Hillsdale, N.J.
JAKOBSON, R. (1964), "Towards a linguistic typology of aphasic impairments", in A.V.S. De Reuck and M. O'Connor (Eds), *Disorders of Language*, Churchill, London.
JAMES, W. (1890), *The Principles of Psychology*, 2 Vols, Henry Holt and Co., New York, Reprinted by Dover Publications: New York, 1950.
JARVELLA, R.J. and HERMANN, S.J. (1972), "Clause structure of sentences and speech processing", *Perception & Psychophysics*, **11**, 381–384.
JENSEN, A.R. (1972), *Genetics and Education*, Methuen, London.
KAY, J. and MARCEL, A. (1981), "One process, not two, in reading aloud: lexical analogies do the work of nonlexical rules", *Quarterly Journal of Experimental Psychology*.
KERTESZ, A. (1979), *Aphasia and Associated Disorders: Taxonomy, Localization and Recovery*, Grune and Stratton, New York.
KERTESZ, A. and McCABE, P. (1975), "Intelligence and aphasia", *Brain and Language*, **2**, 387–395.
KINSBOURNE, M. and WARRINGTON, E.K. (1963), "Jargon aphasia", *Neuropsychologia*, **1**, 27–37.
KOLERS, P.A. (1978), "On the representations of experience", in D. Gerver and W. Sinaiko (Eds), *Language Interpretation and Communication*, Plenum, New York.
KREINDLER, A., MIHAELESCU, L. and ALEXANDRU, S. (1974), "The thinking process in aphasics", in Y. Lebrun and R. Hoops (Eds), *Intelligence and Aphasia*, Swets and Zeitlinger, Amsterdam.
LACHMAN, R., LACHMAN, J.L. and BUTTERFIELD, E.C. (1979), *Cognitive Psychology and Information Processing: an Introduction*, Lawrence Erlbaum Associates, Hillsdale, N.J.
LEBRUN, Y. and HOOPS, R. (Eds) (1974), *Intelligence and Aphasia*, Swets and Zeitlinger, Amsterdam.
LESSER, R. (1978), *Linguistic Investigations of Aphasia*, Edward Arnold, London.
LHERMITTE, F., DEROUESNE, M.-F. and LECOURS, A.R. (1971), "Contribution a l'etude des troubles semantiques dans l'aphasie", *Revue Neurologique*, **125**, 81–101.
LOW, A.A. (1931), "A case of agrammatism in the English language", *Archives of Neurology and Psychiatry*, **25**, 556–569.
LURIA, A.R. (1976), *Basic Problems of Neurolinguistics*, Janua Linguarum, 73, Mouton, The Hague.

LURIA, A.R., TSVETKOVA, L.S. and FUTER, D.S. (1965), "Aphasia in a composer", *Journal of Neurological Science*, **2**, 288–292.
LYONS, J. (1977), *Semantics*, 2 Vols, Cambridge University Press, Cambridge.
LYONS, J. (1981), "Language and speech", *Philosophical Transactions of the Royal Society*, London.
MARIN, O.S.M., SAFFRAN, E.M. and SCHWARTZ, M. (1976), "Dissociations of language in aphasia: implications for normal function", *Annals of the New York Academy of Science*, **280**, 868–884.
MARSHALL, J.C. and NEWCOMBE, F. (1973), "Patterns of paralexia: a psycholinguistic approach", *Journal of Psycholinguistic Research*, **2**, 175–199.
MARSHALL, J.C. and NEWCOMBE, F. (1980), "Response monitoring and response blocking in deep dyslexia", in M. Coltheart, K. Patterson and J.C. Marshall (Eds), *Deep Dyslexia*, Routledge and Kegan Paul, London.
MORTON, J. (1980), "The logogen model and orthographic structure", in U. Frith (Ed.), *Cognitive Processes in Spelling*, Academic Press, London.
NEISSER, U. (1976), *Cognition and Reality*, Freeman, San Francisco.
NEWELL, A. (1981), "Physical symbol systems", in D.A. Norman (Ed.), *Perspectives on Cognitive Science*, Lawrence, Hillsdale, N.J.
NORMAN, D.A. (Ed.) (1981a), *Perspectives on Cognitive Science*, Lawrence Erlbaum Associates, Hillsdale, N.J.
NORMAN, D.A. (1981b), "Categorization of action slips", *Psychological Review*, **88**, 1–15.
ORGASS, B., HARTJE, W., KERSCHENSTEINER, M. and POECK, K. (1972), "Aphasie und nichtsprachliche Intelligenz", *Nervenarzt*, **43**, 623–627.
PATTERSON, K.E. (1981) "Neuropsychological approaches to the study of reading", *British Journal of Psychology*, **72**, 151–174.
PATTERSON, K.E. (1982), in preparation.
PATTERSON, K.E. and MARCEL, A.J. (1977), "Aphasia, dyslexia and the phonological coding of written words", *Quarterly Journal of Experimental Psychology*, **29**, 307–318.
POSNER, M.I. (1978), *Chronometric Explorations of Mind*, Lawrence Erlbaum Associates, Hillsdale, N.J.
RAVEN, J.C. (1958), *Standard Progressive Matrices*, H.K. Lewis, London.
REASON, J. (1979), "Actions not as planned: the price of automatization", in G. Underwood and R. Stephens (Eds), *Aspects of Consciousness*, **1**, Academic Press, London.
ROSENBERG, S. and SIMON, H. (1977), "Modelling semantic memory: effects of presenting semantic information in different modalities", *Cognitive Psychology*, **9**, 293–325.
SACHS, J. (1974), "Memory in reading and listening to discourse", *Memory and Cognition*, **2**, 95–100.
SAFFRAN, E.M. and MARIN, O.S.M. (1975), "Immediate memory for word lists and sentences in a patient with deficient auditory short-term memory", *Brain and Language*, **2**, 420–433.
SAFFRAN, E.M. and MARIN, O.S.M. (1977), "Reading without phonology: evidence from aphasia", *Quarterly Journal of Experimental Psychology*, **29**, 515–525.
SAFFRAN, E.M., MARIN, O.S.M. and YENI-KOMSHIAN, G.H. (1976), "An analysis of speech perception in word deafness", *Brain and Language*, **3**, 209–228.
SAFFRAN, E.M., SCHWARTZ, M. and MARIN, O.S.M. (1980), "The word order problem in agrammatism. II. Production", *Brain and Language*, **10**, 262–280.
SANFORD, A.J. and GARROD, S.C. (1981), *Understanding Written Language*, John Wiley, Chichester.
SCHANK, R. (Ed.) (1975), *Conceptual Information Processing*, North-Holland Press, Amsterdam.
SCHANK, R. and ABELSON, R. (1977), *Scripts, Plans, Goals and Understanding*, Lawrence Erlbaum Associates, Hillsdale, N.J.
SCHWARTZ, M.F., MARIN, O.S.M. and SAFFRAN, E.M. (1979), "Dissociations of language function in dementia: a case study", *Brain and Language*, **7**, 277–306.
SEARLE, J.R. (1980), "Minds, brains and programs", *The Behavioral and Brain Sciences*, **3**, 417–450.
SHAFFER, L.H. (1975), "Multiple attention in continuous verbal tasks", in P.M.A. Rabbitt

and S. Dornic (Eds), *Attention and Performance,* **5**, Academic Press, New York.
SHALLICE, T. (1979), "Case study approach in neuropsychological research", *Journal of Clinical Neuropsychology,* **1**, 183–211.
SHALLICE, T. (1981), "Neurological impairment of cognitive processes", *British Medical Bulletin.*
SHAPIRO, B.E., GROSSMAN, M. and GARDNER, H. (1981), "Selective musical processing deficits in brain damaged populations", *Neuropsychologia,* **19**, 161–169.
SILVERBERG, R. and GORDON, H.W. (1979), "Differential aphasia in two bilingual individuals", *Neurology,* **29**, 51–55.
SYMONDS, C. (1953), "Aphasia", *Journal of Neurology, Neurosurgery and Psychiatry,* **16**, 1–6.
TIERNEY, M. (1973), "Dual task performance: the effects of manipulating stimulus-response requirements", Unpublished B.A. Thesis, University of Reading.
VAN HARSKAMP, F. (1974), "Some considerations concerning the utility of intelligence tests in aphasic patients", in Y. Lebrun and R. Hoops (Eds), *Intelligence and Aphasia,* Swets and Zeitlinger, Amsterdam.
VERNON, P.E. (1960), *Intelligence and Attainment Tests,* University of London Press, London.
WAPNER, W. and GARDNER, H. (1981), "Profiles of symbol-reading skills in organic patients", *Brain and Language,* **12**, 303–312.
WARRINGTON, E.K. (1975), "The selective impairment of semantic memory", *Quarterly Journal of Experimental Psychology,* **27**, 635–657.
WARRINGTON, E.K. (1981), "Neuropsychological studies of verbal semantic systems", *Philosophical Transactions of the Royal Society* (London), **B295**, 411.
WARRINGTON, E.K. and SHALLICE, T. (1969), "The selective impairment of auditory verbal short-term memory", *Brain,* **92**, 885–896.
WARRINGTON, E.K. and SHALLICE, T. (1979), "Semantic access dyslexia", *Brain,* **102**, 43–63.
WECHSLER, D. (1955), *Manual for the Wechsler Adult Intelligence Scale,* The Psychological Corporation, New York.
WEIGL, E. and BIERWISCH, M. (1970), "Neuropsychology and linguistics: topics of common research", *Foundations of Language,* **6**, 1–18.
WELMAN, A. and LANSER, J. (1974), "Intelligence or intellectual tests in aphasic patients", in Y. Lebrun and R. Hoops (Eds), *Intelligence and Aphasia,* Swets and Zeitlinger, Amsterdam.
WHITAKER, H. (1976), "A case of the isolation of the language function", in H.A. and H. Whitaker (Eds), *Studies in Neurolinguistics,* Vol. 2, Academic Press, New York.
WINOGRAD, T. (1972), *Understanding Natural Language,* Edinburgh University Press, Edinburgh.
WINOGRAD, T. (1981), "What does it mean to understand language?" in D.A. Norman (Ed.), *Perspectives on Cognitive Science,* Lawrence Erlbaum Associates, Hillsdale, N.J.
ZANGWILL, O.L. (1964), "Intelligence in aphasia", in A. De Reuck and M. O'Connor, *Disorders of Language,* Churchill, London.

Chapter 5
Language and Truth

MICHAEL DUMMETT

In the early years of this century, the notion of truth was the subject of vigorous philosophical dispute. The two principal philosophical theories of truth were known as the "correspondence theory" and the "coherence theory". According to the correspondence theory, a proposition is true provided that it corresponds to reality; more exactly, if there is a fact to which it precisely corresponds. This appears at first sight as little more than a platitude: it captures the intuitive idea that our thoughts relate to a reality which is independent of them, that the language in which we express our thoughts describes such a reality, and that what we think or say is true provided that external reality is as we think or say that it is. But an account along these lines was rejected by the supporters of the coherence theory on the ground that a proposition cannot be compared with, or found to correspond or not to correspond with, anything so unlike itself as an objective fact. When, according to them, we establish the truth or the falsity of a proposition, we always do so on the basis of other propositions which we accept as true; we can relate a proposition only to other propositions, and therefore the truth of a proposition should be taken as consisting in its coherence with some overall system of propositions.

An argument very popular with the linguistic philosophers of the 1950s and 1960s purported to demonstrate the absurdity of any philosophical theory of truth which, like the correspondence and coherence theories, offered a general characterization of what it is for a proposition to be true. According to this argument, to attempt to say what it is for an arbitrary proposition to be true is absurd in the same way as to attempt to say what it is to win an arbitrary game. If a general characterization of what it is to win any game were possible, then one would be able to apply this characterization to a particular game, say chess, to determine what, specifically, constituted winning that game. In order to do this, one would of course have to know what the game in question was; and now the absurdity of the project becomes apparent. Knowing in what winning the game consists is an essential *part* of knowing what the game *is*. There is no way in which one could derive, from a description of the game that omitted to state what counted as winning it, a knowledge of how that omission ought to be rectified. This is apparent from the fact that it is possible to have two games whose rules agree in everything except what counts as winning—what counts as winning in the second game may even be precisely that which counts as losing in the first one. Thus, if you know what the game is, you do not need any criterion for determining what counts as winning it, and, if you do not know what the game is, you cannot possibly decide what counts as winning it. In the same way, according to this argument, you cannot possibly determine in what circumstances a sentence states the truth unless you know what it means; and, in order to learn what it means, that is, what proposition it expresses, you have to be told explicitly in what circumstances we count it as true. Hence, just as before, if you know what the sentence means, you do not need any criterion for its truth, and, if you do not know what it means, you cannot possibly apply any such criterion.

This argument does not, as its original propounders believed, demonstrate that there is no philosophical problem of truth, or that no philosophical theory of truth is required. It does, however, point rather accurately to what was wrong with the classical theories of truth such as the correspondence and coherence theories. What the argument shows is that the concept of truth is intricately bound up with the concept of meaning; no philosophical elucidation of either concept is to be had which does not at the same time provide an elucidation of the other one. The classical theories of truth were at fault in taking the notion of meaning for granted, as if we could first know what it was for a sentence to have the meaning that it does and then go on further to enquire what it is for it to be true. The classical theories did not, of course, purport to explain the condition for an arbitrary sentence to be true, independently of its meaning. The characterizations of truth which they offered applied, not to sentences, but to propositions; a proposition being what a sentence expresses, indeed what can be expressed in different ways by sentences of different languages. To start with an arbitrary proposition and seek to say what it is for it to be true is, in effect, to assume that we know, of some arbitrary sentence, what it means, in advance of raising the question what counts as its being true. This is indeed a fruitless procedure; if we approach our task in this way, the best that we can hope for is a characterization both banal and unexplanatory. In order to arrive at any genuine elucidation of the concept of truth, we must make our enquiry part of an attempt to elucidate the concept of meaning. We must find an answer to the perplexing question what it is for a sentence to bear the meaning that it does and, therefore, what a language is. It will be a condition upon a successful outcome of this enquiry that the terms in which we answer it also enable us to frame an answer to the question what it is for a sentence to be true.

The analogy between language and play, or between sentences and games, is illuminating but not exact. Even if it were exact, it would show that there can be no informative general characterization of the condition for a sentence to be true, but it would not show that there is nothing to be said in a philosophical elucidation of the concept of truth. In order to know what it is to win a game, that is, what it means to say of someone that he has won a particular game, it is by no means *necessary* to know, for each particular game, what counts under the rules as winning it; more importantly, it is not *sufficient* either. When someone reads the rules of a game hitherto unfamiliar to him, his understanding of the rule which states under what conditions a player or side has won the game depends upon his prior understanding of what it is, in general, to win a game. If, for example, in a statement of the rules of chess the word "win" was not used, but it was merely stated that in such-and-such a position a player was said to have checkmated his opponent and the game then terminates, that would not be enough to convey in what playing a game of chess consisted. To grasp the general concept of winning a game is to understand the role that that concept plays in a general account of the activity of playing games; crudely stated, that each player undertakes to attempt to play in such a way that he or his side wins. (We are so familiar with games-playing that we often fail to notice how complex a notion it is. The presence of a player who is merely observing the rules but making no attempt to win will render it impossible for the other players to play the game in anything but a purely formal sense. On the other hand, one does not yet fully grasp the concept of playing a game if one thinks, as I have heard a young child say, that "there is no point in my playing if I don't win".)

Exactly the same applies to the concept of truth. If to grasp the meaning of a sentence involves knowing when it, or a particular utterance of it, is true, then this knowledge must involve knowing what it is, in general, for a sentence or an utterance to be true. To know this it is neither necessary nor sufficient to know, of every particular sentence, under what conditions it is true. It must, rather, involve knowing how in all cases the concept of truth is related to that of meaning. To be more exact, we ought here to speak of an implicit grasp of the connection between the concepts of truth and of meaning, rather than of a knowledge of it. For we all recognize that a difference between the conditions for the truth of two sentences must reflect a difference between their meanings, and this recognition rests upon our apprehension of a connection between the two notions; but we should be hard put to it to state what the relation between them is, this being a typical case in which it is the task of philosophers to bring to light and render explicit a conceptual connection which formerly was no more than implicit. This involves, therefore, precisely what was stated before: an elucidation of the concept of truth requires a detailed account of what it is for a sentence to have a meaning, an account against the background of which it would be possible to state explicitly how the concept of truth is related to that of meaning.

So much would be evident even were the analogy between games and language exact; but, as already remarked, it is far from being exact. To understand how a game is played, you have to have an explicit statement of the rules, which indeed will include a statement of the conditions for winning the game; but, to understand a sentence, you do not normally have to have any explicit statement of the meaning of that sentence. On the comparatively rare occasions when we are concerned to give the meaning of an entire sentence, we usually do so by offering a paraphrase; but, in case of a more ordinary kind, if someone says that he does not understand a sentence, it is legitimate to ask him what in that sentence he does not understand. It may then appear that he does not understand some particular word, or, perhaps, some construction; and the meaning of the whole sentence will become apparent to him when that particular word or construction is explained. If you understand the words contained, and the grammatical constructions employed, in a meaningful sentence, then you will normally understand the sentence; there is no need for a separate explanation of its meaning. Moreover, there is an evident sense in which you cannot be said genuinely to understand the sentence unless you know the meanings of the individual words and understand the grammatical constructions according to which they are put together. If I hear someone utter a sentence in a language of which I am wholly ignorant, say Burmese, and ask a companion who understands that language, "What did he say?", I shall be given an equivalent sentence in English. In one sense, I now know what the sentence that I heard means; if I remember the sentence phonetically, I may be said, in this sense, to know the meaning of a specific Burmese sentence. But I do not know it of my own knowledge, as the lawyers say; to know it in that way I should have to grasp the articulation of the sentence, how it splits up into words, what the meanings of those words are, and how they are put together to form the sentence, and only by knowing that should I have a genuine understanding of the sentence. It thus does not appear to be in any way literally true that, in order to understand a sentence, I have to have been told what it means; still less that, in the course of having its meaning explained to me, I must expressly have been told under what conditions an utterance of it would be true.

Nevertheless, there is a sense in which sentences, not words, may be said to be the primary bearers of meaning. To understand a paragraph or a speech, in the sense of a continuous utterance by one speaker, is, to a first approximation, to understand in succession the sentences composing it. This is true only to a first approximation: it must be qualified in two distinct ways. First, there are the manifold respects in which an understanding of what is being referred to depends upon what has been said previously. This, though a pervasive and practically important feature, is a relatively superficial one. It would be easy to transform any given speech in such a way that the content of each sentence was rendered independent of its linguistic context; the result would be stylistically intolerable, and the transformation would therefore make a significant rhetorical difference, but the content of the speech would remain unaltered.

The second qualification concerns our apprehension of the relationship between the different sentences composing the speech. Some statements are made by way of illustration or example for what has preceded or is immediately to follow; some by way of concession or qualification to the principal contention; some are advanced as following logically from, or rendered probable by, those preceding it. To take in the contents of the individual sentences without perceiving any of these relationships would be to fail to understand the speech as a whole. Nevertheless, the thesis that an understanding of the speech consists of the successive understanding of the sentences composing it remains true as a first approximation, precisely because the question how the speaker was presenting the different statements that he made as related to one another arises only if an understanding of the individual sentences he uttered is attainable in advance of settling that question.

By contrast, it is not true, even as the roughest approximation, that to understand a sentence is to understand in succession the words that compose it. One can extract a sentence from a speech, and, after supplying whatever is necessary to determine what the speaker was referring to, one can assert that he said *that*. The result may be misleading, in that it gives a quite false impression of his drift, but the assertion is none the less true. One cannot in the same way extract a word, phrase or clause from a sentence that someone uttered, and assert, in the same sense, that he said *that*. In the relevant sense, one does not, by the utterance of a mere word or phrase, say anything at all; one does not, in Wittgenstein's phrase, "make a move in the language-game". Though a clause of a certain kind may convey something that it would be possible, in this sense, to say, the mere utterance of the clause does not constitute saying it; the clause might be being uttered as one half of a disjunctive sentence, or as the antecedent of a conditional sentence.

To understand a word is to grasp its potential contribution to the meaning of any sentence in which it may occur. This is not to say that one cannot explain the meaning of any individual word without explicit reference to sentences containing it. It is to say that any explanation of its meaning rests upon a tacit understanding of the way in which a word whose meaning has been so explained can be used in sentences. For example, the meaning of a proper name can be given by saying that it is the name of a particular object; but such an explanation rests upon a prior understanding of what it is for a word to be a name, that is, how it can be used in a sentence in order to say something about the object for which it stands. In a similar way, one can state what a bishop's move in chess is without overt reference to its occurrence as part of a whole game of chess; but the explanation is significant only because it is understood against the background knowledge that a game of chess consists of alternate moves by the two players. Although the meaning of a particular word can be stated without overt reference to its occurrence in sentences, the adequacy and correctness of any such explanation can be judged only in terms of whether it gives a satisfactory account of the contribution of the word to the meaning of any sentence in which it may occur; if it does, no more can be asked of an explanation of the word's meaning, and if it does not, the explanation fails. For this reason also, we cannot say what it is in general, for a word to have a meaning save by explicit reference to sentences containing it.

Any general account of meaning must therefore take as its fundamental notion some feature possessed by sentences and intuitively connected with their meanings. At first sight, the great variety of our sentences—by means of which we ask questions, give commands, make requests, offer advice, voice our hopes and do many other things—makes such a programme appear impracticable. It appears less so if we follow the great majority of philosophers in believing the assertoric use of language to be primary; if we can once explain in what the meanings of assertoric sentences consist, we shall, they think, be able to explain the meanings of sentences by which we perform these other types of linguistic act in terms dependent upon our prior explanations of the meanings of assertoric ones. A variation on this approach is to distinguish, within the overall meaning of any sentence, its *sense* and its *force*: the sense of the sentence yields a description of a state of affairs, its force constitutes the conventional significance we wish to attach to our giving such a description. Thus an assertoric, an interrogative and an imperative sentence may have the same sense in common; they differ in that the first is used to say that that state of affairs obtains, the second to ask whether it obtains and the third to command that it be made to obtain. The task of providing a systematic account of meaning thus splits into two: that of explaining the sense, or, as we may say, the specific content, of each sentence, and that of explaining the different kinds of force that a sentence may carry. Most words are neutral as to force; a word like "sheep" can occur indifferently in an assertoric, an interrogative or an imperative sentence, and bears the same meaning in whichever type of sentence it occurs. Such a word therefore contributes to the sense or the content of the sentence, and does not in any way determine its force. Force, on the other hand, relates only to the sentence taken as a whole. It is therefore within the theory of sense that we shall find the explanation of how the meaning of the sentence is determined from its composition out of individual words; the explanation of each particular kind of force must be such as to apply uniformly to an arbitrary sentence expressing a given sense. That is not to say that the theory of sense is required to be intelligible in isolation from the theory of force.

The distinction between sense and force is often criticized on the basis of a misunderstanding, namely that the proponents of the distinction believe that there can be such a thing as simply expressing a sense, devoid of any force, or even an entire language whose speakers utter sentences which carry certain senses without having any particular force attached to them. Such critics make observations of the kind, "When I say, 'It is going to rain', I am not doing *two* things, expressing the thought that it will rain *and* asserting that that thought is true: I am doing only *one* thing". Since there is no general criterion for counting "things that I do", they support their dictum by psychological considerations: I am not giving external expression to two distinct mental acts, that of conceiving a thought and that of judging it to be true. We had better refrain at this point from remarking that there is no rule for counting mental acts, either: even if there were, it would not matter, since the distinction between sense and force is not intended as a contribution to any psychological theory, but as a strategy for giving an account of what it is for a sentence to have a meaning, and hence for it to be an utterance in a *language*. The whole point of the theory is that, for an utterance to effect a linguistic act, or to constitute a "move in the language-game", or, in the appropriate sense, for it to be an instance of *saying* something, it must carry some force or other: for this very reason, there can be no such thing as simply expressing a sense without any force attached to the utterance. The ground of distinction lies, not in discerning two things that the speaker does, but in recognizing two types of ways in which he might be misunderstood. If, when a policeman says, "Come along with me", I were to reply, "Thank you very much, but I'm afraid I don't have the time", I should have mistaken an order for an invitation; but a foreigner might very well understand that he was being given an order, without knowing what he was being ordered to do. The strategy of making this distinction seems fruitful, indeed unavoidable, precisely because the specific content may be common to utterances of different types: if it were not possible for one person to invite me to do what another orders me to do, it would not be possible to mistake an order for an invitation.

The distinction between sense and force appears valuable just because there are so many different kinds of utterance we make, or of linguistic acts that we perform: we make assertions, ask questions, give orders, advice, instructions, make requests, express wishes. There could hardly be a language adapted to human beings by means of which it was possible to do only one of these things: but perhaps there could be beings very different from ourselves who employed such a language, something to which, however defective, we should not deny the title "language", as Wittgenstein imagined people who used language only to give commands. Apropos of such an impoverished language, would the distinction between sense and force be otiose? In an obvious respect, it would be: utterances would differ in meaning only along one dimension. For this very reason, however, an account of the practice of using that language would fall into two distinguishable parts, that which explained how various sentences differed in meaning and that which explained the common ingredient in the significance of all sentences. Consider a language used only to give commands. It would be part of the tacit understanding of the language by the speakers that, when any of them heard a sentence uttered by one in authority over him, he had to take appropriate action in accordance with the particular sentence uttered. One part of any account of the use of the language would therefore consist in a specification of the dependence of the action to be performed by the hearer on the composition of the sentence; but another part would explain the general background. It would state the relationships of authority recognized in the community, spell out the correlation between an utterance and the response of the hearer, and say whether this response was invariable or not, and, if not, what were the consequences of disobedience.

This more general part of an account of the functioning of such a language might be said to explain the force uniformly attached to all sentences. The meaning of a sentence does not reside solely in that which differentiates its meaning from that of other sentences of the language to which it belongs, but also in that complex of linguistic and non-linguistic behaviour which renders it significant at all. The meaning of any sentence may be said to consist in the potential difference made by any utterance of it to what subsequently happens; and a full account of a language must spell this out. Since we have the concept of a command, we could give an account of the language in which all utterances are commands by saying just that: having stated that every sentence has the force of a command, we could then go on to the other part of the account, in which the specific content of each such command is shown to depend upon the composition of the sentence. Such an account would be correct, but it would fail to *display* that in which the significance of each utterance consisted: what is needed, in order to do so, is an account which would be intelligible even to people who were previously unfamiliar with the institution of giving commands.

The notion of a command is not altogether clear-cut. "Get out of my room" and "Take your hands off me" may be allowed among us to be commands, because we recognize everyone as having a certain authority over who may enter his room and who may touch him; but "Look where you are going" and "Stop making such a horrible noise" are not properly called commands and yet are not phrased as requests. Despite such uncertainties, it does not seem deeply problematic to give an account of the practice of giving commands, precisely because they are utterances which call for a quite specific response and because their failure to elicit that response has fairly well-defined consequences. The assertoric use of language stands in the sharpest contrast to this. We hardly know how to begin to characterize the use of sentences to make assertions without employing the verb "to assert" or some synonym, such as "to say" or "to tell", used in the appropriate sense. This has little to do with the fact that, in order successfully to convey to someone that a certain utterance was assertoric in character, we should have to give him to understand what we were saying as being itself assertoric, so that he would have already to have an implicit concept of assertion. We experience no similar difficulty in saying what it is for someone to apprehend (hear or read) a sentence, even though, to communicate our formulation to anyone, we should have to bring him to hear or read it. Our difficulty is, rather, that we do not know how to say what it is that anyone must believe about the significance of an utterance if he is to take it as assertoric; and this means that we do not know how to say what it is to have the concept of assertion. It is for this reason that we are so prone, when it is the assertoric use of language that we have in mind, to appeal to the notion of truth in order to characterize meaning.

It was Frege who first drew the distinction between sense and force, and it was he who first made the notion of truth central to the explanation of sense. That is not to say that Frege had a theory of truth of that same kind as the correspondence and coherence theories. On the contrary, he argued that such a theory was impossible in principle, a thesis he expressed by saying that truth is indefinable. There is some obscurity in the claim that truth is indefinable. There is a persistent dispute over what sort of thing we should take the predicate "is true" as applying to, if, indeed, we ought to take it as a *predicate* at all. Now whatever it is that is properly said to be true or false, it certainly cannot, in general, be a sentence, since many sentences can be used now to say something true, now to say something false—such a sentence as "It is raining", for example. We ought, therefore, to speak in this connection of particular utterances of sentences. The dispute may then be phrased thus: should "true" be applied to utterances, or to what utterances express, or to what they stand for? Frege was well aware of the existence of sentences like "It is raining", but preferred, as have many other philosophers when discussing these issues, to write as if all sentences resembled "Water is a compound" in being true on all occasions of utterance if true on any. This proves highly convenient in avoiding long-winded formulations, and is usually harmless provided that we remember that it is strictly incorrect; we may therefore follow Frege's example, and ask whether it is of a sentence, or of what it expresses, or of what it stands for, that we should say that it is or is not true.

What a sentence expresses is a thought or proposition: it is that which is in common to all sentences, in the same or in another language, which have the same meaning. At first sight, it is odd to speak of what a sentence stands for, as if it were related to anything as the phrase "the capital of Denmark" is related to the city of Copenhagen. Frege, in his mature period, believed exactly that about sentences; but it is not necessary to adopt that view in order to allow of the expression "what a sentence stands for". If we regard an expression as standing for whatever it is both necessary and sufficient to associate with it in order to determine every sentence in which it occurs as true or otherwise, then, if we set aside certain occurrences of it as deviant, "the capital of Denmark" indeed comes out as standing for Copenhagen; but, since sentences can occur as parts of more complex sentences, they too will stand for something. In Frege's own formalized language, and in any for which a classical two-valued semantic theory holds good, sentences stand for truth-values, that is, either for truth or for falsity.

It lies to hand to say that the dispute over what "true" applies to is of no significance. A sentence cannot be called "true" unless it is understood as having a certain meaning. If, then, we regard "true" as applying primarily to sentences, there will be a derivative sense in which the thoughts they express may be called "true", since, if a sentence is true, any other sentence that expresses the same thought must also be true. Conversely, if we take "true" as applying primarily to thoughts, there will be a derivative sense in which a sentence can be called "true" if it expresses a true thought. Moreover, whether we adopt classical semantics or not, it is evident that, on the interpretation given of the phrase "to stand for", what a sentence stands for must be sufficient to determine whether or not it is true: for a sentence can certainly occur as part of a more complex sentence in such a way that, if it were replaced by another sentence with a different truth-value, the truth-value of the complex sentence would thereby be altered. Hence, if we have a sense, primary or derivative, in which a sentence can be called "true", there will also be a further, derivative, sense in which what it stands for can be called "true". Conversely, if we take "true" as applying primarily to that for which sentences stand, there will be derivative senses in which sentences themselves, and the thoughts they express, can be called "true". In something of the same way, the predicate "human" applies to what, say, "Charles the Fat" stands for, and not to that expression or to its sense; but there are corresponding predicates, "personal name" and "sense of a personal name", which apply to the phrase and to its sense.

It does not follow from this that nothing is really at issue in this dispute. What follows is that what is at issue is not: given that "true" is a predicate, to what sort of thing may it *legitimately* be applied? It is, rather: given that "true" is a predicate, to what sort of thing ought we, in the order of explanation, to take it as *primarily* applying? Frege held strong, and slightly confusing, views on this question. He repeatedly said that it is a thought which is, in the first instance, said to be true or false, and that it is only in a derivative sense that we can say of a sentence expressing that thought that it is true or false. One of his reasons was that he regarded thoughts as existing timelessly and independently of whether we have any means of expressing them and of whether they are grasped by us or any other rational creatures; and part of his reason for *that* was that truth itself is timeless, since whatever is properly said to be true must be true or false absolutely, rather than true at any particular time. If it were sentences that were, in the primary sense, true or false, then we could not say of a natural law that it was true before it was formulated, whereas, Frege argued, it would still have been true even if it had never been formulated. All this appears to rank Frege with those who hold that "true" primarily applies to what sentences express; but this is only part of his view. He argued, further, that truth is not a property of thoughts, but, rather, stands in the same relation to them as that in which the city of Copenhagen stands for the sense of the phrase "the capital of Denmark". His ultimate view was, then, that truth primarily attaches to what sentences stand for; more accurately, in the light of his semantic theory, that truth just *is* what certain sentences stand for (the true ones), while falsity is what others stand for.

It is a peculiarity of Frege's mature theory that he did not regard the relation between a sentence or a thought and its truth-value as a mere *analogue* of that between a proper name or its sense and the object named, but as an *instance* of that relation. This was not part of any general assimilation of all expressions to names: he insisted that the relation between, say, a predicate or its sense and what it stands for is only the analogue of the relation between a proper name or its sense and its bearer. It is due, rather, to a special doctrine of Frege's concerning the grounds on which expressions could be categorized into distinct logical types, one that did not permit the discernment of a distinction of this nature between singular terms and sentences. This peculiar doctrine of Frege's is not important for our purposes: I mention it only to explain an unusual feature of Frege's formal language. This is, namely, that a sentence may meaningfully occur within a more complex sentence in any position in which a singular term might meaningfully have occurred. This makes the formal language very different from natural languages, as it already is in other ways; the divergence is justified by Frege on the ground that sentences stand, on his view, for one or other of two abstract objects, truth and falsity. As I already remarked, to hold that sentences stand for truth-values is not, in itself, to adopt this more radical view that truth-values are objects and sentences therefore a particular kind of complex singular terms: I do not mean to explore this perplexing claim, but needed to mention it in order to render some later remarks about Frege's formal language intelligible.

It is evident that, while Frege took a definite position in the dispute over what "true" primarily applies to, he was vividly aware of the possibility of explaining it as applying to any of the three types of candidate. Truth is not, for him, in the first instance a property of thoughts. There is nevertheless a property that a thought may have which is naturally expressed by saying that it is true. It might seem, from the foregoing exposition, that this property has to be explained in two stages, by invoking a sentence expressing the thought: a thought is true, in this sense of "true", if any sentence expressing it stands for truth. This is not so, however. Just as Frege held that the sense in which a sentence may be said to be true is derivative from that in which the thought it expresses is said to be true, so he also held that the sense in which an expression may be said to stand for something is derivative from a more primitive sense in which it is what the words express—their sense—which stands for that same thing: "the capital of Denmark" stands, in the derivative sense, for Copenhagen because the sense of the phrase stands, in the primary sense, for Copenhagen. What matters, however, is, first, that there *is* a sense in which a thought may be said to be true, and, secondly, that this is a sense to be explained in terms of the more primitive notion of truth as what a sentence or a thought stands for: a thought is true in this derivative sense if it stands for truth, just as a sentence is true in a tertiary sense if it expresses a thought which is true in the secondary sense.

The doctrine is one about the order of explanation, or, at any rate, the order of understanding. We could not grasp what it is for a sentence to be true if we did not regard it as expressing a thought and understand what it is for a thought to be true. In the same way, according to Frege, we cannot grasp what it is for a thought to be true unless we regard it as standing for something, and can distinguish, among the two things for which it can stand, truth from falsity. But we cannot go further than that: we have reached the basic level, beyond which explanations are impossible. Awareness of truth and falsity is implicit in the assertoric use of language: "these two objects", Frege wrote, "are recognized, if only implicitly, by everyone who judges something to be true".

It is not my purpose to resolve the question to what "true" primarily applies: it was introduced here only as bearing on the meaning of Frege's thesis that truth is indefinable. To say that, in a certain language, the number 0, for example, is indefinable is to say that one cannot construct in that language a singular term standing for the number 0, or, more broadly, that one cannot construct a one-place predicate true, under the intended interpretation of the language, of, and only of, the number 0. It was certainly not in this sense that Frege held truth to be indefinable. Nothing is easier than to construct, in his formal language, a singular term standing for truth: any true sentence of the language will serve this purpose. Nor is it difficult to construct a predicate true of, and only of, truth: "$x = (x = x)$" will fulfil that role, as Frege himself in effect pointed out. Indeed, there is no need to *construct* such a predicate: the horizontal stroke, one of the primitive predicates of the language, is interpreted precisely as being true of truth and false of everything else. In this sense, Frege's formal language may be said to have contained its own truth-predicate.

The horizontal stroke is not a truth-predicate in the sense in which that term is ordinarily used by logicians, namely a predicate true of, and only of, true *sentences* of the language. (The term "truth-predicate" is normally extended to cover an arithmetical predicate true of just those natural numbers which correspond, under a certain type of coding of expressions by numbers, to true sentences; for simplicity of formulation, we may here ignore such "Gödel numbering".) Frege's horizontal stroke is not true of true sentences, but, rather, of, and only of, what all true sentences stand for. Within a formal language, it is no longer a trivial matter to pass from a predicate representing "true" as applied to what sentences stand for to another one representing "true" as applied to sentences themselves. Even if Frege's formal language were supplemented by a vocabulary for referring to expressions of that language, we could not define from the horizontal stroke a truth-predicate in the standard sense, since we should lack any means of expressing in the language the relation between a sentence and what it stands for. This indeed preserves Frege's system from an additional ground of inconsistency, since it debars us from constructing within it semantic paradoxes such as that of the liar: but our present concern is to understand in what sense Frege held truth to be indefinable. "True" in the sense which Frege considered primary, as a predicate of what sentences stand for, is expressible in his formal language, and, even if not taken as primitive, would be definable in it. "True" in what he considered the derivative sense, as a predicate of sentences, is not expressible in it, principally because the language does not contain a means of expressing the relation between symbols and what they stand for: but it hardly seems that it can be to this that he was referring in calling truth indefinable. The derivative character of the notion consists precisely in its being explicable in terms of the more primitive one, an explanation we can give once we are freed from the constraints of the formal language and can avail ourselves of the notion of an expression's standing for something.

The notion of truth may be encountered, in connection with a formal language, in two different ways. We may be concerned, as in the foregoing discussion, with its expressibility within the language; or we may use the notion in order to lay down how we intend the language to be interpreted. The importance of the latter role is entirely independent of the degree to which, or the sense in which, truth is expressible *within* the language. Even though the language does not itself possess the resources for expressing the notion of truth, we may want to use that notion in order to characterize the intended meanings of its sentences; conversely, if we decide that we do not want to use the notion for that purpose, our decision need not be altered by its expressibility in the language. The distinction does not depend upon its being a *formal* language with which we are concerned. We should not be debarred from applying the predicate "true" to utterances in a natural language by the fact that that language contained no word translatable as "true" and no form of sentence equivalent to an ascription of truth to an utterance. It was plainly that notion of truth which we employ in speaking *about* a language, in order to characterize the meanings of its sentences, rather than that which is expressed *within* the language, that Frege held to be indefinable.

Why should we so much as think of employing the notion of truth in order to state the intended interpretation of a formal language, or the received interpretation of a natural one? In explaining the meanings of the words and expressions of a natural language, our usual method is to give rules for translating them into the language in which the explanation is given, and, in doing so, we have no need of the word "true" save as the translation of a word of the object-language. It was in connection with formal languages that this method was first replaced by a different one: partly because a formal language may have a syntax so different from the natural language used for explaining it that only approximate translations would be possible; and partly because, when we want to prove something *about* a formal language, the notion of one expression's "meaning the same as" another is a flabby instrument. For these reasons, it is preferable to state the intended interpretation of the formal language *directly*, rather than via the corresponding expressions of English or German. To state its interpretation directly involves eschewing the phrase "means the same as" or even, when speaking of whole sentences, its equivalent, "means that . . .", in the *oratio obliqua* construction: the object is to specify the meanings of expressions of the language without *using* the notion of meaning, but, rather, by laying down those properties of expressions in virtue of which they have the meanings that they are to bear. The result is a semantic theory for the language; and Frege, the first to devise a formal language in the modern sense, was also the first to construct such a semantic theory. A semantic theory for a formal language is not, however, merely a convenient alternative means of specifying an interpretation for a symbolic system which we wish to handle in a more precise mathematical manner than that in which we treat of natural languages: it is a model for what might in principle be done for all languages.

To put a speaker of, say, English in a position to interpret some other natural language, a system of translation is unquestionably the most efficient means. To the extent that the modes of phrase- and sentence-formation in that language differ from those of English, a few grammatical notions, such as that of a transitive verb or of a subordinate clause, will be needed: but they will still be used to frame rules of translation. In knowing English, the student thereby knows what English expressions mean; and, if he does not already understand the phrase "means the same as", he is likely, in the process of learning the other language, to come by a grasp of the concept it expresses. His having grasped that concept would be shown by his asking a question like, "How (in the other language) do I say, 'i shouldn't do that if I were you'?"; here "say" means "say something meaning the same as". Just because this process rests upon a tacit grasp of the concept of meaning, however, it can throw no philosophical light on what meaning is: as Davidson has insisted, to explain an expression as having the same meaning as another is not to say what it is to have that common meaning. If we want to attain a clear view of what it is for the words and expressions of a natural language to have the meanings they have, we must know, in principle, how to specify the correct interpretation of such a language without appeal to the notion of meaning; to do so will require us to single out and characterize those features of its expressions their possession of which constitutes their meaning what they do.

Such a theory of meaning for a natural language fulfils a role similar to that of a semantic theory for a formal language. It will, however, be very much more complex. The least important reason for this is that natural languages themselves are vastly more complex than formal ones; other reasons spring from the fact that a theory of meaning must be explicit in a way that a semantic theory need not. A semantic theory for a formal language serves as a practical means for laying down the intended interpretation of that language; it may therefore take for granted whatever the reader may be presumed already to know. A theory of meaning for a natural language is, by contrast, a purely hypothetical entity. No one proposes actually to construct one, or to use one for teaching a foreign language: the only point of considering what form such a theory would in principle take is the philosophical one of throwing light on the concept of meaning and that of a language. A theory of meaning must therefore be conceived as taking nothing for granted: to the extent that it did, it would be failing to provide the elucidation that constituted its entire purpose.

There is a further evident difference. A semantic theory for a formal language is used to *stipulate* the intended interpretation of the language; but a theory of meaning for a natural language purports to explain how it is actually understood. The semantic theory conveys the intended interpretation of the formal language by laying down what determines as true any given sentence of that language. A reader unfamiliar with the word "true" would not gain from those stipulations a knowledge of how to interpret the language, or even a realization that it served as a *language*: an actual reader will do so precisely because he has a tacit grasp of the connection between the meaning of a sentence of any language and the conditions which determine it as true. That this connection cannot be left tacit by a theory of meaning for a natural language, but must be spelled out, follows from the general necessity that the theory of meaning be fully explicit; but it also follows from the need to explain when such a theory counts as being correct. We could not decide the correctness of a theory of meaning for a natural language simply by asking the speakers. The speakers will certainly not know a theory of meaning for their language in advance; they cannot even be presumed to be able to recognize one as correct when presented with it. It is useless to discuss what form a correct theory of meaning would take if we do not know what would justify us in judging it to be correct: we have therefore to determine the relation between such a theory and the observable practice of the speakers in using the language.

Some philosophers and linguists attribute to a speaker of a language an implicit or tacit knowledge of a theory of meaning which constitutes his knowledge of the language and from which he derives his understanding of its expressions, that is, his knowledge of their meanings. Others reject the concept of tacit knowledge altogether. Three distinct positions are commonly advanced:

(i) Knowledge of a language is a genuine piece of knowledge, albeit tacit or unconscious knowledge, which issues in and explains its possessor's practical competence in using the language.
(ii) We may legitimately attribute to a speaker a tacit knowledge of a theory of meaning, but, in doing so, we are not *explaining*, but merely *characterizing*, his practical competence, his possession of which simply constitutes his tacit knowledge of the theory.
(iii) Understanding a language does not amount to knowing anything at all, in the sense of knowing something to be the case: it is simply a practical ability, namely to use the language and to respond appropriately to the utterances of others when couched in it.

Between (ii) and (iii) there appears little more than a difference of terminology; (i), on the other hand, is puzzling. Unconscious knowledge can explain an ability only if its possessor is able to avail himself of it; how, then, can he avail himself of knowledge that he is unaware of possessing? In common discourse, we indeed speak of knowing a language, and treat "knows the meaning of . . ." as synonymous with "understands"; but it is natural at this stage to enquire why we should be disposed to invoke the notion of knowledge in connection with the ability to speak a language. A proponent of position (iii) might reply that it is due solely to the empirical fact that no one can speak a language unless he has learned to do so, just as it is likewise an empirical fact that no one can swim unless he has learned to do so (although this is not the case with dogs); we therefore have the same justification for speaking of "knowing how to swim". Now it is common to all three positions that they ascribe to a speaker a certain practical competence lacked by those who do not know the language. Within a practical ability there may, in general, be distinguished a theoretical as well as a practical component. The skill of a ballet dancer, for example, involves not only the ability to perform certain movements of which those not so trained are incapable—the practical component—but also a knowledge of which movements to perform, which is the theoretical component; someone who was a natural ballet dancer in the sense that he could, without any training, execute fouettés and the like as soon as he was shown them would, until he was shown the steps, possess only the practical component of the ability and not the ability itself.

One might be tempted to assimilate the practical component to the theoretical one by representing it as a knowledge of what strictly bodily movements—what muscular contractions—would bring about certain desired effects on the motion of the body. The picture here is of an agent as operating the efferent nerves as a signalman operates his levers, the muscles corresponding to the signals on the track and the limbs and torso to the trains controlled by them. The temptation to make this assimilation should be resisted: the dancer is largely unaware of the muscles he is using, but knows, in a straightforward, conscious manner, what steps he has to execute.

Some practical abilities, no doubt, have only a practical component, and others only a theoretical one (for example, the ability to solve Rubik's cube). Speaking a language has a small practical component, namely the ability to pronounce it correctly; but what interests us is the theoretical component—knowing *what* to say, in the sense of what sounds to utter, rather than knowing how to make those sounds. It is precisely the large theoretical component in linguistic competence that prompts us to describe it as an instance of knowledge. The practical component of a skill could not be acquired by reading a book or otherwise gaining theoretical knowledge; but, by its nature, the theoretical component can be so acquired. It does not follow from this that anyone who has the theoretical component in question actually has the relevant explicit knowledge; someone may be able to "see" what rotations are needed to bring one of the small cubes into its correct position on Rubik's cube without disturbing certain others, and yet be unable to explain the principles he follows. What cannot be supposed is that he does not follow a system capable in principle of being codified and so known explicitly.

This explains why it is so compelling to refer to the ability to speak a language as "knowledge", in a sense more serious than that in which we talk of "knowing how to skate", and to characterize it as implicit knowledge, as on position (ii), or to postulate unconscious knowledge to account for it, as on position (i). It may nevertheless seem remarkable that proponents of none of the three positions attempt any direct characterization of linguistic competence, but speak only of the theory of meaning for the language, a theory which is the object of possible knowledge. This failure might seem the least reprehensible on the part of proponents of position (i), since they after all believe that a speaker actually does know the theory of meaning, although only unconsciously; but in fact the failure weakens the credibility of their claim. On their account of the matter, the speaker's tacit knowledge of the theory *explains* his linguistic competence; to evaluate such a claim, we need to be told what are the deliverances of that unconscious knowledge. To exercise a practical ability with an exclusively theoretical component is not, after all, to engage in a species of automatism; the subject, even if unable to state the principles that guide him, is acting quite consciously. We therefore need an account of how unconscious knowledge is supposed to operate; and, to judge whether or not it would explain linguistic competence, we need a description of what precisely linguistic competence consists in.

At first sight, the appeal to knowledge by proponents of position (iii) is even less defensible, since they deny that linguistic competence involves knowledge in any sense whatever. If, however, ability to speak a language were just like an inarticulate skill with Rubik's cube, their appeal to knowledge would be entirely justified. Someone who has a skill of this kind acts *just as if* he had a certain body of knowledge: there is therefore nothing problematic in characterizing his skill in terms of the knowledge which would be one means of acquiring it. This is precisely what advocates of position (iii) propose as a means of characterizing linguistic competence: namely by stating what body of knowledge someone would have to have if he were to possess such competence by virtue of having that knowledge. If someone explicitly knew a correct theory of meaning for a given language, he would be able to understand any sentence of the language, and hence, if he could apply his knowledge with sufficient rapidity, could use the language himself and comprehend the utterances of others. Speakers do not normally have such knowledge, explicitly or implicitly: but, by stating what someone would have to know if he were thereby to be able to understand the language, we characterize what it is that a speaker is able to do.

This would in most cases be an indisputably reasonable procedure, precisely because there would be no difficulty in converting the enunciation of the given body of knowledge into a description of what someone who has the ability actually does. Thus a description of a sequence of dance steps may serve equally as a means of stating what someone does when performing that dance and as a representation of the body of explicit verbalized knowledge which would enable anyone with the requisite agility to perform it. The same applies to a statement of a strategy, or set of strategies, for solving Rubik's cube. These cases differ from that of language, in that either, as with the dance, there is no purpose requiring explanation, or, as with Rubik's cube, the purpose is independently statable and is known explicitly to the agent.

This may also be said to hold for someone's knowledge of a second language: the object is to produce in that language equivalents of sentences of his mother tongue. So regarded, his knowledge of the second language is explicable as a mastery of a scheme of translation; it is therefore comparable to the other instances of a skill with a largely theoretical component which we have been considering. The same does not hold for his knowledge of his mother tongue. It is constitutive of its being a language that his production of sentences in it is not, like skat singing, devoid of further purpose. The purpose of uttering a sentence, for instance, "I seem to have lost my spectacles", is not, however, one that can be grasped independently of the means used to attain it, namely the use of language. One may first grasp the objective of making every face of Rubik's cube uniform in colour, and subsequently discover or learn a means of doing this; but we do not begin with a conception such as that of informing another of a fact, and then, when we learn language, acquire a method of doing so. Rather, the general purpose and effect of each utterance are part of what we learn when we learn our mother tongue.

For this reason, it is difficult to resolve the dispute about the role of knowledge in an account of linguistic competence: the dispute will be easier to resolve when we have a better understanding of the relation between what is, or might be, known and the practice it explains or characterizes. It is precisely because linguists and philosophers of language do not know how to cast a theory of meaning into such a form as to yield a direct description of linguistic practice that they feel compelled to appeal to the conception of the speaker's knowing such a theory, actually but implicitly or hypothetically and explicitly. The question how such a theory could be converted into a description of the speaker's practice is the same question as that which we asked earlier in a slightly different form: how are we to judge from the observable practice of the speakers of a language whether a proposed theory of meaning is correct?

A semantic theory issues, as we have seen, in a specification of the condition for any sentence of the language to be true; but it leaves the connection between truth and meaning tacit. Theories of meaning for natural languages are usually conceived of in the same way. They may be, as in my opinion they ought, more explicit in their accounts of individual words of the language, though not all philosophers of language would agree with that requirement. They may also contain means of differentiating sentences according to the type of force attached to them, which a semantic theory for a formal language does not need. But they are ordinarily thought of as distinguishing the specific contents of sentences—their senses, in Frege's terminology, as opposed to the force attached to them—by what determines them as true. When so conceived, the connection between truth and meaning has been as much taken as already understood as for a semantic theory of the usual kind. We have to make this connection explicit in explaining how such a theory is to be evaluated by reference to linguistic practice. A natural suggestion is that the theory is confirmed if competent speakers come, by and large, to recognize sentences as true by steps that match those by which they could be determined as true by someone similarly placed but with an explicit knowledge of the theory of meaning. The qualification "by and large" is needed in order to allow, on the one hand, for errors and inattention, and, on the other, for hunches and guesses, wild or inspired; the consequent vagueness is unavoidable. It has, however, to be explained what is meant by a speaker's "recognizing a sentence as true": the language need not itself contain a word for "true", and, if it did, there would be a question about the appositeness of so translating it.

On the face of it, this poses no very great problem. The theory of meaning will presumably indicate a basis on which certain utterances are to be classified as assertoric, either by the form of the sentence uttered or by the tone, manner or circumstances of its utterance. Independently of his personal motives, a speaker makes an assertion by uttering an assertoric sentence in the appropriate circumstances and manner; his asserting a sentence is to be taken as expressing his recognition of it as true. Hence we may simply equate a speaker's recognition of a sentence as true with his willingness to assert it. Of course, we shall not always know which sentences a given speaker would be willing to assert, other than those he actually does assert and those to which he gives some conventional sign of assent when asserted by others; but such an uncertainty is intrinsic to any inductive enterprise rather than an objection on principle to the matching of theory with practice. The theory of meaning has, indeed, so far been correlated only with assertoric utterances, but it may be presumed that this lacuna can be filled: the utility of the sense/force distinction appears to depend upon its being relatively easy to explain the significance of non-assertoric utterances once the meanings of assertoric ones are known.

To many philosophers of language, an account along these lines offers the definitive solution to the problem of meaning. A theory of meaning takes the form of one laying down what determines any sentence of the language as *true*: and the notion of a sentence's being true is connected with the linguistic behaviour of the speakers in that an assertoric utterance of it is to be construed as expressing that the speaker takes it to be true. Whether or not we view this as a satisfactory solution depends upon what ambitions we conceive on behalf of a theory of meaning; and that in turn depends upon what we regard as being "the problem of meaning". It is indeed arguable that a theory of meaning confirmed in this manner by the practice of the speakers determines the meaning of each sentence uniquely and correctly. It is clear, on the other hand, that it falls far short of giving an account of what is involved in speaking a language: it is not an adequate theory of the phenomenon of language.

To see this, imagine first two sheepdogs, each of which, when guarding the fold on his own, has been trained to emit a distinctive kind of repeated bark if any of the sheep escape; he then tries by himself to round up the sheep, continuing to give the bark until the shepherd arrives with the other dog. To the shepherd, this special bark means "Sheep have escaped from the fold; come and help": but does the sheepdog mean this by the bark? That would depend upon how he would behave if he were off duty and he heard his colleague giving the same bark. If he was completely unresponsive, he could surely not be said to attach that meaning to the bark: it would be significant only for the shepherd. If, on the other hand, in the absence of the shepherd, he went to give aid to the dog raising the alarm, or, in his presence, prepared to do so, then we could reasonably say that he understood the bark just as the shepherd did.

The same would apply to a small child beginning to acquire language. Suppose him to have acquired the habit of responding to certain observable situations by suitable one-word utterances: others can then use his exclamations as an extension of their own sensory equipment. If, for example, the child says "Pussy", his mother, in the next room, will know that the cat is in there with him. Now can we say that, in saying "Pussy", the child means "There is a cat here"? If the child cannot respond suitably to that utterance when made by others, we cannot say so. Suppose, for instance, that the child is afraid of the cat: before he enters a room, his mother tries to warn him that the cat is there by saying "Pussy", but he takes no notice, comes in and then becomes alarmed on seeing the cat. In such a case, he does not take "Pussy" as meaning "There is a cat here", but has merely acquired the habit of saying that in response to the sight of a cat.

Now we can imagine a set of adult speakers who are capable of handling assertoric sentences of arbitrary complexity. Let us suppose them capable of going through all the procedures of observation and theorizing, including deductive and inductive inferences, which we employ in ascertaining the truth of sentences; but all they ever do, having established a sentence to be true, is to assert it; in no other way does it affect their behaviour. Here the content of any of their sentences is taken as determined by the manner in which they establish it, in accordance with the proposal already made for justifying a putative theory of meaning. Though these speakers arrive quite correctly at conclusions, they never apply them: they may, for instance, assert a substance to be poisonous, but show no reluctance to eat it. We must suppose that, having established a sentence as true, one of these people will retain it as a truth for use in subsequent inferences; but, while in this respect a *judgment* will have an effect, we may take the principle that an *assertion* has no effect on them in a stricter or a laxer sense. Taken strictly, it will entail that an assertion made by one of them will not add to another's store of truths; taken in a weaker sense, it will allow one speaker's assertions to affect the purely linguistic behaviour of another, in that he accepts it as true and uses it in deriving further truths, provided that each individual's stock of truths in no way affects any of his non-linguistic behaviour: he never acts on what he knows.

Obviously the individuals in this strange community do not speak a language in any ordinary sense: their utterances do not engage with the rest of their activities. Evidently, then, the practice of the speakers of a language, properly so called, must satisfy a further condition if a proposed theory of meaning is to be an adequate representation of the meanings of its sentences. Alternatively expressed, in taking a theory which specifies what determines each sentence as true to constitute a theory *of meaning*, we are presupposing that the speakers satisfy this further condition as well as that concerning how they establish their sentences as true. This further condition is that the speakers act in accordance with the truth of those sentences they take to be true. Our problem is now to explain what "acting in accordance with the truth of a sentence" may be.

The apparent intractability of this problem is due to a subtle illusion. If we set aside sentences containing so-called evaluative expressions, we can say that what counts as establishing the truth of a sentence is independent of the speaker's particular desires and motivations. It has been repeatedly observed, by contrast, that there is no one course of action consequent upon accepting such a sentence as true: how that affects someone's behaviour will depend crucially upon what his aims are. If we continue to ignore the matter of "evaluative" expressions, this is perfectly true: but it is a confusion to see it as posing an obstacle in principle to explaining the effect upon action of accepting a given sentence as true. The confusion is due to the error of thinking that any explanation must treat each sentence on its own in isolation from the rest of the language.

It has come to be widely accepted that it is an error to do this when treating of how sentences are recognized as true; the first philosopher to point this out clearly and cogently was Quine in his celebrated article "Two Dogmas of Empiricism". The logical positivists had committed precisely this error. Holding that the meaning of a sentence is to be explained in terms of the means by which it can be verified, they applied this principle to each sentence taken by itself, as if it could exist, and have the significance that it has, without the language in which it is embedded. The means of verification must therefore be described independently of the use by the subject of any other sentences; it had accordingly to be taken to consist of one of a set of sequences of sense-experiences. This obviously yielded an account of meaning bearing no recognizable relation to what is actually involved in a speaker's understanding of a sentence. In particular, it allowed no basis for a distinction in meaning between any two analytically equivalent sentences, that is, sentences whose equivalence is demonstrable by deductive reasoning, however complex. It also created a problem about the meanings of logical and mathematical statements: the positivists solved this problem by declaring them to have a meaning of a kind so different that it became little more than a pun to ascribe meaning both to them and to empirical statements.

It was Quine who showed the way out of this impasse. A speaker understands a sentence because he understands the language: we shall therefore arrive at an accurate account of his understanding of the sentence only by appeal to his understanding of other parts of the language. In general, a sentence is recognized as true on the basis of inferential reasoning of some kind, involving the use of other sentences. Hence inference must be treated as an integral part of what in practice counts as the verification of a sentence: logical and mathematical statements are therefore not a special case, but, at most, a limiting one, in which nothing but deductive inference enters into the verification. Furthermore, in explaining the meaning of any given sentence, we do not need to describe the entire route from the infantile *tabula rasa* to the establishment of that sentence, but have only to explain it relatively to the understanding of those sentences from which it can immediately be inferred. If the understanding of a mathematical statement be said to consist in a knowledge of what would count as a proof of it, it becomes obscure how we can understand such a statement without knowing whether, and how, it can be proved: but if our understanding resides in our ability to arrive at it by means of a single inferential step, it ceases to be perplexing that we often do not know whether it is possible to construct a sequence of such steps leading ultimately to it from what we have already established; and the same holds for empirical statements.

An account of this kind looks as though it might be entrapped within language, allowing no place for the impact of sensory perception; but that is a danger Quine has always guarded against. According to him, the language will contain a small class of sentences constituting a limiting case of the opposite kind, namely ones for which the original positivist account is more or less correct: the verification of these observation sentences will consist solely of the occurrence of certain sense-perceptions (including, we may add, observations of the result of some procedure of testing, measurement or counting. Another danger in such an account is that of circularity: the meaning of a sentence is explained in terms of the meanings of other sentences, whose meanings will in turn be explained in terms of those of yet further sentences; there is an evident risk that a path in this tree will lead back to the original sentence. Quine himself does not see this as a serious danger: he inclines to a holistic view of language, according to which the full explanation of the meaning of any sentence will involve an explanation of the entire language. It is far from obvious that such a holistic thesis can avert the danger of vicious circularity; but circularity can be avoided if we adopt a hypothesis that would probably not be to Quine's liking, namely that sentences are to be graded by degree of complexity. On such a hypothesis, an explanation of the meaning of a sentence may presuppose the meanings only of sentences of lower complexity, and will perhaps be given simultaneously with the explanation of certain sentences of equal complexity: it will never involve explaining or presupposing the meaning of any sentence of higher complexity. On this hypothesis, an understanding of any sentence will involve an understanding of some fragment of the language, a fragment which could, moreover, exist as a language on its own; but an explanation of the language as a whole could be constructed without circularity by starting with sentences of minimal complexity (the observation sentences) and completing the explanation of sentences of any degree of complexity before proceeding to the explanation of those of the next degree.

If this conception is clearly borne in mind, it will be apparent that there would be no greater difficulty in giving a corresponding explanation of meaning in terms, not of how we establish sentences as true, but of what are the consequences for a subject of accepting them as true. To construct such an account, we do not have, for each individual sentence, to survey all the ultimate consequences acceptance of it may have for the actions of an individual, any more than, in explaining meaning in terms of verification, we had to survey all the steps which in any one case might ultimately lead to establishing it. All we need to do is to explain the *immediate* consequences of accepting the sentence as true, again presupposing the meanings of other sentences. Dually to the former case, the immediate consequence of accepting a sentence as true will most usually be the inferential derivation, from it and other sentences already held to be true, of the truth of yet further sentences. Just as, on the verificationist account, the connection with observation was made only at certain particular points, so here the connection with action will be made only at certain points. The judgement by a given individual that a particular sentence is true may not, even in the long term, influence any of his actual actions, possibly including linguistic ones: its only actual consequences might be further judgments which he does not communicate. It always has, however, a potentiality for doing so.

The duality is, indeed, imperfect. Let us call a sentence the acceptance of which has as an immediate consequence an action or sequence of actions by the subject an "action sentence", by analogy with "observation sentence". Many quite ordinary sentences, such as "If you touch the stove, you will burn yourself", would qualify as action sentences under this characterization; but it is easier to think of them as taking a special form, such as expressions of intention like "I will not touch the stove". An observation sentence is determined as such by its meaning, given the character of our perceptual faculties, though there is some variation between individuals, as with the blind, the deaf, those literate in various scripts and the altogether illiterate.

The important difference between the two cases lies in the fact that the point at which a chain of consequences terminates in action depends in large part on the aims and objectives of the individual subject.

It would not be so if all our desires were basic common ones—to avoid pain, preserve our life, and the like; but different people obviously have varying projects and ideals that cannot be accounted for as alternative strategies for reaching common goals. For this reason, the quality of being directed towards action cannot be restricted to the action sentences. The subject's objective may be statable only in a sentence of some complexity, incapable of being directly acted upon: actions result only when recognized as means to the end. We might, therefore, think of the action sentence as expressed, rather, in normative form, say as "The stove is not to be touched": if so, such normative sentences may have figured in several previous steps of the deduction, not themselves action sentences. Thus, in a manner to which there is no analogue in the case of verification, this normative character may be thought of as injected by a sentence expressing an objective of the subject at a stage that may be comparatively remote from the point at which the chain of consequences terminates in action.

This disanalogy with the earlier case is no impediment to the explanation of meaning in terms of consequences. The meaning of a sentence, as understood alike by all the speakers, is, when so explained, a function with arguments of two kinds: the subject's desires, and the other truths he accepts. Its value is a set of consequences, in action and in judgment, both factual and normative. The arguments vary from one speaker to another; the function itself remains the same for all. We are not, in this context, concerned with the celebrated inductive problem of determining beliefs and desires from actions, a problem residing in our having to solve simultaneously for two unknowns. Quine and Davidson have dramatized the philosophical problem of language by imagining how one might arrive, from observation of the speakers, at an interpretation of a hitherto unfamiliar language. The practical difficulties of doing so are, however, only obliquely germane to the philosophical problem how we may elucidate what it is for utterances in a language we in fact understand to have the significance we know them to have. We know what beliefs and what desires our fellow speakers have, in so far as they express them, because we understand the language; our problem as philosophers is to say in what our understanding it consists. Quine's well-known indeterminacy thesis suggests that, if we can find one theory to elucidate this, then we could find a distinct theory which would fit the observable behaviour of the speakers equally well, but would involve attributing to them different beliefs and desires. Now, given any two such theories, the speakers could be asked if either represented their understanding of the language better. If they preferred one, it seems unlikely that they could not give grounds for their preference in terms of what they would say or how they would respond to what others said; if they found them equally acceptable, it seems likely that analysis could reveal a sense in which they were equivalent. If neither of these two resolutions of the dilemma were available, the situation would indeed reveal that both rival theories of meaning had some superfluous content in excess of what is required for characterizing the speakers' understanding of the language; but it seems better to deal with such a crisis only when it actually occurs than to draw morals from a conviction of the possibility of its occurrence.

If we want to avoid circularity in an account of meaning in terms of the consequences of accepting a sentence as true, we must observe the same principle as in the other case: relative to suitable assignments of degrees of complexity, an explanation of the meaning of any sentence can presuppose the meanings only of sentences of lower complexity, and can be given simultaneously only with the meanings of those of the same complexity. Assignment of degrees of complexity is severely constrained by the principle that an understanding of a sentence is derived from its composition: we understand a sentence because we know the meanings of the words and the significance of the ways in which they are combined. This principle is not only intuitively evident, but inescapable in view of the fact that a theory of meaning cannot give the meaning of each sentence outright, since there are potentially infinitely many sentences of the language and the speakers are able to understand sentences they have not previously encountered: the theory therefore has no option but to lay down rules governing the individual words and the various modes of phrase- and sentence-composition from which the meanings of all possible sentences can be derived. For this reason, a compound sentence must always have a higher degree of complexity than any subsentence occurring in it; there is only limited latitude in the assignment of degrees of complexity.

From this it follows that, when the meaning of a sentence is explained in terms of the manner in which we establish it as true, the only inferences that can be taken into consideration are those that lead from premisses of lower complexity to conclusions of higher complexity. Conversely, when we explain meaning in terms of consequences, the only inferences considered are those leading from sentences of higher complexity to those of lower. It may be objected that we often come to recognize a sentence as true by means of an argument not all of whose steps are of the first kind, from less complex to more complex; indeed, if it were not so, there would be no such thing as drawing from a given sentence accepted as true the consequence that some simpler sentence is true, as is demanded for an account of meaning in terms of consequences. The converse objection can likewise be made to the restriction upon an account of the second kind. What reply is to be made to these objections?

What we have been considering are two alternative ways of explaining the meanings of the sentences of a language: in terms of how we establish them as true; and in terms of what is involved in accepting them as true. They are alternative in that either is sufficient to determine the meaning of a sentence uniquely; but they are complementary in that both are needed to give an account of the practice of speaking the language. Because either fully determines the meaning of a sentence, these two features of the use of a sentence cannot be assigned independently: given either, the other should follow. There ought, that is, to exist a harmony between these two features of use: it is principally because in the actual practice of speakers such harmony may be imperfect that customary linguistic practice is not sacrosanct or self-justifying, but may be open to criticism.

When the meaning of a sentence is given in terms of the manner in which that sentence may be verified, what is cited is the most *direct* means of verification. A direct verification, in the sense here intended, is one which corresponds step by step with the way in which the sentence is built up out of its constituents, and so with the way in which the truth-value of the sentence is represented by the theory of meaning as being determined in accordance with its composition. For example, if the meaning of the connective "or" is taken as given by the rule of disjunction-introduction, a direct verification of a disjunctive sentence will involve the verification of one of the two disjuncts. Likewise, a direct verification of a sentence like "There are nineteen eggs in the basket" will consist of counting. No one asked to explain how we verify this latter sentence would cite anything else; and yet one can certainly establish it as true in a variety of indirect ways; for instance, from the fact that the shopper who bought them and nothing else started with £9.73 and has £6.12 left, together with the fact that the eggs were of uniform price and cost more than 1p. and less than £1 each.

For all sentences other than observation sentences, we have seen that inferential reasoning will play an indispensable part in establishing their truth; but all that are strictly needed for this purpose are inferences leading from simpler to more complex sentences. Once the meanings of sentences are given in terms of the most direct means of verifying them, however, the meanings so given themselves justify the use of indirect means, because of the interrelation between the means of verifying different sentences. If the direct verification of one or more sentences would involve the verification of some simpler one, then if, on whatever basis, say that of testimony, someone has accepted the former sentences as true, he is entitled to accept the simpler one as true also. More generally, if we have a recipe for transforming the verification of one sentence into the verification of another, we are entitled to conclude the truth of the latter from that of the former; such a recipe is precisely what is supplied by a constructive proof.

For this reason, to explain meaning in terms of direct verification is not to deny that indirect verification is possible, but to indicate why it is justified.

In particular, it allows us to derive, from the meaning as so given, what is involved in accepting a given sentence as true: for to derive consequences from its truth is just a special case of an indirect verification of those consequences, up to the point when they issue in action. The converse also holds good. An explanation of meaning in terms of consequences takes into consideration only the most *direct* consequences, in an analogous sense. Such an explanation will, however, justify the drawing of indirect consequences: given certain sentences, accepted as true, we shall be entitled to infer any other sentence, any consequence of which would already be a consequence of the given sentences. Among such indirect consequences will be inferences, from less to more complex, of precisely the kind that occur in a direct verification. Hence, if the content of each sentence is given in terms of the consequences of accepting it, that will determine, for each sentence, what should count as verifying it. In this manner, whichever of the two features we take as constitutive of meaning, we can explain the harmony that ought to exist between them and, in virtue of that harmony, derive the other feature.

In the course of the foregoing discussion, a shift of perspective occurred which the attentive reader will have noticed. We began by considering a theory of meaning as laying down the condition for each sentence to be true, and our question was how, by appeal to the observable behaviour of the speakers of the language, such a theory might be judged correct. Identifying someone's taking a sentence to be true with his willingness to assert it, we distinguished two criteria of correctness: how the speakers establish or come to recognize sentences as true; and how so recognizing them affects their subsequent course of action. In discussing these two features of linguistic practice, however, we passed from treating them as providing the standard for evaluating a theory of meaning to regarding them as supplying its substance. From this second viewpoint, we have, not two complementary ways of validating a theory of meaning couched in terms of a sentence's being true, but two alternative types of theories, one couched in terms of a sentence's being established as true and the other in terms of its being treated as true.

The advantage of a theory of either of these last two kinds is that we do not need to ask how to connect it up with linguistic practice: it is framed in terms of linguistic practice. Hence, if a theory of either kind can be devised so as to yield a faithful account of our actual practice, it is preferable to one for which the connection needs still to be made. In such a case, we do not need, for the purposes of a theory of meaning, any such predicate as "is true", but only the predicates "is established (as true)" and "is accepted (as true)", where the parenthesized phrase has no independent meaning. We may very well continue to have a use for the predicate "is true" *within* the language, something easier to explain but of much less philosophical interest. But could a successful theory of either of the two kinds be devised? We cannot say, because we are a long way from solving the many problems of devising a workable theory of meaning of any kind. But, if it should prove impossible to construct a theory of meaning of either of the two kinds, that will almost certainly be because either type of theory would give an inadequate account of our deductive practice: it would license some, but not all, of those forms of inference we customarily treat as valid. If so, and if our deductive practice is to be vindicated, there will be no choice but to fall back on a theory of meaning of the first kind we discussed, one in which essential use is made of the predicate "is true".

To my mind, such an outcome would pose a deep and perplexing problem. We should be falling back on such a theory precisely because we found it impossible to construct one framed directly in terms of a feature of actual linguistic practice. It would seem to follow that the truth-conditional theory on which we had fallen back could not be fully justified by reference to that practice: it would, of its essence, reach beyond it. The theory would, indeed, supply an explanation of our practice, both of what we take as establishing our sentences as true and of what we treat as being the consequences of accepting them. Inasmuch as it explained these features of our linguistic practice, they in turn could be claimed as confirming the theory: but the fact that, by hypothesis, we could not recast that theory in terms of either of these two features would show that its content comprised more than a systematization of our practice.

It might be retorted that, on the hypothesis considered, it would have been yet another feature of our linguistic practice, namely the forms of inference we employ, that had forced us to fall back on the truth-conditional theory of meaning. This, however, is precisely the difficulty. We are not free to employ whatever forms of inference we choose, by convention, to count as valid: our linguistic practice will be incoherent unless we use only those forms of inference for which the assertion of the conclusion is as justified as the assertion of the premisses, according to the meanings of those sentences, however their meanings are thought of as having been given to us. Inferential practice must be faithful to meaning. The hypothesis is that we cannot justify all the forms of inference we use in terms of meaning taken as given in terms of verification. It follows that meaning cannot be taken as so given, unless we are in error in using certain forms of inference: for, by using them, we arrive at conclusions which we could not verify directly even given direct verifications of the premisses. Further, according to the hypothesis, we cannot justify all the forms of inference we use in terms of meaning taken as given in terms of consequences. It again follows that meaning cannot be taken as given in this way, unless our reasoning is, in part, in error: for, by using certain forms of inference, we shall be drawing conclusions the consequences of which would not flow from the premisses. The hypothesis therefore entails that, although deductive reasoning is part of our practice, it cannot without modification be justified by appeal to that practice: it can be justified only by imputing to us a grasp of meaning amounting to more than a grasp of the principles governing our use of the language.

The understanding of the language thus imputed to us will rest upon the notion of a sentence's being true, a notion which, by hypothesis, is not fully explicable in terms of what we actually learn to do when we learn to speak. We, as speakers of the language, will be presumed to have, for each sentence, a conception of what it is for it to be true: it will be in our grasp of that conception that our understanding of the sentence will consist. In applying this assumption to any one particular sentence, say "There are intelligent beings on a planet in the Andromeda galaxy", we do not need to employ the word "true" itself: to grasp what it is for that sentence to be true is just to grasp what it is for there to be intelligent beings on a planet in the Andromeda galaxy. This observation is sometimes made with an air of dissolving any difficulty there might seem to be in imputing such a conception to us; but this is to miss the point in two separate respects. For, first, the word "true" is not eliminable in stating the general assumption, which is what is required in characterizing our understanding of the language as such; and, secondly, the elimination of the word "true" in the particular case does not dissolve the difficulty. The difficulty is one of which some people find it hard to become aware: surely, they think, there can be nothing tendentious or paradoxical in ascribing to someone who understands the sentence quoted above a grasp of what it is for there to be intelligent beings on a planet in the Andromeda galaxy; asked if you knew what it was for that to be so, you would reply "Yes" simply on the strength of your understanding the sentence. To dismiss the matter thus is to ignore the hypothesis under which the whole of the present discussion is proceeding. That hypothesis, applied to the particular case, was that knowing what it is for there to be intelligent beings on a planet in the Andromeda galaxy cannot be exhaustively explained in terms of knowing what would establish that there were such beings, or in terms of knowing what consequences would follow from accepting that there were such beings, or from any other feature of our employment of the sentence: it would be a substantial conception, but no further explicable. It is in the context of that hypothesis that the assumption that we have such a conception of what it is for a sentence to be true becomes opaque; for my part, rather than accept that assumption, I should prefer to believe that some of our accustomed modes of reasoning are unjustifiable and ought to be abandoned.

I do not wish to be misunderstood. I am not asserting that the notion of truth, as employed in the theory of meaning, cannot be wholly explained in terms of those of verification and of consequences. I hope very much that it will prove to be able to be so explained; that would constitute a final resolution of the philosophical problem of truth. If, however, the notion of truth can be explained in terms of those notions, it can also be *replaced* by them, and would be better so replaced. More exactly, in such a case a truth-conditional theory of meaning could, and preferably should, be replaced by one in terms of verification or of consequences. If this cannot be done, we have the alternative of accepting, as essential to an account of our understanding of our language, a notion of truth which in principle resists complete elucidation, or of admitting radical error in accepted modes of reasoning. Perhaps fortunately for our peace of mind, we are not yet in a position to say whether we need face this choice or not.

Chapter 6

Language and Social Action

R. HARRÉ

Introduction

In considering how an understanding of speech can support an understanding of social action there have been two fruitful ways in which the relations between speech and action can be considered. First of all, one might look at complex social actions such as, for example, negotiating amongst the fellows of a college as to who ought to be the next Master, followed by the electoral process by which that person is selected, together with the ceremonial confirmation and installation of the new Master in his post. All of this could be considered as a complex social event. Within it there are component actions and speeches which are plainly social in their effect; for instance, performing them brings about changes in the social order. In considering speech instances with which we effect changes in a social order, one must consult some theory which will allow us to conceive of an utterance as something other than factual communication. The installation of a Master is a social event involving speech, in which there is a minimal communicative intent, perhaps at the most a way of showing members of the institution who the new Master shall henceforth be.

I shall be exploring in a little more detail in the body of this paper, the ways in which Austin's "theory of speech acts" can be developed to give an account of speech as part of social action. It will turn out that social functions of speech are much more complex than the simple example of parish politics I have mentioned would suggest. There are cases where speech ostensibly seems to be a description, or explanation of action, presenting some kind of theory about why the action occurred. This kind of discourse has come to be called accounting (Lyman and Scott, 1970). However, an examination of the occasions on which accounting is resorted to in real life suggests that not only is it a form of theorizing about action, but it is part of the action itself. To account for something, justify it, or excuse it, is itself to make a move in the social world, a move which has consequences for one's standing in that world. Consequently, such speech must be considered with respect to its social effectiveness and expressiveness, as well as its explanatory power.

In recent years speech production and the forms that speech takes, have been used in a different way by social analysts. They have been used as analogues of social action, so that the analysis of social events has been undertaken by developing techniques and concepts which have already earned a place in linguistics. In the body of this paper I shall be examining one of the many ways in which speech and speech analysis serves as an analogue of social action and its analysis.

Speech as an Analogue of Social Action

The introduction of linguistics into social science as an analogue science arose through the decline of confidence in the old-fashioned behaviourist way of thinking about social action. Although behaviourism as a general theory of psychology has been long since dead, it lives on in many of the unformulated assumptions of those who attempt to study social action experimentally. In order for a social experiment to be plausible, the action itself must be seen as partitionable into atomic events in such a way that the variables describing events can be separated one from another and to control the manipulation of treatment and outcomes. This condition can be met only if it is further assumed that the atomic events and the independent variables in terms of which they are analysed display merely Humean regularities. That is, statistical concomitances are treated as evidence of the existence of causal relations. It is not my purpose in this paper to rehearse once again the criticisms of the naive experimentalist approach, but it is worth pointing out that the most chilling of these involves the realization that the partition of a real episode into components where, as is inevitable in social action, those components are internally related one to another, leads to a fundamental change in the nature of the components as they are separated out. For example, a kiss has several distinctive social meanings, depending on the episode within which it is defined. So an experiment which would investigate the social effect of kissing or not-kissing when all other variables are maintained constant, must necessarily fail to capture anything of importance. Reflection on this criticism and the assumptions that lay behind the attempt to construct a psychology in the experimentalist mode serve to emphasize the fact that the structural properties of social activities are quite crucial to their reality and to their being determinately what they are.

Ethogenic analysis tends to see social action as a structured product, the component parts of which come into being by virtue of the relationship in which they stand to other component parts (Harré, 1979). In short, the elements of the structure are internally related. In the natural sciences the identification of structure and the teasing out of the definitive and constructive relationships between the elements of the structure, is a quite central form of empirical investigation, found alike in chemistry, anatomy, geology and so on. In the natural sciences, when a structured product is identified, the problem of its origin is immediately posed. In what way does it come into existence? Is it the result of the realization in new matter of some pre-existing structure which we could conceive of as a kind of template? In biology the biochemical foundation of genetics is conceived of in just such a way in that a gene is not a particular molecular realization of a structure but a structure that is realized in chemical material as DNA replication continues.

Sometimes, however, a structured product is not a result of the realization of a pre-existing structure but comes into being because the component elements that make it up fit together only in certain characteristic ways. The structure of a diamond is a product of the structured electronic fields of its component carbon atoms. There is no overall plan for a diamond which is realized by coming to exist in new matter. In traditional terms, form can be the product of form, or form can come into existence through the fitting together of particular component parts. In general the ethogenic approach to social psychology presumes that when a structure has been identified in the product social action, there must be some structured template to be found somewhere in the antecedent conditions of that action which is realized in the action.

Sometimes the structure may be individually founded, as for example in the linguistic knowledge which an individual has in the utilization of which the grammatical structure of his speech is produced. But sometimes this structure may exist only distributed somehow in the collectives to which a person belongs. It is the interaction of the collectives that provides the structural antecedent of some structured form. For instance, the way that a discussion develops, the turn-taking, the deference that is shown to speakers, and so on, can sometimes be shown to be a reflection of pre-existing hierarchical social structure of status that exists among the discussants. So to understand the structure of the conversation we may need to refer to the structured hierarchy of the persons engaged in it.

In thinking of social action as a structure of elements one must examine the complementary notion to structure, that of elements or components of that structure. In order for one's analysis to have any generality it is essential that the level of analysis at which elements are revealed should identify component parts with respect to the types or categories to which they belong. So one looks at a sequence of actions to ask what *kind* of action follows what kind, and is the antecedent of what kind. It is of no social interest that this or that particular set of coins is passed over to that particular person but rather that in passing over these particular coins a payment is made for a service. "Payment" and "service" are social elements conceived at a higher level of category or type than is say "57p". So the generalization that payments normally are subsequent to services is a description of a structured sequence which is defined at what I shall later call the level of *act*.

Any scientific enterprise involves theorizing, and any theorizing involves going beyond experience, to formulate hypotheses about causative processes which are rarely able to be observed by the scientific community at the time the theory is first formulated. How, then, are theoretical concepts to be developed and theoretical discourse to be kept on the rails, so to speak? In old-fashioned positivist philosophy of science it was thought sufficient that a theory should be logically related to the descriptions of matters which it was being introduced to explain. However, it was realized as long ago as 1600 by Christopher Clavius that that requirement left infinitely many rival theories in the field, in principle, for any given factual matter that had to be explained. In recent years attempts have been made by philosophers of science to understand how the specific theories that are formulated in explanatory contexts are controlled, so that one, or at most a very few theories, are in the field as plausible candidates for explanation. The most advanced thinking on this subject suggests that the content of a theory has much to do with whether that theory is or is not acceptable as a plausible explanation. However, in examining typical theory-content, it turns out that the explicit discourse of the science refers to only some of the components that an intuitive content analysis would suggest are crucial to theoretical undertaking. In general, the source of theoretical concepts is not explicit in the finished theoretical discourse. Nor, indeed, are the analytical models in terms of which the empirical work has been done, explicitly formulated either.

Once again, the ethogenic approach tries to take into account the ways in which theories are formulated and to make explicit what would be the source of theoretical content if we took the structured template point of view seriously. Suppose that one looked around the social world for kinds of events which were quite obviously orderly and structured—one type of action that was regularly followed by an action of another kind in such a way that common-sense understanding would allow us to see how in the totality of the action some social effect, such as a change of status for instance, was brought off.

Typically, ceremonies are such events. At a degree-giving, there are quite distinctive actions performed, quite specific linguistic formulae are recited (in Oxford, happily, in Latin, a language with which few contemporary scholars are acquainted, thus preserving its purely ritual quality). The formulae of presentation and admission follow one another in a sequence together with deferential and confirmatory actions. Common-sense understanding enables us to see how it is that doing these things are the ways in which a person's status is transformed from undergraduate to Bachelor of Arts to Doctor of Philosophy. How is it that several times a year, in the Sheldonian Theatre in the University of Oxford, a succession of Deans of

Degrees, Vice-Chancellors, Proctors, Marshals, and candidates, have, for the last seven hundred years, successfully replicated the same ceremony over and over and over again? The answer is simple but instructive. The order of service, as it were, is laid down. There are statutes which define the ceremony in terms of the kinds of things that must be done in order for the ceremony to have been properly performed. There are constitutive and regulative rules which define who may appear, what they must wear in order to be seen to appear, and the kind and sequence of formulae which are required to bring off the social change which is at the heart of this particular activity.

In this example there is a structured product and there is also, in plain view, a structured template, namely the printed order of service which defines the sequences which make up the ceremony. Suppose we choose this kind of social event as a source-model for developing concepts, for explaining (and analysing) social events of a more informal kind. For example, the behaviour of a group of friends who after a meeting of a local protest committee go to the local pub for a drink or two, and if my experience is anything to go by, behave in a remarkably orderly and structured way in distributing responsibility for ordering and paying for drinks, as the event gets under way. How should we explain this? If we take the ceremony and its rules as a source-model, then we would postulate that the social knowledge of individuals includes constitutive and regulative rules. An individual would then be competent to pay for and receive drinks in a pub without offence, displaying appropriate forms of deference, so that the *amour propre* of everyone is preserved.

In general, rules represent in linguistic mode whatever entities function as templates in cognitive processes of which we are normally not conscious. Only if we have a foreigner with us, or if we begin to go badly wrong, or someone behaves unfortunately in refusing to accept a subordinate status in the payment business, then we may consciously reference the rule and perhaps publicly state it. The fact that this can be done and that the rule is recognized as *the* rule, suggests that once stated it has become part of public social reality. Its mandatory force is manifest, and the offender shuts up. All of this goes to show how, supposing a process representable as following rules is a powerfully explanatory idea as representing a possible mechanism for understanding, when we are not paying attention, nevertheless we do shape our actions cognitively. It is no part of my theory to suggest that the rules are themselves efficient causes of action.

This analogy can be taken a little further and amplified by a second conceptual system introducing a second more general analogy into the story. It has often been remarked that ceremonies have a dramatic quality, if performed properly on a ceremonial occasion. A person behaves somewhat in the same manner as an actor. A person is to be seen as playing a part and the parts are quite distinctive. Indeed in most ceremonies there is a script, there are costumes, there is an audience, and there may even be producers, directors and the like. We can look at the ceremonial analogue as suggesting a version of a more general dramaturgical analogy. This might suggest looking for settings, props, and other features of staging, for instance. We might go so far as to propose that in certain kinds of social actions people should be seen to be related to their actions as actors are related to the performances they put on, on the stage. This further step in the analogy needs to be taken with the greatest caution. It does not follow that because we can usefully look for props and costumes, even for directors and producers, that we are thereby committed to saying that the person in this performance is always or even generally psychologically related to his action as an actor is to the playing of his part. That would be a serious over-stretching of the analogy.

It may sometimes be the case that the psychology of a human agent is just that of the human agent as stage actor. Lyman has made one or two interesting comments on the occasions in married life when this kind of relation to action seems to be appropriate. Goffman (1972) too has pointed to the peculiar state of mind of someone who finds it necessary to deliberately create an appearance of normality. The adulterous wife returning from an evening with her lover and making the evening cocoa in such a way as to provide for a reading of the events of the evening as normal, is *skillfully* maintaining what is ordinarily an unattended orderliness.

We can now take a further step. The analysis and explanatory system that I have been outlining has introduced the idea of types of social elements in structured sequences. These structures must be preserved for the social force of component actions to be maintained and the intelligibility of the whole activity to be sustained. This final requirement suggests an explanatory hypothesis—that much social activity is the product of a system of templates which human beings follow consciously as rules, or unconsciously in the active formation of structured sequences.

It should be clear now how the linguistic analogy is immediately suggested. Words are defined for grammatical purposes at the level of types and grammar is expressible in one way or another as a system of rules. Furthermore, no one supposes that a native speaker consciously pays attention to the rules of grammar unless he is instructing a foreigner, or dealing with some manifest error or uncertainty as to how he should go on. Access to rules is normally not conscious. Rules are the linguistic representations of cognitive templates. It follows, then, that we should explore the idea of a social syntax in which we should look for relational invariants between types of actions at the level of social significance or social effectiveness; and that we should look for an analogue of semantics in which we would identify the significance of the units which might have their existence in various different physical modes, for example as speeches, or movements or stances, or orders of procession, and so on.

In order to work out this thought in detail, I need to introduce a vitally important distinction between the *social force* of a human performance and the *shaped reality* in which that force is manifested by an actor. For example, the social force of something somebody says or does may be an insult. Obviously unless someone does or says, or deliberately refrains from doing or saying something, neither insulting nor any other social act can be performed. We have to look, then, for the realization of the intention to insult in some action or speech, as for example, cocking a snook may be the action by which an insult is performed. Common-sense understanding suggests that there are many ways of insulting someone, of which cocking a snook is only one. Some of these ways may be pre-empted by the kind of event by which the insult is to be delivered, but others are a matter of choice and personal style. The importance of this distinction lies in the fact that our social syntax must be conceived of at the level of types of action, that is where the type is defined in terms of social effectiveness or force. Thus, the level of generality at which we should expect to find structure in social action would be that at which we identify insults, apologies, requests, pleas, promises and so on, rather than that at which we identify cockings of snooks, wavings of hands, sayings of "thanks", and so on.

My argument depends upon the assumption that social analysis is necessarily top-down, that is, we first identify a social episode in terms of the social sequence of acts performed and then secondarily, look for the public actions in and by which those acts are carried out. At both levels the concept of intention has a part to play. It seems clear that in most cases it would be proper to speak of acts as intended in a straightforward and simplistic way, that is that someone should be thought of as having formed an intention to insult as part of the conditions of his producing a public insult. We would also want to say, I believe, that the actions with which the acts are performed, are themselves intended actions, that is that they do not occur by accident, or unintentionally, and so on. It does not necessarily follow that a person will have formed a prior and conscious intention to perform this or that action. However, by saying that these actions are intended, does open up the possibility of cases arising in which for one reason or another, for instance social uncertainty, conscious choice would have to be made as to the material realization of a particular social act. And then indeed we might want to say quite literally, that he intended to cock a snook when he raised a hand to his nose, and what is more, that he intended to raise his hand to his nose when he started to raise his hand. And all of that is intended in his primary intention too.

One further theoretical remark is required at this point. While we would give a social occasion explanation in terms of *amour propre* and the like, as to why he felt inclined to insult someone we would have to give an account in terms of the local communal rules for performance of social acts in order to see cocking a snook as an action appropriate to the performance of that insult. We must take account, then, of two levels of normative material. The first level is concerned with the protection of personal or collective honour. The second is concerned with the means by which the acts required at the first level can be successfully brought off.

We can now consider the possibility of making explicit the implicit social syntax, an empirical investigation which explores order at the level of acts. Having identified a structure in a social interaction the normative principles of that structure can be linguistically represented as rules. We are now in a position to ask a further question about the status of those rules, that is the rules that we have presently extracted from our syntactical analysis of the situation conceived as typical of the situations of this sort. Normative statements might have three different implications.

(i) They may be regulatory principles which are consulted or followed by actors in the production of the action. In a society of a highly formalist cast we would expect there to be many such rules. Court circles, for instance, as described in one of the Japanese Pillow Books, require behaviour which is highly stylized and which is acquired by quite explicit processes of conscious rule-following. The rules are very near the surface of life in that they are regularly referred to in commentary upon action and planning future events.

(ii) The rules may, as we express them, reflect normative principles, though perhaps "principles" is too propositional a way of talking in this context, which represent our linguistic formulation of habits and conventions through which people define and control actions in a certain society. It may be that never in that society's history has a convention been formulated, so that knowledge of it, though expressible propositionally, ought not to be thought to be propositional in the way it is known to competent actors. A social habit, for instance, may be of that kind. An example of this sort of thing would be the regularities which are found in the highly distinctive bodily adjustments of males to females in different human societies. There are different conventions as to how one should walk, sit, etc., relative to a member of the other sex, and only rarely will such conventions be propositionally formulated at any time. We should still wish to speak of these habits and conventions as normative, that is, action which violates them would be felt in some way to be inadequate, wrong, rude and so on, but the commentary upon such inadequacies would not, of necessity, involve explicit formulation in the social settings of the rule as propositionally expressed.

(iii) There is a third possibility that the rules which are formulated by the ethogenic investigator on the basis of his use of folk understandings to identify the social acts that have been performed, have no further status but that of the description of regularities. We may have no idea on what those regularities are based—whether something explicit, something implicit but culturally idiosyncratic, or something universal and biological, perhaps encoded in the genes. Collett (1974) discovered a clear pattern of behaviour, in the way people pass each other in the street. The principles of propriety for "passing", have never before been formulated and have this unresolved and ambiguous character. It is no part of the ethogenic viewpoint to argue that all patterns of social interaction must be determined by normative principles, be they propositional or merely habitual. It is an empirical question whether a certain regularity in behaviour is to be related to a prior existing normative template in the cognitive structures of the collectives or sometimes even the individuals in that society.

However, having formulated the rules, we may then ask why it is that those rules have survived in the society. Questions of that sort asked in these contexts, have to be very carefully controlled to avoid implying teleological processes for which we have no evidence. The most cautious approach is the one I wish to advocate in this paper, namely that the explanation of the continued existence of a practice on the grounds of its capacity to sustain some social property such as stability, must be taken with a considerable degree of caution. The only safe way is to argue that the functionality, for example, of a practice is seen to be sustaining of human dignity—such a functional remark must be taken in a strictly evolutionary (Darwinian) sense, that is, the explanation of the continued presence of a custom is not teleological, but rather that in the absence of any alternative it remains the human practice. Variations, mistakes, etc., are weeded out because for one reason or another they do not subserve human dignity so well as existing alternatives. We do not need any teleological explanatory framework in which there is an unreduceable "in-order-to" linking a practice with its social effects.

I shall return in the last part of this paper to a consideration of how the material arrived at by ethogenic analysis can form the basis of a psychological theory of action.

The elements or units which form the material basis of the syntactical structures that we have now seen ways of identifying, could be analysed at any one of three levels—social acts, social actions, or individual behaviour. The argument of the last section concerning the level at which structure is to be discerned, suggests that analysis in terms of individual behaviour is worthless. The minimal level at which elements relevant to the structure can be identified is that of action. If we are talking of social semantics, in what way is the notion of meaning to be introduced into our analysis? I believe that it is in accordance with contemporary usage to identify acts as the meaning of actions, so that the question "What did he mean by that?" requires an act-description as an answer, and it is an action to which the "that" refers. "What did he mean by waving at me?" "What did he mean by jamming on the brakes?" "What did he mean by that enigmatic smile?" and so on.

Meaning is, at least on the face of it, a concept which has a place in both linguistics and social action analysis. The second phase of the linguistic analogue I wish to examine is how far a linguistic theory of meaning would help us to understand how it is that acts can be the meanings of actions. The first point to notice is that any referential theory of meaning is applicable. Characteristically, sentences which are used to perform social acts such as committing oneself, do not refer to a commital which is, as it were, something external to the use of that sentence, as for instance, a horse is external to the use of the sentence "My horse is brown". So, for example, the oath in the marriage ceremony "I will" does not refer to an act of oath taking; it is one. Now this point is familiar to linguists and philosophers from speech act theory. Clearly, a non-referential theory of meaning will be required to understand such speeches. As far as I can see, the non-referential theory that makes the most sense in this context is a modified form of the *valeur/signifié* theory of Ferdinand de Saussure (1974). In that theory we have an intra-systematic element in meaning (*valeur*) and an extra-systematic element in meaning (*signifié*). Whatever the merits of this theory may be for understanding linguistic meaning (and I think they are great), it certainly seems to systematize our own intuitions in social semantics quite successfully.

De Saussure's conception of intra-systematic meaning has to do with the location of a meaningful item, such as a word or a gesture, in two kinds of structures. A meaningful item is located in a syntagmatic dimension by reference to relations to other meaningful items which occur, for instance, in a sentence, or in a social ritual, or whatever. So the first step in expressing the social meaning of a kiss, say, is to describe the location of the kiss relative to other socially meaningful actions in various interactional events. But in order to grasp the point of there being a kiss, rather than something else, at that point in the ceremony, say a wave or a handshake, we have to represent the presence of a kiss as excluding certain other kinds of interactive actions. For example, a kiss on the cheek excludes a kiss on the lips. A kiss excludes a handshake, and so on. So our understanding of social significance is amplified by representing alternatives on paradigmatic axes, normal, as it were, to the axis upon which the syntagmata in which that item appears could be laid out. The totality of these structures expresses the intra-systematic element in the meaning of the kiss. Paradigmatic axes represent not only alternatives that might have the same meaning, but alternatives which would involve a change in meaning, if inserted into the syntagmata in the place of a kiss.

The second, or extra-systematic element in de Saussure's linguistic theory is, if I have understood him aright, some form of referential relation. However, we have seen that in social semantics the idea of there being a referential relation seems implausible. What then, could stand in for the extra-systematic elements in such a meaning-analysis? Clearly, in the case of social acts it is the social consequences that are crucial to our understanding of what it is that the act means. If we understand the act as a commitment, then it is the commitments which constitute the meaning of having performed that act. Similarly, it is the preservation of dignity that is the consequence of the performing of certain acts in what Goffman has called "face-work", the mutually supportive activity in which we remedy the social infelicities of members of our set, securing our honour by preserving their face. The act of commitment, etc., points beyond itself to its consequences. One can hardly be said to have delivered an insult if no one is thereby insulted. At the most one can have tried to insult someone and failed. In sum, then, social semantics can be developed with a theory parallel to a linguistic theory, provided that a plausible substitute for referential meaning can be found.

The theory required to express social meaning in all its detail needs to be somewhat more complex than the sketch I have proposed here. There are various other levels of meaning involved in social action. This is largely because, once we reach the level of acts, it becomes apparent that acts form hierarchies, concatenate into larger structures in which more molar kinds of acts are engendered by the performance of the acts which are lower in the hierarchical sequence. For instance, there is a structured sequence of specific acts such as the signing of documents, the witnessing of those signatures, the transfer of money, and so on, by which the higher order act of the winding up of a company, let us say, is performed. Finally, though in this paper I wish only to note the point, there are acts of yet higher orders which are performed by all the more subordinate kinds of acts. These have to do with the expression of the very nature of the society itself. Only a subtle hermeneutical analysis can bring to light those acts in the rapid and often glaringly illuminated flow of acts and actions which constitute everyday life.

Speech as Part of Social Action

I pointed out in the introduction the extent to which speech forms part of social action sequences. Now this role is complex. Indeed, as I hope to demonstrate there are two quite distinctive roles played by speech in the course of social action.

(i) *Speech as part of the action:* this idea has been well known since Austin's discovery of the performative force of utterances which has been generalized into speech act theory. However, I would like to draw attention to a recent development that has raised some interesting issues about the form of speech act development. The context is Bruner's (1978) work on the way in which young children acquire the capacity to make requests in what he calls "request-formats", and to respond to what they recognize as requests made by adults. Bruner has shown that grammatical form, at least as adults recognize it, is no guide to performative force. Indeed, it would be fair to say that he has demonstrated that performative force is prior to grammatical form in infant understanding. For example, the question-form "Why don't you eat up your greens?" is used by parents in English-speaking cultures, to make a request or perhaps sometimes even to issue an order. Bruner has been able to demonstrate that an infant understands the performative force rather than the grammatical form. Indeed, the capacity to identify a grammatical form as a specific representation of performative force, is a rather late stage in the development of linguistic capacity. Infants recognize questions by their performative force rather than by reference to their grammatical form. The idea that the question-form, a grammatical form, is linked to performative force is a late acquisition.

To connect this kind of analysis with the social semantics/social syntax suggestions that I made in the first section, one can use Austin's distinction between illocutionary and perlocutionary force. The refinement and development of speech act theory since Austin's original formulation of the idea has left the distinction between the social forces of speech acts unimpaired. The illocutionary force could be identified with the social act performed in the course of the speech act performed in doing some appropriate social action, as for example, the illocutionary force of saying that one promises is promising. Perlocutionary force of a speech act includes the social consequences created by the action. This notion has been generalized, indeed, was generalized already by Austin, to include consequences other than the social ones. But for our purposes these are not of singular importance. So, for example, in the social act of promising, there is commitment, the social consequences of which may include subsequent actions (Austin, 1965). So while the illocutionary force of "I promise" is a promise, its perlocutionary force is to effect some consequential fulfilment of that promise. With respect to our analysis of meaning, the illocutionary force represents one level of meaning, that by which the act is identified as such, and perlocutionary force represents that level of meaning which we define in terms of consequences. All of this is very well known and hardly needs great elaboration on my part. Refinements in speech act theory have had to do more with the structure of speech acts than with the underlying social hypotheses concerning the uses of speech upon which it is based.

(ii) *Speech as accounting for the action:* i.e. the creation by speaking of a certain socially desired construal of events in question, a construal in terms of which they are seeable as justified or unjustified, excusable or inexcusable. Accounting, it turns out, involves two levels of interpretation. In the first, what one might call the existential level, ways of speaking create social facts.

For instance, in investigations of the way football fans talk about their ritual encounters, it becomes clear that there is a definitional process involved in which the events in question are described as "fights" and fights in this sense have all the implications of fights in the real world, i.e. as physical encounters which are likely to involve some sort of physical damage. In this way, an event is created in a certain category (Marsh, Rosser and Harré, 1978). It is irrelevant, therefore, whether or not blood has actually flowed. The social consequences of the redefinition of the encounter as a fight in the way that fans discuss these matters is what is relevant to the social effects of the event in question. So existential redefinition is a ritual creative process in the construction of a social order, and this is done primarily by speech of various kinds.

Recent work in the sociology of science has shown that there are comparable redefinitions in which hypotheses are converted into facts by being expressed in a fact-stating kind of language (Latour and Woolgar, 1979). However, existential transformation is not the only way in which accounting can function. It is necessary for human beings engaging in social events of various kinds to show to themselves and to each other that they are proper, right, worthy, dignified, moral, rational, etc. That involves embedding the action, as existentially redefined, in a system of normative propositions (and implications) in which whatever is done is seen as the actions of a rational being within a well-understood moral order. Once again we are indebted to Austin for the initial impetus in this investigation, with his famous distinction between excuses and justifications, forms of talk in terms of which actions are construed within a moral order (Austin, 1961). In an excuse, an action is reckoned to have the moral quality assigned to it by the complainer, but a reason is given by which what was done was construable as inevitable. And in claiming the inevitability of the action, the actor is clearly making a claim about his own moral standing. On the other hand in justifications a form of speech is employed in which the moral quality originally imputed to the act by the complainer is denied. Once again, the speaker, if his account is accepted, has succeeded in altering not only the moral quality of the action but his own moral standing as well, since he now appears, relative to the act, as one who might or could, commit it.

Backman (1977) has added a third category of great practical importance to Austin's list—the process that he calls normalization. In accounts that normalize an event, the event is seen as something for which there is no call for any kind of moral judgement since it is amongst the ordinary activities of mankind. For instance, the activity of mild, middle-class smuggling, is justified on the grounds that everyone does it. Now this is neither an excuse nor justification in Austin's sense. The issue of its moral quality does not enter into the discourse since it is, after all, just normal. It is easy to see that in all these linguistic activities, the issue of the moral standing of the speaker is central so that one could look upon these forms of speaking as addressed to the maintenance of the position of the speaker in the moral order and the challenges to which he or she is responding as attempts to alter that standing. Furthermore, if we regard the position of the human being in the expressive orders of his society as of central concern, then it is no other than accounting that accounts for a great deal of human social talk.

By analysing accounts one can discover the system of meanings, rules, etc., that competent members must be capable of developing since it is in terms of those normative propositions that the entire apparatus of accounting works as a way of demonstrating one's moral qualities and impugning those of other people. The basic hypothesis which the linguistic analogy suggests to one is a generalization of the classical "competence/performance" distinction which, perhaps of all the theoretical notions introduced by Chomsky, has survived with the least modification. The principles involved in the production of action (those principles which were the product of ethogenic analysis of action) can be organized in terms of their power to reveal the social syntax and social semantics of a culture. By testing the results of "outsider" analysis of action–act performances against the material that is revealed in accounts, the most general hypothesis of all could be tested: that social competence of members as speakers and actors is to be identified with the totality of normative material that is found by conjoining the ethogenic analysis of action with the existential and moral analysis of accounts. In this way, one can put together a set of hypotheses about the cognitive foundations of competence. Of course, nothing whatever follows from this about how a performer on a particular occasion employs that knowledge to generate a particular sequence of actions having a specifiable meaning.

Finally, it is worth pointing out that a great many human activities are constructed so as *not* to have a precise and univocal reading. Those actions which I have used as examples inevitably suggest *precise meanings*. However, many actions are produced in such a way as to allow a multiplicity of readings. They are deliberately vague. One can see immediately, on common-sense grounds alone, why it is that much of social action has a less well-defined form than linguistic performances generally. Since any social action whatever is liable to come up for criticism and to require accounting, it is clear that an action which offers scope for redefinition is in many contexts a more useful kind of action than one which is susceptible to only one interpretation. Therefore, the analytical stages that I have defined in this section, namely the use of Austinian performative theory to identify action and then the use of account analysis to locate that action, in a normative system, is in practice frequently reversed. The action is sufficiently vague for the actor to be able to wait upon the specification of the moral order in which it is to occur before he sets about the remedial task of redefining it as a performative of a particular kind. In this way, vague statements are made which only in certain circumstances are construed as and refined into promises. Much of this has been identified by anthropologists as phatic speech. For example, "Why don't you join me for lunch sometime?" opens up the possibility of, and prepares the way for, a genuine invitation. The function of such talk is to leave matters unresolved so that as the social world changes actions and acts become more or less defined one way or the other. These open matters can be made more specific, and so can function as having particular illocutionary force, for example, being genuinely inviting.

In this paper I have explored two ways in which aspects of the study of language can be used to throw light on human conduct. By judicious borrowings from linguistic theory, a social syntax and a social semantics can be constructed by which forms of order are identified and the social meanings of actions defined. Linguistic structures, such as sentences, are here treated as analogues of social act–action structures, such as ceremonies.

But in many contexts social action is realized in the very medium of speech itself. Speech act theory opens up the possibility of a level of understanding which makes the study of the social force of talk a species of social semantics. But we are frequently required to account for our actions. On those occasions a skilful social actor may seize the opportunity not only to "get himself off the hook", but to present himself to those around in the most favourable possible light. In this way giving an account not only explains an action but serves to reveal the character and accomplishments of the speaker.

References

AUSTIN, J.L. (1961), "A plea for excuses" in Urmson, J.O. and Warnock, G.J. (Eds), *Philosophical Papers*, Clarendon Press, Oxford, Chapter 6.
AUSTIN, J.L. (1965), *How to do Things with Words*, Oxford University Press, New York, p. 101.
BACKMAN, C. (1976), "Explorations in psycho-ethics: the warranting of judgements", in Harré, R. (Ed.), *Life Sentences*, Wiley, London, Chapter 12.
BRUNER, J. (1981), "The organization of action and the nature of adult–infant transaction", in von Cranach, M. and Harré, R. (Eds), *The Analysis of Action*, Cambridge University Press.
COLLETT, P. (1974), "Patterns of public behaviour: collision avoidance on a pedestrian crossing", *Semiotica*, **12** (4), 281–299.
DE SAUSSURE, F. (1974), *Course in General Linguistics* (translated Baskin, W.), Fontana, London.
GOFFMAN, E. (1972), *Relations in Public*, Penguin Books, Harmondsworth, Chapter 6.
HARRÉ, R. (1979), *Social Being*, Blackwell, Oxford, Chapters 2, 3 and 4.
LATOUR, B. and WOOLGAR, S. (1979), *Laboratory Life*, Sage, Beverley Hills and London, Chapter 3.
LYMAN, S.M. and SCOTT, M.B. (1970), *A Sociology of the Absurd*, Appleton-Century-Crofts, New York, Chapter 5.
MARSH, P., ROSSER, E. and HARRÉ, R. (1978), *The Rules of Disorder*, Routledge and Kegan Paul, London, p. 97.

Chapter 7
Social Anthropology, Language and Reality

EDWIN ARDENER

The study of classification has a long history in social anthropology.[1†] At many points this interest has closely paralleled and overlapped with the interests of linguists, both in its general and its particular applications. A classical instance of common endeavour has, for example, been in the field of colour classification. Hjelmslev (1963: 52–53), for example, long ago noted the discrepancies in colour labels between different languages. Anthropology has multiplied such instances, so that both the numbers and kinds of colours discriminated by unit category terms have been shown to be of considerable variety. Later, some order was brought into the variation by (among others) Berlin and Kay (1969). There are some general principles underlying the cultural choices.

These studies raised the issue of relativism versus universals in social anthropology. Thus, insofar as all classifications partake of this feature exemplified by colour classification it became legitimate to ask whether all cultural systems were in principle *sui generis*, even implying in some sense "separate realities". Whorf, as generally represented at least, took this question to the point of appearing to argue that cultural perceptions were not simply mediated by language, but that language determined the way in which we experience reality. His examples were drawn in part from the kinds of classification differences referred to already, such as the famous three kinds of snow of the Eskimo (Carroll, 1964: 210). He referred also to other more general features of language—for example, presence or absence of grammatical "tense" or of "mood" or "aspect"—as being some kind of determinant of views of time or process in particular cultures. Thus, again putting the matter very simply, a Hopi physics (for reasons of this sort) would differ from a European physics.

I think that Whorf has been misunderstood, but there is no doubt that the misunderstanding itself has a firm place in specialist thinking about this

† Superscript numbers refer to Notes at end of chapter.

knotty combination of language, classification, and reality. Consequently much of this work has been judged to have painted itself into a corner, appearing to favour: (a) extreme cultural relativism; (b) separate cultural realities; (c) the cultural determination of both knowledge and "experience"; and even, as we have seen, (d) linguistic determination of cultural experience. These extreme positions (if actually held) would obviously make arguments for the existence of cultural universals more difficult, and stand in opposition to ideas of cultural change, as well as to more subtle views of the relation of language to culture and of culture to reality.

Berlin and Kay's work on colour classification was seen by many as restoring universals to the centre of discussion. Thus cultures were "relativistic" in detail but there was some kind of limit to their arbitrary, reality-shaping powers. Some went so far as to argue that at a commonsense level cultural differences were greatly exaggerated, and that the major differences were mystifications deriving from ritual specialists (Bloch, 1977). For people with any idea of a universal truth to be taught to all mankind, the exact nature of cultural difference is a serious question. Thus at times, both missionaries and historical materialists have led violent attacks on the merest hint of cultural relativism. In Miss Mandy Rice-Davies's phrase, "They would, wouldn't they?" If there are self-evident truths that are to be taught these truths cannot themselves be subject to any law of cultural relativism. "Cultural realities" must then be rejected on two grounds: (a) if the observer's vision is the truth, then it cannot just be part of the relativity of the observer's culture; (b) if that truth is to be transmitted to others, then cultural "worlds" that differ from it or reject it must be obfuscations of some kind, obscuring the truth. Whether or not one goes on to attribute the obfuscations to simple error, or to self-interest on the part of some portion of the population concerned, is a detail. Fundamentalist missionaries and some development economists have vacillated between both interpretations, while Marxists and historical materialists often tend to favour the latter. That is after all the more universalistic position: cultural classifications thereby become the secondary result, or "artefact", of human universals like power and dominance. As for any kind of role for language—those of "running dog", or at best of "handmaiden" or "lackey", seem to be the most conveniently vacant! So much for any short-lived Whorfian linguistic dreams of empire.

I do not wish to caricature this debate—I think that the oppositions implied are simply false, although it is easy to see why they should arise. It is, for example, quite obvious that "mystifications" do occur. The literature on the social manipulation of discourse is quite well established: there is really nothing controversial about it. Indeed, it probably seems less problematic to linguists even than it does to social anthropologists.

Let us, as it were, assert that when the issues are big enough there is no recourse but to firmly universalistic principles. Yet cross-cultural (or subcultural) misunderstanding on supposedly trivial issues (whatever the possibilities on greater ones) is a very real problem at the level of close interactions between individuals, so much so that it is itself a human universal, and whether we like it or not language looms very large in these situations. This does not only arise in the obvious limiting case, in which the interactors do not share a language. On the contrary, it often seems that the more they *think* they share, the more those "Whorfian" characteristics arise, and in comes the whole baggage of cultural classifications and the rest, all clothed in rich linguistic detail. It is my opinion (see Ardener, 1971: xix–xxvii), not perhaps widely understood, that this is the point on which Whorf's original insight rests. The self-taught fire-insurance assessor was in the possession of the basic facts of the interpenetration of "language, thought and reality" (Carroll, 1964) before he was tempted into the world of the professionals and learned bad habits. The famous programme for linguistic determinism is correctly named the "Sapir-Whorf Hypothesis", for there was no reason why Whorf in his untutored state should have taken that road.

Whorf's problem as a fire-insurance assessor was a *material* one. The insurance company lost if a fire broke out. Any interpretation of the cause of a fire that reduced the incidence of such fires and the amount of such payments was "cost-effective". It might even reduce premiums. We are used to such causes being cast in terms of the physics of combustion. Whorf's insight was to see that the disposition of flammable materials in vulnerable places was often due to a set of underlying linguistic classifications. For him "empty gasoline drums" exploded because they were classed as "empty" (so that people smoked near them) instead of "full" (of gasoline fumes). He found that "spun limestone", and "scrap lead" from condensers (both highly combustible materials), burst into flames when left near rubbish fires, because they were heaped wrongly with non-combustible waste. The mistake was due to the classifications with "lead" and "stone". Whorf's "reality" was inextricably intertwined with human classifications. Physical explosions (he appeared to say) were produced by a careless mixture of categories as well as of chemicals (Ardener, 1971: xxii). It is the *material* nature of Whorf's basic problem that contains the interesting antidote to his own, and other people's flight into debates on cultural reality. Of course, Whorf's failure to develop an adequate language to discuss his original insight does not absolve him from serious criticism. From any modern point of view it is a great pity that time has frequently to be wasted in denying that this or that study of language and categories of classification embodies merely a culturally relativistic position (Ardener, 1971). Meanwhile, from the point of view of linguistics this often leads to the study of cultural classifications being represented as the collection of cultural curiosities.

Some of these points, including the materiality feature, are here illustrated from the classification of bodily parts. It is well known that the human body is divided by different criteria in different languages. In the present exposition I shall treat part of such a classification through a simultaneous analysis of thought, language and action, in order to make clearer my arguments.

Let us consider the shaking of hands in England and among the Ibo of south-eastern Nigeria.[2] In both languages there are apparently inter-translatable terms for the gesture (Ibo: *ji aka*). Although *aka* is usually translated "hand" the boundaries of the parts concerned are, however, quite different. The English "hand" is bounded at the wrist. The Ibo *aka* is bounded just below the shoulder. The fingers and thumb are called *mkpisi aka*, in which *mkpisi* is "any thin somewhat elongated object" (cf. "a stick" *mkpisi osisi*—*osisi* "tree"; "a match" *mkpisi okhu*—*okhu* "fire") (see Fig. 7.1). The more open-gestured nature of the Ibo handshake compared with the English handshake is linked in part to this difference of classification. For the English-speaker the extreme, "formal" possibility of presenting an only slightly mobile hand at the end of a relatively stiff arm becomes a choice reinforced by language. For the Ibo-speaker, even if that is a possible gesture it has no backing from language. On the contrary, for him, gripping the forearm and other variants of the gesture are still covered by the concept of shaking the *aka*, and are, as it were, allomorphs of the common gestural morpheme. For the English-speaker such arm-grips are gesturally (that is, not merely linguistically) separate from shaking hands—they are gestures of a different "meaning".

We do not resort to any linguistic determinism if we argue that the gestural classification rests to a certain degree on the labeling of bodily parts. The possibility of a different classification of greetings exists for the English speaker because of the particular placing of a conceptual boundary, which does not exist in Ibo. Thus, on the average of observations, an Ibo in "shaking hands" may involve the movement of an area greater than the "hand" more often than does an English person. Consistently shaking the hand alone, with articulation only at the wrist, might therefore seem to the traditional Ibo a slightly incomprehensible restriction of movement, equivalent perhaps in flavour to being, in the English case, offered only two or three fingers to shake. From the opposite point of view, to the English-speaker "shaking hands" and "arm-grip" are two *kinds* of greeting. To the Ibo they are degrees of intensity, demonstrativeness, of warmth, of "the same" greeting. As a result even a "warm" handshake in the English sense may seem relatively "cool" as a greeting to an Ibo.

Further light is shed by another collocation. The English "help" is translated *nye aka* in Ibo, which appears to mean "give a hand" and thus to be a directly parallel metaphorical usage. Yet in close face-to-face cases when a physical "hand" is appropriate, such as when assistance over a large

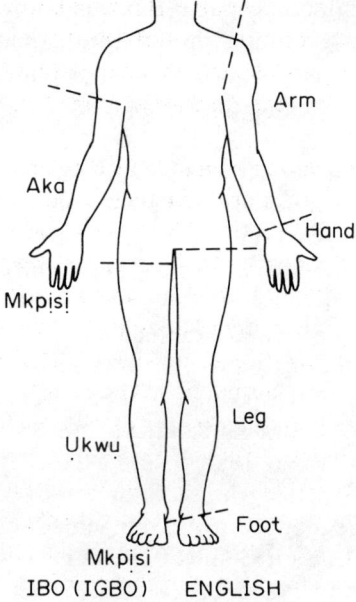

FIG. 7.1. Diagram to show the different boundaries of various parts of the body in English and Ibo.

fallen tree-trunk on a path, or up a steep slope, is asked for (*nye m aka* "give me a hand"), a forearm may be offered to be gripped as often as the hand, if in practical terms either may suffice. In an English language context the request "give (or lend) me a hand" in those exact circumstances would only rarely fail to result in the offer of the literal "hand". With regard to the "degree" of helpfulness it is a "warmer" gesture for the English-speaker to be offered a hand than a forearm. The apparent deficiency is thus now on the opposite side of the cultural-linguistic divide.

We may easily ask here, following a respectable anthropological tradition, whether the bodily classifications are not simply determined by the social events the body mediates. One chain of argument might develop from the observation that when the hand is engaged in work, or in preparing palm-oil or food, there is a polite reluctance to offer help or greeting with it. The offering of a portion of the "arm" is, however, still conceptually the "same" gesture, and not a completely "substitute" gesture, as it would have to be in English. Thus, in such circumstances, where an Ibo will offer another part of his *aka*, the English person will have to say "I'm sorry, I can't shake hands". Socially speaking the more extended Ibo *aka* may be determined, let us say, by an overriding requirement that a physical gesture of greeting be made in the maximum number of circumstances.

We shall have cause to revert in a different way to this statistical feature. This view implicitly argues that conceptual boundaries are modified like rules: as if a rule with too many exceptions (anomalies) is replaced by a revised rule to accommodate the exceptions. Douglas (1966) was very helpful in relating the idea of category anomaly to the study of social categorization. But as she herself shows, the existence of anomalies does not lead necessarily to the revision of categories—ambiguity at boundaries, she argues, is, for example, commonly marked by taboo.

It is nevertheless proper to consider our case through the eyes of those who see the body as a map of social interactions. For Douglas and for several other theorists the body is viewed as a main image of society. For them, we would be adding a further reason why the images of the body and of society should be able to coincide. It is possible, on the other hand, to accommodate quite extreme pragmatism, or a kind of behaviourism. For example, to take now the particular use of the *aka* as a "helping hand" it might be that the use of the *aka* as a "rope" to be gripped in an emergency, with the "hand" portion clenched, offers more security, the helped one's "hand" being less likely to slide off—in a hot, sticky and often raining environment in which all helping hands are likely to be slippery (Fig. 7.2). Such pragmatic interpretations are not uninteresting. They lead us, indeed to enquire why two English-speakers' hands should have to make those wild grasping movements towards each other in a similar circumstance. Perhaps a helping *aka* is really more often needed, and the help more often required in more messy and mildly dangerous conditions, than a helping "hand" is.

We should encourage all such lines of discussion, in order to show that the material and statistical side of this question is a normal subject for examination. It would be misleading, however, to argue from this pragmatically that the "behaviour determines the language classification". The *aka* classification ignores a possible intermediate conceptual boundary and

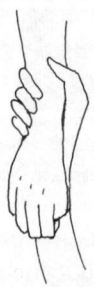

FIG. 7.2. A "helping hand".

thereby, we can argue, removes a linguistic criterion that might introduce the possibility of an unwanted choice into the material situation. Once the classification exists, however, it is part of the total experience of unreflecting individuals. There is no "arrow of causation" from behaviour to category, since they cannot be separated. They form a "simultaneity".

It is quite clear then that the *aka* is not a "mere" taxonomic label. Some would echo certain philosophers and say: there are not first of all "objects" and then they are "used"—they are objects *because* they are used. There is a Yoruba proverb which may be translated: "In a forest no-one need fail to fight because of the lack of a cudgel" (Ojo, 1966: 34). The forest here is defined as littered with cudgels—that is a social classification, not a botanical one. We cannot define "use" in a pragmatic sense therefore (by the way, I am not speaking of the use of *words*, for that would be to prejudge the fundamental question). It seems that *aka* is not a "mere" word in some nineteenth century lexicographical sense. It is attached to the upper limb, but it is a mnemonic for conceptualizations which are not conventionally linguistic or psychological, and which are actualized almost unconsciously as far as the individual is concerned. This is undoubtedly part of the distinction known by the terms "signifier" and "signified" (Saussure, 1916). Nevertheless, such a "signified" is too complex for the traditional "linguistic sign" to encompass.

It does seem that persons bilingual or partially bilingual in Ibo and English are prepared to tolerate the rough translation of *aka* as "hand" rather than "arm". The reason lies perhaps in a partly statistical judgment of the relative importance of certain kinds of error. The English "hand" does not easily bear classification as an "arm", but, as we have seen, it is perhaps surprisingly easy to use "hand" for some "arm" interactions. The basic misunderstandings emerge in failed interactions of the rather subtle but materially important kinds that we have been discussing. Different, simpler, more narrowly "linguistic", misunderstandings also occur when (as is usual) animal front limbs are called "hands" by untutored English-speaking Ibo ("hand of dog"). This makes a double misclassification, from an English-language view, since animal front limbs are generally classed as "legs", that is as "rear" not "front" limbs from a human point of view.[3]

I would distinguish between cases of misunderstanding of this sort, which are experienced as apparent if puzzling "misidentifications" (from the point of view of one or other speaker), and the cases of deeper misunderstanding that I have in mind. In the one case the solution is, figuratively, to call for a dictionary (or to make one if it does not exist). In the other the material problem is not experienced as a "misidentification". It is experienced as a social error or a social puzzle, even as some kind of wickedness. Who should be sent for? The difference lies in the fact that only parts of the language–category–object simultaneity are defined as language problems by natural language users. Underestimated as this latter group commonly are, it is worth stressing that such natural users have got the hang of lexical translation. They recognize that there is a common comprehension problem due to using a "wrong" label. They reach frequently for the nearest lexical solution ("That is not a dog's hand but its leg"). The problems we started with, on the contrary, are not seen as linguistic, but as lying in the realm of action. Whorf tried to call them "linguistic", but confused everyone including, very often, himself.

I do not wish to add to the complexities of this case. It is, however, important now to take up the further matter of the "density" of a category. For Ibo-speakers the forearm or lower part of the *aka* is engaged in more socially significant activity than the upper part—as if, as Berlin and Kay argue for colours, the category has a centre of gravity, or a zone most characteristic of its qualities. It may be noted that the Ibo "shoulder" (which we are not discussing here) bounds the top of the upper limb as does a vest or undershirt with a short sleeve, not (as with the English word) as does a garment without a sleeve; in other words, the *aka* is not quite as long shoulderwards as the "arm". It is a fact of common experience that "unit" categories commonly exhibit conceptual subgradings (or shadings). We are, for example, clearly aware of this feature with some "unit" kinship terms covering various genealogical specifications. Thus the Ibo *nwa nna* ("father's child") refers to "half-sibling" as well as various "patrilineal relatives". There is always felt to be some degree of semantic density about half-siblings within the category even though half-siblings are also indelibly marked as kinds of patrilineal relative, in virtue of their membership of the unit category. It is worth noting that this is not quite the same as saying that the term *nwa nna* is "extended" from half-siblings to other patrilineal relatives. That is now seen as an ethnocentric error, compounded though it is by the common Ibo-English translation of *nwa nna* as "brother" or "sister".

The "density" gradients of categories must be related to frequency in some way—perhaps we may put it as frequency of association or interaction with reality. Categories thus contain or coexist with a statistical feature—it is part of their materiality, and we see that the earlier discussion of the possible influence of certain frequencies of social interaction involving the *aka* category has prepared us for such a view. Our perception of the gradients of semantic density, or the possibility of such a perception, is a main reason for denying any simple view that all reality is exhausted by sets of categories. The statistical feature marks irregularities in experience which are not flattened out by unit categories. This is an important point, accounting as it does for the existence of ways of incorporating experience into the category system. We shall wish to recall this later.

To return to our case, the *aka* is more *aka*-like, the lower down the limb we travel. The denser *aka* of the Ibo still includes the forearm, not just the "hand". The next named subdivisions, as we have seen, are the *mkpisi aka*, the "fingers". The biological pragmatist would draw attention to the undoubted saliency of the fingers (and thumb) for all humans. This merely leads us to reflect that the wrist is not anything like so important a subdivision pragmatically, and we may be ready to concede that the real problem may be why the wrist became a boundary in (say) north-west Europe, and not why it fails to be in some other areas (perhaps we shall look forward to a full historical account of these questions from the pens of experts). To subdivide *aka* into "arm" and "hand" is then to reinforce the density gradient at the active end of the limb, but the declaration of terminological independence of the "hand" still does not eliminate a possible perception of the ambiguity of the wrist boundary. For the moment, we may note that the "social" extends so far into the "semantic" here, that the case for a "semantic anthropology" in these terms (Crick, 1975) is only a case for a more delicate social anthropology.

For help in making further important distinctions I will allude to the "leg" word *ukwu*, which in a parallel fashion includes the English "foot". Again there are *mkpisi ukwu* ("toes") to match *mkpisi aka* ("fingers"). I have no absolutely equivalent data that bring the *ukwu*/"leg + foot" relationship into prominence, but it is my impression that the classification is susceptible of an equally detailed analysis. The social interventions of the *ukwu* are not subtle, but the "foot" part of the *ukwu* rarely suffers any fate not shared by at least the lower "leg". There is a strong possibility that the uneventful *ukwu* classification reinforces the *aka* classification by the example of a classificatory symmetry. But conversely the forelimb may provide the lively model for the classification of the lower limb. The English system, if we use the new perspective gained from our analysis, is surely *over*symmetrical? The terminological specification of the "hand" and its "fingers" must be the model for the elaborate separation of "foot" from "leg", and the further provision of "toes" as a separate lexical term to balance the "fingers". We detect here the entry into categorization of a symmetry feature. The failure to provide a unit category term equivalent to "thumb" for the appropriate (big) toe strengthens rather than weakens this impression. The big toe is the only one worth singling out ("I stubbed my toe"), so that the limit to the application of classificatory symmetry is marked by ambiguity.

As we examine the *ukwu* classification beside the *aka* one, new suggestions concerning the different experiential gradients of different terms even inside the same set have arisen. Kroeber long ago (1909) noted the tendency for a classificatory symmetry to tidy up such sets. This is important as indicating that some categories may be "emptier", more decorative, more intellectual, more "cognitive" perhaps, or just more "linguistic" than others. It cannot therefore be the case that the statistical ("frequency") feature we have discussed already, actually determines the categories. On the contrary, through at least the symmetry feature, a certain autonomy appears in category sets. Thus we have been able to catch even bodily terms already taking off into realms of abstraction, their materiality giving way to ideality. In all respects, however, the Ibo system is relatively less advanced than the English one on that road.

I started my account at a point where *aka* was neither behaviour nor text, neither social nor linguistic, but a simultaneity, a unit in total experience. It is now possible to see why Levi-Strauss's structuralism was able to stumble on the discovery that society *is* text, or that the social is homologous with the textual. As we know, the failure of structuralism in practice was to have no theory to account for the homology. Only a microscopic focus enables us to track the way in which "textuality" peels away from experiential unity. Language is in large measure responsible, no doubt. It is a hybrid medium, its map being partly interior, subjective and rooted in regularities of the "human mind", and partly exterior, objective, and rooted in materiality. Left to itself it intrudes its own arabesques into the perception of materiality: as if a fungus on a lens were to add a galaxy to a record of the universe.

In making an analysis such as the foregoing, I have no opinion on whether other systems which contain a unit "arm + hand" category would have similar detailed features. No other has been made in exactly this way. However, Professor Mihai Pop, on hearing a version of this paper, stated that Romanian usages were remarkably similar. *Mînă*, although from Latin *manus* "hand", is a "forelimb" (the pattern is common in Eastern European languages) and *da mînă* "to give a hand" also (he stated) differs in its realization from the English manner. Dr. Andrei Pippidi, the historian, tells me that the use of *braţ* ("arm") has overlaid the *mînă* classification only in the recent history of the standard Romanian language. The *aka*-like features of *mînă* emerge in many standard collocations. The spread of *braţ* is a westernizing feature, exemplified by an indeterminacy about the bounds of the member, as well as by the lack of a symmetrical feature in the lower limb. The "foot + leg" term *picior* is even today undifferentiated. The terms for "finger" and "toe" are also not separated: *degetul mîinii* and *degetul piciorului*. Such parallels are, when attested, a bonus, but are also in a sense diversions, as the realities must be explored *de novo* in each case. It is interesting, however, that Roman imperial interactions resulted in the Dacian limb, like the Ibo *aka*, receiving in translation the foreign "hand" term. We cannot pursue these issues here. Even the French terminology bears signs of several reconstructions (cf. Ullman, 1951; von Wartburg, 1969: 118; Ardener, 1971: xxvii). The common Romance "leg" word is a loan in several modern Romance languages (*gamba* > Greek *kambe*). The "finger" and "toe" words remain undifferentiated. The *aka*-type terminology is to be detected in Gaelic and Welsh despite the confusions of English models. Certainly linguistic collections of cultural classifications should be dusted off and restored to the social mixtures from which they were untimely ripped. Many rich results lie in wait for the researcher.

The purpose of this paper has, however, been to illustrate what is meant by the study of "simultaneities". I wish to indicate that it is possible to derive a multiplicity of social, epistemological, linguistic and psychological theories from a single case. No prizes are offered for their discovery. I am particularly desirous to stress the material features of the reality demonstrated, being tired of the naive assumption that we must here be in an "idealist" discourse. A multiplicity of interpretations is possible because all interpretations start off together in a point source. Certain familiar oppositions take on a healthily problematic air: category/object, structure/event, relativistic/universalistic, collective/individual, and yet there is no collapse by this method of analysis into abstraction.

It will be evident that choosing one part of a body classification instead of a whole body classification (let alone a whole social space) reduces the amount of exotic description, so that it can easily be seen what the anthropology is like.[5] The total social space is composed of an infinite series of subtleties of that order. It is also important to demonstrate the very close mesh with reality that I have in mind. The particular case has also some useful corrective features embodied in it. Handshakes and the like belong to an area of human social life which are commonly taken to be the most "observable". Such behaviour can, it is often thought, be relatively objectively described in much the same way as is expected (not always safely) to be done with animals. Indeed, "greeting" in animals is even considered by some to be the same *sort* of phenomenon. Yet even in this simple zone it is clear that the critical humanization has taken place—such that the handshake and the helping hand are "sicklied o'er with the pale cast of thought" mediated by language. We may think the actual instance socially trivial, but in fact the relations of naive English-speakers with naive Ibo-speakers have no more characteristic a framework than this. It is commonplace to draw attention to differences between cultures in complex domains (colour terms and the like). The excellence of such work has perhaps led to the too abstracted view of "cognitive" processes. The classification of the event and the "event" itself are simultaneous. That is why language penetrates the social. That is also why, by a paradox, linguistics, including sociolinguistics as commonly practised, does not seem to exhaust its significance.

My treatment of Whorf is introduced to show how the absence of a discourse through which to tell of his insights led him ultimately up one of the many blind alleys that start from his initial position. I have often puzzled over why people tend to see only text *or* life, as if each rules out the other. Malinowski too may have started from a similar insight but his blind alley was the theory of context of situation, and the equation of meaning with function (Henson, 1974).

Category contains a statistical feature which I have called a "density". This feature accounts for the mathematical possibilities implied in many theories. Start with the extreme view that the cultural categories, linguistically expressed, are the only way we can register experience. Unit categories are then matched to a pattern of frequencies of occurrence which introduces discrepancies both within and between the categories. Thus the *aka* is more involved in interactions the further one travels towards the fingers from the shoulder. The *nwa nna* is realized as "half sibling" with a particular experiential frequency, within the general pattern of frequency for other patrilineal relatives.[5] The importance of the statistical feature can be illustrated from its bearing on the Berlin and Kay statement concerning colour universals: that colour shades described by subjects as the most typical within unit colour categories are more similar cross-culturally than are the colour *ranges* covered by the categories. The statement is not without methodologically controversial problems, but it matches the notion of frequency and density.

The biological features of perception are not abolished by the grid of category: they appear in the density gradients of categories. For the "language is reality" people the existence of the gradients does not change the fact that they are not "present" in the inventory of categories. In addition, as we have seen, the category boundaries intrude their own effects upon the perception of frequency gradients. They are themselves a kind of statistical feature. On the other hand, the "reality is universal" people will pick up frequency gradients corresponding to pan-human experiences which cannot be held therefore to be culturally derived. The important point is, however, that there is in experience no subdivision. For that reason worlds set up by categories bear all the signs of materiality to the untutored human being.

The major contribution of anthropology results from the experience of trying on a multiplicity of cultural spectacles: the illusion of total truth is amended by the revealed discrepancies. Where all the spectacles agree we have a universal. Is it simply a universal of spectacle construction? To find out we try to deconstruct the spectacles. We have added a semantic materialism to the approaches available for such purposes. It is inevitably in part linguistic, for our worlds are inescapably contaminated with language. It is an important advance to learn that the contamination extends into materiality, for that has long been for some the last refuge from language. Conversely, for others language has been a refuge from materiality.

Notes

1. See Ellen and Reason (1979) for recent contributions, and bibliographical references. Durkheim and Mauss (1963) was a founding study.
2. The Ibo live in south-eastern Nigeria, the erstwhile Biafra, and number some 7 millions. The language is conventionally rendered *Igbo*. This spelling is not used here. The *gb* phoneme is not a labiovelar but an imploded bilabial. The spelling *Ibo*, although strictly non-phonetic, thus leads to a less misleading English pronunciation than *Igbo*, which is often mispronounced *Ig-bo*. Ibo is also the normal Nigerian-English spelling. The spelling of examples is simplified here, and is not the official one, in which certain vowels are distinguished by subscript dots, nor an IPA rendering. In the examples, *nye* has an open *e*, the vowels of *mkpisi* are both *i* with subscript dot (a close *e*), *okhu* has dotted *o* (approximately as in *not*) and a dotted *u* (roughly as in *put*), *ukwu* has dotted *u* in both syllables. Tones are not marked here. *Aka* and *ukwu* both have two high tones. See also Green and Igwe (1963).
3. When English butchers classify the carcasses of (dead) animals a series of separate usages appear, including a distinction between front and rear limbs. Thus:

	Front	Rear
Beef	shin	leg
Mutton	shoulder	leg
Pork	hand (or spring)	leg

 The shift of human categories is very notable in butchery terms. The "hand" of pork is not strictly like an *aka* of dog, because the "hand" of pork excludes the "pig's feet" or "trotters" which are attached to it.
4. The body has different categories for different classes of classifier. "The 'polite' body has many fewer subdivisions than the 'sexual' body. The 'medical' body may have more divisions than either and can be ambiguously polite or sexual." (Ardener, 1971). Victorian polite "throat" included much of the female trunk, and "limb" replaced "leg". Traces of such phenomena can still be discovered in the history of body labelling.
5. This presentation is not the occasion to take the matter further, but a hint of the dynamism of the processes concerned may be further exemplified. *Nwa nna* (see above) is contrasted with *nwa nne* ("mother's child" or "full sibling"). This is also used for "patrilineal relative" when closeness of relationship is emphasized. These usages are totally context dependent, but in a regular manner (see Ardener, 1954, 1959). We have then two unit categories each with its own frequency gradient, transferred as a pair to represent relative "nearness" and "distance" of patrilineality. At this new "meta"-level of categorization, the old frequency gradients are now symbolic only. Put oversimply the close associations of *nwa nna* with "half-sibling" and of *nwa nne* with "full sibling", are reduced to degrees of patrilineality defined by other criteria, in different contexts. Here again we catch a category peeling away from materiality with no indication in the linguistic terminology to warn us.

References

ARDENER, E. (1954), "The kinship terminology of a group of southern Ibo", *Africa*, **24**, 85–99.
ARDENER, E. (1959), "Lineage and locality among the Mba-Ise Ibo", *Africa*, **29**, 113–133.
ARDENER, E. (Ed.) (1971), *Social Anthropology and Language*, Tavistock, London.
BERLIN, B. and KAY, P. (1969), *Basic Colour Terms, their Unversality and Evolution*, University of California Press, Berkeley and Los Angeles.

BLOCH, M. (1977), "The past and present in the present", *Man*, (N.S.) **12**, 278–92.
CARROLL, J.B. (Ed.) (1964), *Language, Thought and Reality; Selected Writings of Benjamin Lee Whorf*, MIT Press, Cambridge, Massachusetts.
CRICK, M. (1975), *Explorations in Language and Meaning: Towards a Semantic Anthropology*, Dent, London.
DE SAUSSURE, F. (1916), *Cours de linguistique générale*, Payot, Paris/Geneva.
DOUGLAS, M. (1966), *Purity and Danger*, Routledge and Kegan Paul, London.
DURKHEIM, E. and MAUSS, M. (1963), *Primitive Classification*, Cohen and West, London.
ELLEN, R.F. and REASON, D. (1979), *Classifications in their Social Context*, Academic Press, London.
GREEN, M.M. and IGWE, G.E. (1963), *A Descriptive Grammar of Igbo*, Oxford University Press, London.
HENSON, H. (1974), *British Social Anthropologists and Language*, Clarendon Press, Oxford.
HJELMSLEV, B.L. (1963), *Prolegomena to a Theory of Language* (2nd edn of translation), University of Wisconsin, Madison.
KROEBER, A.L. (1909), "Classificatory Systems of Relationship", *Journal of the Royal Anthropological Institute* **39**, 74–84.
OJO, G.J.S. (1966), *Yoruba Culture: a Geographical Analysis*, University of London Press, London.
ULLMAN, S. (1951), *The Principles of Semantics*, Jackson, Glasgow.
VON WARTBURG, W. (1969), *Problems and Methods in Linguistics* (translation of 1943 German edn), Blackwell, Oxford.

Chapter 8

Language and Communicational Efficiency: The Case of Tok Pisin[†]

PETER MÜHLHÄUSLER

Introduction

For a long time linguists have not only been very reluctant to make value judgements about language but have also denied that such judgements could be made in principle. From the point of view of the ordinary speaker this seems strange indeed. But there is a gradual realization among linguists today that the assumption that all languages and all linguistic forms are equal is by no means a sign of objectivity and scholarship. Instead, the refusal to comment on qualitative matters has made linguistics a less useful source of information to those who need it most, the language planners. The insistence of many linguists that their job was to describe some abstract linguistic system underlying the actual utterance of everyday speakers has also led to a neglect of external factors such as attitude studies.

In this paper I will try to propose ways in which the lack of information in this area could be lessened. I will concentrate on two main tasks:

(i) the discussion of general principles of language evaluation;
(ii) a history of judgements about varieties and individual constructions found in Tok Pisin.

I have chosen Tok Pisin for a number of reasons:

(i) Both the language itself and judgements about its merits have undergone considerable change over the hundred or so years of its existence.
(ii) The fact that Tok Pisin is the principal medium of communication in a nation where over 700 languages are spoken means that language attitudes can crucially affect the functioning of cross-linguistic communication.

[†] Reprinted from *Language & Communication*, Vol. 1, 1981.

(iii) Tok Pisin has become one of the best documented pidgins and creoles in recent years, and has attained a certain prominence in the discussion of linguistic development. Tok Pisin has also attracted the attention of sociologists of language because of its dominant role in private and public life in Papua New Guinea.

Among the many English-based pidgins and creoles of the south-western Pacific Tok Pisin is both the linguistically most developed and the socially most firmly institutionalized variety. It is the major lingua franca of Papua New Guinea, being spoken by some 750,000–1,000,000 speakers as a second language and in about 20,000 households as a first language. The total population of Papua New Guinea amounts to slightly more than 2,000,000. The language has been known by many names, among them New Guinea Pidgin, Neomelanesian and Tok Boi. Its present name Tok Pisin (literally: *talk pidgin*) reflects the linguistic independence of this language as well as the political independence of its speakers.

Evaluating Linguistic Systems

Among the criteria proposed by the experts on language planning, the following are the most important:

(i) *referential adequacy*, i.e. "the capacity of the language to meet the needs of its users as an instrument of referential meaning" (Haugen, 1966);
(ii) *systematic adequacy*, i.e. a language should be structured in such a way that its rules are maximally general and natural;
(iii) *acceptability*, i.e. a form must be adopted or adoptable by the majority of whatever society or subsociety is involved.

Subordinate to these considerations are others, such as euphony, brevity, and symmetry between expression and content, which are listed and discussed by Tauli (1968).

(i) With regard to Tok Pisin, referential adequacy would not have to be the same for all of its users. Whilst a small minority who speak this language as a first language have to express all ideas and feelings in Tok Pisin, for the majority of speakers Tok Pisin is used in a limited number of functions and domains. Thus, referential adequacy has to be judged against the background of the communicative needs of a specific group of speakers. There are indications that Tok Pisin is not an adequate means of communication in a number of areas of discourse relating to recent technological and sociological change, but this can be said of virtually any language, including English. Because of Tok Pisin's productive word formation component and its relatively high syncretic capacity, most referential inadequacies can be repaired quite easily in principle.

Whilst the notion of referential adequacy is most often used to refer to deficiencies in the lexical area, it is also found on other levels of grammar. Wurm (1977) stresses that syntactic differentiation is not equally developed in all varieties of Tok Pisin. Thus, in some of the older second-language varieties,

(a) grammatical categories such as tense, aspect or number are either absent or under-represented;
(b) the system of prepositions is rather rudimentary;
(c) discourse-structuring grammatical elements are rare, making it difficult to express the difference between important and less important information.

However, since most of these deficiencies have been repaired in creolized and newer second-language varieties of Tok Pisin, language planners could easily resort to internal borrowing if it was felt that such distinctions were needed in the language.

A lot of claims have been made about the referential adequacy or inadequacy of Tok Pisin and such claims have often formed the basis of value judgements. It must be remembered, however, that very little empirical research has been done in this area and that the question needs to be treated with great care. To claim that either Tok Pisin or one of its varieties is good or bad because of its referential potential ignores the fact that the potential of all varieties is continuously changing.

(ii) The systematic adequacy of a language is concerned primarily with its internal consistency and regularity. Ideally, grammatical rules should be maximally general. Contrary to certain claims that pidgins are extremely simple, it can be shown that this statement has little meaning unless seen against the background of the continuous grammatical development of these languages.

As a general rule it can be stated that, in its initial stages, a pidgin grammar is full of exceptions and relatively minor or unproductive grammatical rules, and that greater regularity is only reached in its more developed varieties, if it develops without external interference. If, on the other hand, contact with its original lexifier language (English in the case of Tok Pisin) is renewed, then language mixing can lead to a substantial increase in grammatical irregularity. I wish to illustrate these two points with an actual example, the signalling of plural in Tok Pisin (full details in Mülhäusler, 1980).

In the early part of this century, speakers of Tok Pisin used the pluralizer *ol* only variably, with nouns referring to living beings and preferably in grammatical subject or direct object position. Today, in a number of creolized varieties, the pluralizer *ol* is used before any noun which is semantically plural. This means that the rule to account for pluralization around 1910 is much more complex than the rule needed to state pluralization in the creolized Tok Pisin of 1980. The latter variety is therefore systematically more adequate.

Contact with English in some varieties of Urban Tok Pisin has led to the introduction of pluralization by means of the formative *-s*, as in *mans* for Rural Tok Pisin *ol man* "men". This new rule is not applied in all instances, however. Instead, one finds combinations such as *ol gels*, *gels*, *ol gel* "girls", often used by the same speaker. It is extremely difficult to state the conditions under which one or other form is chosen. This means that the systematic adequacy of the grammar has been reduced considerably under the influence of language contact.

Systematic adequacy also refers to the notion of linguistic naturalness. In second-language Tok Pisin, because it is a second language, linguistic strategies which optimalize perception are more favoured than those promoting production. As a result, natural phonological processes (e.g. processes reducing sounds or converting sound segments into more readily pronounceable sounds) are suppressed, and natural morphological processes, i.e. processes favouring the optimalization of perception, are favoured. This means that there is a strong tendency in Tok Pisin for one form to have one meaning and for the same meaning to be expressed by the same form. An example of morphological naturalness would be in the formation of derived words. Compare the irregular English examples with the regular ones of Tok Pisin:

Tok Pisin		English	
taun	*bilong taun*	town	urban
kantri	*bilong kantri*	country	rural
pisop	*bilong pisop*	bishop	episcopal
meme	*bilong meme*	goat	hirsute
plisman		policeman	
draivman		driver	
paniman		joker	
woksaveman		specialist	
hos man	*hos meri*	stallion	mare
sipsip man	*sipsip meri*	ram	ewe
kakaruk man	*kakaruk meri*	cock	hen
pikinini man	*pikinini meri*	son	daughter
pik man	*pik meri*	boar	sow

Tok Pisin's high degree of morphological naturalness makes it an easy language to learn as a second language. It is for this reason that borrowing from both internal and external sources may have to be carefully controlled if this advantage of the language is not to be lost.

The case of morphological naturalness illustrates that the terms good or bad Pidgin cannot be discussed outside a social context. To have a maximum of morphological naturalness makes the language good from a learner's point of view. On the other hand, it reduces its stylistic flexibility and can make it rather monotonous, as has been illustrated by Mead (1931).

(iii) Whilst linguistically naive speakers may make reference to the referential and systematic adequacy of Tok Pisin in discussing its merits, this is typically done in a haphazard way. Their main concern, and this goes particularly for New Guinean speakers of the language, is its social acceptability. This factor depends to a large extent on external circumstances and may change considerably over time. Some of these changes will be discussed below.

To begin with I want to discuss a more context-independent principle of social acceptability, namely whether expressions in a language are iconically encoded or not. There seem to be language-independent reasons for saying for instance, that:

(a) Reduplicated lexical stems should stand for concepts centring around childhood experiences and lighthearted personal emotions. Applying this criterion, the Tok Pisin items *tingting* "to think", *toktok* "to talk" and *lukluk* "to look" would be badly encoded. In fact, educated speakers of the language tend to replace them with unreduplicated forms.

(b) Concepts which are central to a culture should be expressed by means of short lexical bases whilst marginal concepts can be expressed by longer compounds or circumlocutions. The difference in the relative importance of concepts can be seen from the following examples:

Tok Pisin	English
laplap	length of cloth worn around the waist like a kilt
kain laplap ol Skots i save pasim	kilt
lala	tailor fish
man bilong samapim klos	tailor

(c) There are limits to the degree of homophony in a language. Laycock (1969) observes that Pidgin already has a relatively large number of words where different English words have fallen together. "To add to this number incautiously could well overload the language with forms that sound the same but have different meanings." Thus, the proposal to translate English "peace" as Tok Pisin *pis* is ill founded, as *pis* can already mean "piece", "piss", "fish", "fees" and (in some varieties) "peas".

In addition to such external or mechanical factors underlying social acceptability there are a number of socio-pychological factors. Among them the following are of particular importance:

(a) Expressions are regarded as socially harmful because they create divisions, e.g. insults, group labels or elite language.
(b) Expressions are regarded as taboo. In this connection it is interesting to observe that conventions for a taboo register in Tok Pisin emerged very early in its development, e.g. the use of *longpela pik* "long pig" for a human being eaten during a cannibal meal.
(c) A number of expressions are regarded as difficult to understand or confusing. Such expressions are particularly undesirable in the case of Tok Pisin, since its main function is that of a nationwide lingua franca.

Tok Pisin is spoken by people of a wide range of social and cultural backgrounds and it is for this reason that one can expect significant differences in the social acceptability of linguistic forms. Let me illustrate this with an example from the lowest linguistic level, that of pronunciation. A group of Tok Pisin speakers objected to the proposal to call Papua New Guinea *Pagini* on the ground that this would sound like *Pakim mi* "fuck me". Had they had a distinction between (p) and (f) in their variety this objection would hardly have arisen. At present, we do not even understand such relatively mechanical processes, and as a result unfortunate and socially damaging new expressions continue to enter Tok Pisin. Thus, the recently introduced expression *selek komiti* "Select Committee" is often interpreted as *slek komiti* "a slack or inefficient village committee member" and *investim mani* "to invest money" is frequently interpreted as *westim mani* "to waste money".

Extensive language attitude studies need to be carried out to test this and other aspects of social acceptability. Without the results of such research no proper language planning can be carried out, since it is the social acceptability of an expression which in the last instance determines whether a proposed new expression will be fully adopted or not.

Historical Notes on Linguistic Value Judgements about Tok Pisin

Judgements about good and bad varieties of Tok Pisin are dependent on the meta-linguistic abilities, i.e. the ability to speak about linguistic matters, of those who make them. This means that, in the early days of development of this language, statements about good and bad Pidgin can only be found in expatriate sources, for it is only fairly recently that Tok Pisin has also become an instrument for talking about language. Thus, expressions such as *tok brukbruk* "incoherent talk or stuttering" are of very recent origin. This, incidentally, poses a considerable problem for fieldworkers who want to elicit linguistic judgements from people living in remote areas or from older speakers of Tok Pisin.

In discussing European pronouncements I am not concerned with attitudes towards the language as a whole since this question has been dealt with elsewhere (Wurm and Mühlhäusler, 1979): I will only deal with pronouncements as to the relative merit of two or more recognized varieties of the language.

Whilst most writers in Tok Pisin's formative years dismiss all varieties of the language as a garbled, grammarless and debased form of English, Friederici (1911) takes a more balanced view. Here follow two extracts from McDonald's translation of his article on Tok Pisin (1977):

> The jargon is capable of a limited flexibility and of strongly-expressed statements when it is spoken by someone who has really mastered it. Being left entirely with natives for many months, I learnt to make speeches of the kind that a company commander really does make to his company. I thought that moderately impressive until hearing the profound speeches that were (*sic*!) between kiap Boluminski of Kavieng and the chiefs at their official meetings and in legal proceedings. I heard him and Herr Rodatz, master of the Aitape station, speaking the best Pidgin English in the colony.

Friederici contrasts this kind of Tok Pisin with the kind spoken by a newly arrived judge:

> I shall not forget the summing-up of a judge which demonstrated exactly the opposite of real ability such as that of Herr Boluminski, praised above, and was officially recorded during legal proceedings . . . I can only say that it produced a miserable situation.

An interesting set of comments on good and bad Pidgin can be found in the *Rabaul Times* in the years between the two wars. Most writers appear to be concerned with the fact that the stable Tok Pisin which had developed during German times was gradually being eroded by the continuous introduction of English vocabulary and grammar. The resulting new variety was considered both less stable and less efficient for interracial and cross-territorial communication. I have selected two articles making this point:

(i) *Rabaul Times*, editorial 13 March 1931:

> Our own pidgin-English . . . is becoming less "pidgin" than what one might term a "corrupted" English or Australianese. For, with the general inrush of Australians and Englishmen since the war who were ignorant of pidgin English as it should be spoken, little attention has been paid to the preservation of the purity of pidgin English as it was methodically learned by the new arrivals from Germany in pre-war days . . .
> It is a pity if our picturesque pidgin-English is to be lost entirely and replaced by a corrupted and distorted English . . .

(ii) *Rabaul Times*, editorial 15 February 1935:

> Before the 1914 holocaust pidgin-English retained an individualism of its own.
>
> ... at the present time, thoughout the territory there is a garbled corruption of English spoken without any rules or limitations of vocabulary interspersed with mispronounced pidgin and native idioms ...

Whilst for most secular writers the loss of communicative efficiency in the anglicized varieties of the language is the main target of their criticism, the missions are concerned with different issues. Their main criticism against Tok Pisin, it appears, is that it is full of crudities and obscenities. One expression in particular annoyed the missions, *goddam*, which according to a number of sources was a very frequent vocabulary item before 1930. Thus, Friederici reports (McDonald's (1977) translation):

> If a Melanesian exclaims: "God dam! He savvee too much!" when he refers to another Melanesian who is magnificently decorated as to look like a negro from Washington or Virginia, he will always create amusement. But it made me really sad when I heard a man from Lamassa, while he was building a *mon* (Boat), muttering: "God dam, work belong kanaka he no good!"

Mead (1931) comments on the initial effort of the missions to remove crude expressions from the language.

> When the missionaries preach and translate the Bible into pidgin, they make some effort to smooth out the crudities of the language, but in the hands of the boys these all crop up again. Pidgin without continual "goddams" and "bloodys" is inconceivable to the boys.

Mission bodies were set up in the 1930s (Hoeltker, 1945) with the expressed aim of

> removing the crude or obscene expressions from approved language use and replacing them with others taken from the existing inventory of expressions.

The attempts of the missions to purify the language in this way are interesting in that they introduce a new, and it would appear quite non-New Guinean, dimension into the discussion of what is good and what is bad language.

Mission publications around 1930 are also concerned with a second "non-New Guinean" question, namely that of establishing standards for the correctness of pronunciation and spelling. In this context, it is interesting that their writers appear to be guided not by local pronunciation, which is described as "vulgar", but by the real or presumed English etymon. Examples include:

bernim/burn/, (vulg. *boinim*)
boks/box/, (vulg. *bokis*)
drift/drift/, (vulg. *drip*)
foldaun/fall down/, (vulg. *pundaun*).

All examples were taken from the *Woerterbuch mit Redewendungen*, published by the Alexishafen missionaries around 1935. Note that the so-called vulgar forms were the only ones used by the vast majority of Tok Pisin speakers at the time.

Whilst language attitudes with Papua New Guinea appeared to change little in the years after the War, and whilst both missions and government continued in their efforts to create a standard Tok Pisin, there was a growing opinion among outside observers, and in particular linguists, that the language should be left alone. One of the best known proponents of this direction in the 1950s and early 1960s is Robert A. Hall (1955a). He argues:

> You can't create a language by fiat, or by deliberate introduction of terms. People will inevitably use words in accordance, not with someone's notion of what is 'correct', but with their own pattern of behaviour and outlook on life . . .
> These considerations have a direct bearing on the proposals that are occasionally made to 'purify' Pidgin by altering the vocabulary. Well-meaning observers are often shocked by one Pidgin word or another, not only terms with erotic or scatological implications, but words which by now have acquired unpleasant connotations of racial discrimination in English . . .

Hall's refusal to be anything other than purely descriptive is symptomatic of a kind of linguistics which tried to be purely "scientific" and which strictly separated between the structure and the use of language. The doctrine of the day was that all languages can express adequately whatever their speakers want them to express and that therefore no planning or interference was called for. Hall's remarks are also symptomatic of the view that language planning is concerned mainly with purifying a language from erotic connotations. It has been shown elsewhere in this chapter that most Papua New Guineans are not concerned with this aspect of language and that planning in this area is not needed. The view that all languages are equal as to their referential potential is not supported by empirical evidence. On the contrary, Scott's (1977) study of agricultural vocabulary in Tok Pisin bears out a principle known to language planners, namely that in times of rapid social and technological change linguistic development lags behind external development. Thus, a more realistic view would be one which takes into consideration the linguistic needs of Tok Pisin speakers in the years immediately before and subsequent to independence.

From the late 1960s onward one can observe a gradual convergence between the attitudes of the linguistically naive users of the language and those concerned with laying down its rules. An important step is the official campaign against socially harmful outdated colonialist and racist expressions. In 1969 the Australian Administrator of Papua New Guinea directed Administration staff not to use offensive Tok Pisin words:

> I believe it is time the Administration initiated some changes to a few words which are tending to be regarded as offensive by some of the educated Papua and New Guineans. For this reason the Administration should officially discourage their use, and encourage the use of suitable alternatives.

The words concerned are discussed in some detail by Healey (undated). They include:

previous socially loaded word	suggested new word	gloss
boi	man	indigene in European employment
meri	wuman, gel	indigenous woman or girl
misis	wuman, gel	white woman or girl
masta	man	European man
mankimasta	domestik	house servant
kanaka	pipol, manmeri	indigene

Common to all judgements about good and bad varieties of Tok Pisin discussed so far is that they are limited to very small subparts of the language as a whole, mainly lexical items. The reason for this is no doubt that lexical items (words) are most readily associated by the layman with good and bad language. Thus, whilst it is possible to have an obscene word, it is hardly possible to have an obscene syntactic structure.

Language judgements about words are thus concerned primarily with the connotative aspects of Tok Pisin and only to a limited extent with its communicative aspects. However, it would seem that the main function of Tok Pisin is that of providing an easy means of inter-tribal and cross-language communication and that judgements about good or bad Pidgin should be concerned primarily with this aspect. Serious attempts to deal with this aspect only began to appear in the mid-1970s.

Apart from the literature concerned with language planning (which will be discussed elsewhere in this volume) there are two articles dealing specifically with the communicative efficiency of Tok Pisin. The first one is a study by Franklin (1975), which illustrates that a large proportion of newly introduced Tok Pisin terms in a leaflet on coffee growing are misunderstood by a significant number of readers, and that the same is true, to a more limited extent, for the understanding of allegedly firmly established Tok Pisin items.

Franklin appears to suggest that Tok Pisin alone is not capable of handling the communicative requirements of Papua New Guinea society and that it should be supplemented by both the vernacular and English. Attempts to make Tok Pisin carry all information result in communication breakdown. It seems to follow that Tok Pisin is good only for a limited number of domains and functions. One could argue on the basis of this article that a distinction could be made between "good" Tok Pisin, i.e. the language used in its proper setting, and "bad" *ad hoc* Tok Pisin, i.e. Tok Pisin used in inappropriate contexts. However, such a view fails to consider the rapid functional and structural expansion of the language for the majority of its speakers.

Franklin does not stand alone with this claim, however, and Chatterton in the *Pacific Islands Monthly* (November 1973) remarks on Tok Pisin as used in the House of Assembly:

> I have suffered too much during long hours spent in listening to Pidgin speeches in the House of Assembly. I am convinced that Pidgin is not a suitable medium for the discussion of political or economic problems.

Chatterton fails to see that the use of a language in a new domain or a new medium will involve certain initial difficulties. The political terminology developed by Hull (1968) for parliamentary procedures and the growing pressure for more efficient communication in Tok Pisin will no doubt increase the value of this language in the parliamentary setting.

A much more serious matter than temporary lack of referential power is the problem of large-scale disintegration of Tok Pisin as a result of continued borrowing from English. This disintegraton is due to two main linguistic principles:

(i) In times of rapid upward social mobility speakers from a lower social class tend to unsystematically borrow forms from socially superior language varieties or languages.

(ii) Whereas normal language development results in more natural and more regular forms of speech, language contact leads to irregularity and unnaturalness. The greater the distance between the linguistic systems or subsystems in contact, the more severe are the structural consequences.

In a programmatic statement Wurm (1976) draws attention to these developments in Tok Pisin:

> It is because of this structural difference between pidgin and English that straight borrowing from English can lead to the distintegration of the pidgin structure and the pidgin lexical system and can cause serious misunderstanding in communication.
> The disintegration process has already assumed fairly serious proportions in a variety of pidgin spoken in the big urban centres . . .

Among those expatriates who are aware of this problem there are three basic schools of opinion:

(i) Those who maintain that the language should be left alone and that any form of Tok Pisin is as good as any other form. Thus, Chatterton (1973) maintains:

> This (i.e. language engineering) is not the way that languages have grown in the past. Usage—the usage of ordinary people, not of academics—has decided what is or is not "correct" . . . "correct" New Guinea Pidgin is what New Guineans actually say when they talk to one another, not what the experts think they ought to say.

(ii) Those who would like to see Tok Pisin preserved in the form of a conservative Rural Pidgin. In a letter to the *Post Courier* (19 July 1973) M. C. Plummer comments on this view allegedly held by A. Balint:

> With a wave of his linguistic wand he would freeze the Pidgin tongue in that wondrous, golden age, when J. J. Murphy was a mere budling, in that era when (to the delight of the

initiates) *baim* meant "pay", *peim* meant "sell", *selim* meant "send", *barata* often possessed mammalia and *sista* wore phallocrypt, and *siubim* meant "push" . . .
To suggest that at any given stage in this process, a language is somehow qualitatively more pure or perfect than at others, plausible though it seems, is a piece of spurious linguistic nonsense.

There are probably only few writers who adhere to such an extreme view, but it is easy to find isolated examples of prescriptive statements about Tok Pisin. A course which abounds in examples is *Untangled New Guinea Pidgin* by W. Sadler (1973). Sadler rejects the use of *taim* to mean "when" remarking that it is "the least desirable" of a number of given alternatives. The justification for his judgements appears to be the fact that to use *taim* in this construction is un-Melanesian. However, it has been in use in Tok Pisin for a very long time and there is no reason for assuming that Tok Pisin syntax is more Melanesian than English. Instead, as I have tried to show elsewhere, it is by-and-large the result of independent development rather than borrowing.

(iii) Those who aim to reconcile the requirement that Tok Pisin must remain an efficient means of communication with the inevitability of linguistic change. Proponents of this view, for instance Wurm and the present author, would distinguish between "good" or natural development which is in agreement with the general developmental tendencies of the language and "bad" or unnatural growth resulting from excessive borrowing of incompatible material. Such a view would imply that borrowing is legitimate as long as the borrowed items can be readily integrated into the existing system. The best chance for linguistic development, as seen by Wurm (1977) is that of internal borrowing, borrowing of syntax and lexicon from more advanced (e.g. creolized) varieties of the language. Such borrowing would strengthen the coherence of Tok Pisin. Instead of splitting up into two separate systems, the traditional and the heavily anglicized, there would be a single system where the less developed subsystems would be genuine subparts of the more developed planned variety. It has been argued elsewhere that it is perfectly possible to anticipate much of Tok Pisin's future natural development, whereas it is much less clear what linguistic consequences would result from "unnatural" borrowing.

Expatriates have been attacked, particularly in recent years, for meddling with a language which does not belong to them but to the Papua New Guineans (e.g. Chatterton, 1973). It would therefore seem interesting to contrast European pronouncements about good and bad Pidgin with those made by Papua New Guineans.

Indigenous Attitudes on Good and Bad Pidgin

General Attitudes

The most remarkable difference between expatriate and indigenous views on good and bad Pidgin is the absence of statements on correctness and, until very recently, words with obscene etymologies. Instead, the bulk of expressed attitudes towards aspects of Tok Pisin are directed towards (a) the communicative efficiency and (b) the social desirability of certain expressions. The situation thus is comparable to that found among the Gbeya by Samarin (1969):

> There is bad speech and good speech, but bad speech is what causes trouble between people.

This is quite different from many European societies where good and bad speech is determined with reference to some abstract system of socially approved norms of linguistic usage. Papua New Guineans, on the whole, tend to be very tolerant in language matters and, whilst it is often assumed that one's own variety of Tok Pisin is the best or purest, other varieties are not looked down upon or called bad, unless they are bordering on the unintelligible.

In recent years, under the impact of rapidly increasing literacy in Tok Pisin, there is a tendency towards recognizing the written Tok Pisin, as found in the *Nupela Testamen* or *Wantok*, as a kind of standard. The influence of written Tok Pisin is also enhanced by the numerous Tok Pisin Skuls (cf. Zinkel, 1977) in all parts of Papua New Guinea. Again, it appears that the positive feelings towards the conservative written form are due to the fact that this lect of the language is most widely understood.

With the arrival of self government and independence there has been a marked trend away from European or Australian values and this has also been felt in the area of linguistic attitudes. Most pronounced is the growing reluctance to recognize Tok Masta, the reduced "kitchen" variety of Tok Pisin (cf. Mühlhäusler, 1981), as a model on which to improve one's performance in Tok Pisin. As no systematic studies on indigenous attitudes towards different types of Tok Pisin are available, I shall present a preliminary classification of observations made on this point.

The attitude of speakers of the more advanced varieties of Tok Pisin towards Bush Pidgin is, as far as I could observe, one of tolerance, but it is generally understood that speakers who *toktok brukbruk nabaut* "to speak in incoherent bits" or whose *maus bilong en i paul* "pronunciation is unclear" are in a transitional state. The difference between idiolectal and communal Tok Pisin is illustrated in the following quotation (Salisbury, 1967):

> Among the Siane of the Eastern Highlands in 1952 I observed the change from there being only one or two Pidgin speakers in each village of two hundred, to there being twenty or more. In the first situation each speaker has idiosyncracies and gets away with unstandard ("bad") Pidgin as no one can check him, and his idosyncracies may be copied. With twenty speakers idiosyncracies are scorned and standardization is the rule.

There are, however, differences in attitudes towards less developed varieties of Tok Pisin, in particular attitudes towards the Tok Pisin spoken by Papuans. In this case, the lack of proficiency in Tok Pisin is often seen by New Guineans as an indication of deficiencies of character. Rew (1974) remarks:

'Papua' versus 'New Guinea' is a recurrent theme in Port Moresby social life. It derives largely from contrasted histories of administrative and economic development and political status. For most migrants from the Trust Territory, the opposition finds its most readily understood expression in beliefs about language differences and differences in economic ethos. It is almost an axiom of daily parlance that Papuans are people who speak Motu and no Pidgin, or at best a highly bastardized form of it, while New Guineans all speak Pidgin fluently and with a flair for idiom. Furthermore, almost every New Guinean I discussed the issue with believed (and was sure that other New Guineans agreed) that Papuans were lazy.

Unfortunately, these observations have not been supported by more formal methods of research. A statistical comparison of changing attitudes about language and character in a situation such as Port Moresby should be of considerable interest to language planners. They should also take into account that language attitudes can change considerably over a relatively short period of time. This is illustrated by the change in attitudes towards Tok Masta.

In the first decades of Tok Pisin's development few indigenous speakers realized that their language differed from that spoken by the Europeans. In fact, for a long time Tok Pisin was called *Tok Vaitiman* by the Papua New Guineans. Judgements about correctness and good and bad varieties can only develop once the speakers of a pidgin see it as an independent language. Reinecke (1937) remarks:

> But when, owing to closer and more frequent contacts with the other party, a group that has been speaking a trade jargon comes to realize that it has been using a sub-standard dialect, it reacts in accordance with its attitudes regarding 'correct' speech, much as do the speakers of a creole dialect. In this case the change to a recognized language is quicker and easier, because they have no attachment to this supplementary tongue. This stage has been reached in the Chinese ports; it was being reached among the Russians who traded to northern Norway; it is beginning to be evident in parts of West Africa; but in Melanesia it is barely apparent among a very few natives of the thousands who speak Beach-la-mar.

Commenting on Reinecke's observations a few years later, Reed (1943) notes a significant change in the pattern of indigenous attitudes:

> We now find, however, that the terms *tok pijin* and *tok boi* are part of the speech and stand in contrast to *tok ples waitman* and *tok ples bilong Sydney* which designate true English. This distinction implies the general acceptance by natives of pidgin's subordinate position. More direct confirmation was given by a Kwoma informant who, laughing at his own naiveté, told how he had believed pidgin to be the white man's speech "true" before he had been recruited. But even before he had learned pidgin for himself, he had been disabused of the notion that the white *masta* had no other speech of their own.

However, it is a long way from the realization that one is speaking an independent language to the development of meta-linguistic abilities. Among the functions in which Tok Pisin is used, the meta-linguistic function developed very late and made itself felt only after World War II, when the first reports of indigenes making a distinction between Tok Pisin as spoken by themselves and that spoken by Europeans are found. In 1956 Mead refers to

> ... *men* who have been away at work for a long time and are able to make fine distinctions between Neomelanesian [= Tok Pisin] as the European speaks it and Neomelanesian as spoken among themselves.

The same author remarks about an interviewee:

> He could answer slowly, with experience of the ways in which Europeans spoke Pidgin English.

The first mention that indigenes actually disapprove of the expatriate variety of Tok Pisin is found in Wurm (1969):

> Indigenes . . . are becoming increasingly critical of the mistakes made by Europeans speaking the language and of the incorrect Pidgin of many Europeans in general.

The name "Tok Masta" appears to be of quite recent origin. It reflects the growing self-awareness of the Papua New Guineans in the years preceding independence and a more critical attitude towards the ways of the expatriate population. The following statement by S. Piniau (1975) stands representative for the views of many educated Papua New Guineans:

> Expatriates are mistaken if they think that Tok Pisin cannot be used to express everything well. If they find difficulty in expressing themselves, it is because they either do not know Tok Pisin well or they still think and formulate their ideas in their own native language.

It is generally realized that the present-day speakers of Bush Pidgin (i.e. the broken Tok Pisin used by the inhabitants of recently "opened-up" outlying areas) will eventually become part of the larger Tok Pisin speaking community. Feelings regarding Tok Masta are different. Thus it is "bad" because it is only marginally intelligible to the average speaker of Tok Pisin, and because it has come to be a symbol of those Europeans who do not wish to integrate with the Papua New Guinean society:

> I cannot help but see the many evidences of bad Pidgin as used by some expatriates as a symptom of their condescending attitude towards people in this country (letter by L. Brouwer, in the *Post Courier* of 9 July 1973).

The attitudes towards Urban Pidgin are much more ambiguous than those towards Tok Masta. On the one hand Urban Pidgin represents a prestige variety, spoken by those who hold desirable jobs and who live in desirable places. On the the hand, Urban Pidgin is "bad" because there is decreasing intelligibility between this and other varieties of the language and consequently the danger of developing social division. The following extract from a letter to *Wantok* (10 July 1976) summarizes this:

> *Planti taim mi save lukim Wantok Niuspepa na sampela man na meri i save tok inglis, taim ol i raitim pas. I no min olsem ol i laik tru long raitim pas, tasol ol i laik soim ol i save inglis moa long tok pisin. . . .*
>
> *Sampela taim, as bilong tok i no kamap gut taim yu putim tok inglis insait . . . Yu no ken putim hap inglis insait. Em i kranki. Orait Tok Pisin em i pisin na tok Inglis em i inglis. Tupela i no ken abusim wantaim. Tupela i mas wanwan stret. No ken paulim nabaut ol wantok.*

> I often observe in Wantok Newspaper that some men and women use English expressions when they are writing letters. They don't really want to write a letter, they just want to show that they know English better than Pidgin.
>
> Sometimes, the meaning of an expression is not clear when you use English words in it . . . You must not put in English words. It is stupid. Well, Tok Pisin is Tok Pisin and English is English. The two must not mix. Each must remain separate. You must not confuse your fellow speakers.

The same complaint is found in many other letters and has often been expressed by my informants. The consequences of unrestricted borrowing from English have been outlined very clearly by Mr. Yaliali in a letter to *Wantok* (3 May 1972):

> *Sapos yumi mekim dispela pasin nogut, bai bihain tok pisin bilong bus na tok pisin bilong taun tupela in kamap narakain tru . . . Nogut yumi hambak nabaut na bagarapim tok ples bilong yumi olosem.*

> If we indulge in this bad habit then Rural Pidgin and Urban Pidgin will become quite different languages. Thus Pidgin will really become fragmented. Let's not mess about and thus ruin our common language.

Good and bad talk for most users of Tok Pisin is closely associated with intelligibility and communicative efficiency. In discussing this problem many of my informants have referred to an earlier period in which Tok Pisin was less clear and less efficient. I want to illustrate this with two quotations:

(i) Raka of Tumam Village, East Sepik Province near Dreikikir, comments on the variable proficiency in Tok Pisin in earlier days and in the present (1973):

> *Brata bilong mipela ol i go long stesin, ol i kisim save long stesin, ol i kam bek, marit, ol i tok pisin. Na mipela save samting i klia long en, mipela i save. Tasol samting i no klia long en, i hat liklik, mipela mas askim ol tok, dispela samting kolim olsem wanem? Orait, ol i tok: Dispela samting em Tok Pisin ol i kolim olsem. Orait, i go i go i go i go, woa i kamap, orait, mipela i klia gut long Tok Pisin.*

> My brothers went to the Government station. They acquired knowledge on the station, they returned, got married, they spoke pidgin. And the meaning of some expressions was clear to us, we knew it. But some expressions were unintelligible, they were difficult, and we asked our brothers: Hey, what do you call this, and they would answer: This is how it is called in Tok Pisin. Well, this went on for some time, then the war came and we knew Tok Pisin pretty well.

(ii) Joseph K. from Lorengau, Manus Province, makes the following remarks about Tok Pisin as spoken in German times:

> *Nambawan toktok long taim Jeman i kam ol i bin iusim, ol i bin iusim taim ples i tudak yet, i no gat man bilong mi i save pren gut long ol waitman. . . . Sampela ol i bin iusim tasol mipela tete laik traiim lainim i hat tumas i olsem planti i no krai gut. Orait, ol i bin lusim dispela toktok bilong bipo tasol, i no gutpela toktok tumas.*

> The first variety of speech was used in German times, they used it when our village was still uncivilized, when there was none of us who made friends with the white man. Some men used this variety but when we today try to learn it it is very difficult and it is as if many things are not expressed properly. Well, they have now given up this speech of the old days, it was not a very good language.

An important consideration in assessing the potential for language planning for Tok Pisin is the acceptability of linguistic change. Attitudes of older speakers towards the rapidly developing creolized varieties of Tok Pisin would provide an interesting test case. At present we only have very limited anecdotal evidence of these. Sankoff (1975) reports that second-language speakers of Tok Pisin in urban areas tend to comment favourably on the linguistic performance of their children who are native speakers. However, I have observed cases of disapproval and active discouragement of innovations by adults in conservative rural areas. The unwritten norms of second-language Tok Pisin appear to exercise considerable pressure. On Manus Island, adult second-generation native speakers of Tok Pisin did not speak very differently from adult second-language speakers, whilst their children spoke a much faster and more complex variety. Thus, the linguistic progress accompanying the nativization of a pidgin is constrained by outside factors, in particular its usefulness as a means of communication with a speech community.

Attitudes Towards Individual Expressions

Whereas in the past reactions against individuals words or expressions were typically those of Europeans who objected against the use of words related to English four-letter words, in more recent times one can observe a dramatic increase in indigenous comments on the appropriateness of Tok Pisin words. Again, the principal criteria of whether a word is good or bad are (a) whether it contributes to social harmony and (b) whether it is understood by a reasonable proportion of the speech community. The following quotations illustrate this:

Remarks concerned with socially damaging words.

(i) The use of *kuk* "cook" instead of *meri* "wife", to signal the inferior status of women.

| Sampela man em ol i save kolim ol meri bilong ol olsem kuk bilong ol. Ating plenti long yufela i save harim dispela kain tok tu? Sori brata, yu husat man yu save kolim meri bilong yu olsem kuk bilong yu, orait ating yu mas baiim em long olgeta potnait long mani. . . . (Unpublished letter to *Wantok* newspaper, 1974.) | Some men call their wives "cook". A lot of you have perhaps heard this expression. My dear brother, if you call your wife your cook you better pay her fortnightly wages. |

(ii) The insults *graslain* "grasscutter, hillbilly" and *smelbek* "someone who fills copra in bags, a smelly person, hillbilly".

| Graslain, smelbek. Planti taim mi save harim hap tok hia: Kolim ol man i no bin i gat gutpela edukesen o ol man i save wok long ol plantesen o ol man i save stap long ples o ol man i save sakim kopra long smel bek na gras lain . . . Dispela kain tok olsem in no pasin bilong bung. Em inap kirapim trabel laka. (Letter to *Wantok*, 15 November 1972.) | Grasscutter and smelly person. I have heard these expressions many times. This is how they call people with little education or the workers on a plantation or the villagers in their home villages or the people who fill copra in bags, smelly people and grass-cutters.
These expressions do not promote unity, they mean trouble, you see? |

(iii) The word *stupit* used as an insult for uneducated Papua New Guineans:

Mi harim sampela skul pikinini I save tok stupit long ol man na meri i no save go skul bipo. Dispela pasin i no gutpela long yumi olgeta skul pikinini. (Unpublished letter to *Wantok* 1974.)	I hear some schoolchildren refer to people with no school education as "stupid". This is not a good thing to say for us schoolchildren.

Remarks on words which are misleading or unintelligible.

(iv) There are significant differences in the various names for motor vehicles. Thus a saloon car may be referred to as *kar*, *sip* (from "Jeep"), or *teksi* in different parts of the country. Many speakers do not distinguish between *trak* "truck" and *trakta* "tractor". The following unpublished letter to *Wantok*, written in 1971, deplores the use of *trakta* "tractor" instead of *taksi* "small car, taxi":

Mi bin halim planti man na meri ol i save kolim taksi long trakta, tasol mi ting dispela pasin i no stret long tingting bilong mi. Taksi i no save givim mani long yumi, yumi save spenim mani long taksi . . . Na trakta i save givim mani long yumi taim em i brukim graun . . .	I hear many people call taxis "tractors", but this is not right to my way of thinking. A taxi does not produce wealth for us, we spend our money on taxis . . . but a tractor gives us money when it is used for ploughing.

(v) The expression *givim bel* in the meaning "spiritual love or devotion" has caused considerable controversy as for most speakers *givim bel* means "to impregnate, cause to be pregnant". This ambiguity could have been avoided if *givim bel bilong mi* "to surrender my soul" has been chosen for spiritual love. One of the many writers dealing with this unfortunate expression is Mr. E. Saragum in a letter to *Wantok* dated 6 November 1974:

Mi save harim wanpela hap tok long Baibel na i no save stret long ting-ting bilong mi. Hap tok hia Givum Bel na tingting bilong mi, i min olsem yu givim bel long meri na bai meri i karim pikinini . . . Mi ting ol bikman bilong sios i mas traiim na senisim. Ol i mas senisim na tok Laikim.	I often hear an expression in the Bible which is not correct according to my way of thinking. This expression is "givim bel" and to me this means to make a woman pregnant so that she will give birth to a child. I feel the "big men" of the church must try to replace this expression with "laikim" (= to like, be fond of).

(vi) The following comment on somebody's use of the loan *anaunsemen* "announcement" instead of *toksave* was recorded at the University of Papua New Guinea in 1976. It illustrates that the use of "prestige" vocabulary can backfire:

Ya, man ya, i tok wanem? *Husat?* *Nogat, em i tok anaunsemen tasol, em i tok a-naun-se-men. Mi laik tokim liklik anaunsemen—i no laik tok-save (general laughter). Kain bilong ol bikman ya dey been hearing it from somewhere, na nau ol i laik yusim it—a, toksave, a! Toksave is good, it explains everything, toksave! Toksave, he laik yusim hat wot ya, anaunsemen, anaunsemen. (Laughter.) I tell you, he doesn't know what it meant.*	And what did this man say? Who? You know who I mean, he said "*anaunsemen*", he said "a-naun-semen". I want to make a little "anausemen", not a toksave (general laughter). It's typical of these prominent villagers—they been hearing it from somewhere, and now they all want to use it—you know, toksave! Toksave is good, it explains everything, toksave; he wanted to use a difficult word, "anausemen, anaunsemen". (Laughter,) I tell you, he doesn't know what it meant.

Other lexical items which have been frequently commented upon by my informants include *harim smel* "to notice a smell" instead of the more widely accepted *smelim mel*, the use of *popi* "Catholic" instead of the more accceptable *katolik* and the use of *pusim* to mean "to push" rather than "to have intercourse with". Some of my educated informants also objected to reduplicated forms such as *toktok* "to talk" or *tingting* "to think". On the whole, however, the number of lexical items of Tok Pisin whose status is in debate remains very low.

I have found that the only reliable statements about good or bad language can be obtained in the area of the lexicon. Testing the grammaticality or acceptability of pronunciations or syntactic constructions is extremely difficult. I personally decided to give up working with test sentences and questionnaires as it was virtually impossible to get judgements about decontextualized sentences. I found it equally difficult to get consistent judgements on taped texts which I played to a number of test persons. It would seem that the meta-linguistic capacity and/or interest of Papua New Guinean Tok Pisin speakers differs considerably from that of an average educated European. However, more detailed and more systematic research in this area is badly needed.

Conclusions

I have maintained that (a) it is possible in principle to lay down a set of linguistic criteria for the evaluation of language and (b) value judgements made by different users of the language at different times are not necessarily identical.

There appears to be a significant difference between the judgements made by professional linguists (in particular language planners) and laymen and there is an even greater discrepancy between the criteria for a value judgement used by the Papua New Guineans and expatriates.

The present study is only preliminary and should be supplemented with more systematic research in this area. Value judgements and language attitudes need to be known to language planners if they want to contribute to the communicational efficiency of a linguistic system and if their recommendations are to have a chance of being accepted.

References

CHATTERTON, P. (1973), "A long hard road for Pidgin", *Pacific Islands Monthly*, Nov. 1973, 24–25.
FRANKLIN, K.S. (1975), "Vernaculars as bridges to cross-cultural understanding", in K.A. McElhanon (Eds), *Tok Pisin i Go We?*, Linguistic Society.
FRIEDERICI, G. (1911), "Pidgin-English in Deutsch-Neuguinea", *Koloniale Rundschau*, 3, 92–106.
HALL, R.A. jun. (1955a), *Hands Off Pidgin English*, Pacific Publications, Sydney.
HALL, R.A. jun. (1955b), "Pidgin English in the British Solomon Islands", *Australian Quarterly*, 27, 68–74.
HAUGEN, E. (1966), "Linguistics and language planning", in Bright (Ed.), *Sociolinguistics*, pp. 50–71, Mouton, The Hague.
HEALEY, L. R. (undated), *Tok Pisin*, Dept of Adult Education, Port Moresby.
HÖLTKER, G. (1945), "Das Pidgin-English als sprachliches Missionsmittel in Neuguinea", *Neue Zeitschrift für Missionswissenschaft*, 1, 44–63.
HULL, B. (1968), "The use of Pidgin in the House of Assembly", *Journal of the Papua New Guinea Society*, 2/1, 22–25.
LAYCOCK, D.C. (1969), "Pidgin progress", *New Guinea*, 4/2, 8–15.
McDONALD, B. (Ed.) (1977), *Georg Friederici's Pidgin Englisch in Deutsch-Neuguinea*, Occasional paper No. 14, Dept of Language, University of Papua New Guinea.
MEAD, M (1931), "Talk boy", *Asia*, 31, 141–151.
MEAD, M (1956), *New Lives for Old*, W. Morrow, New York.
MÜHLHÄUSLER, P. (1980), "The development of the category of number in Tok Pisin", in P. Muysken (Ed.), *Generative Studies on Creole Languages*, Foris Publications, Dordrecht.
MÜHLHÄUSLER, P. (1981), "Foreigner talk: Tok Masta in New Guinea", *International Journal of the Sociology of Language*, 28, 81–113.
PINIAU, S. (1975), "Tok Pisin—Wanapela tok i nap Karimapim yumi olgeta, in K.A. McElhanon (Ed.), *Tok Pisin i Go We?*, Linguistic Society.
REED, S.W. (1943), *The Making of Modern New Guinea*, Memoir No. 18, American Philosophical Society, Philadelphia.
REINECKE, J.E. (1937), "Marginal languages", unpublished Ph.D. thesis, Yale University.
REW, A. (1974), *Social Images and Processes in urban New Guinea*, West Publishing Company, St. Paul, M.I.
SADLER, W. (1973), *Untangled New Guinea Pidgin*, Kristen Press, Madang.
SALISBURY, R.F. (1967), "Pidgins respectable past", *New Guinea*, 2/2, 44–48.
SAMARIN, W. S. (1969), "The art of Gbeya insults", *International Journal of African Languages*, 35, 323–329.
SANKOFF, G. (1975), "Wanpela lain manmeri ibin kisim Tok Pisin i kamap olsem tok ples bilong ol", in K.A. McElhanon (Eds), *Tok Pisin i Go We?*, Linguistic Society.
SCOTT, R.P. (1977), "New Guinea Pidgin teaching: agricultural problems and Pidgin", in S.A. Wurm (Ed.), *New Guinea Area Languages and Language Study*, vol. 3, pp. 723–731, Pacific Linguistics C-40, Canberra.
TAULI, W. (1968), *Introduction to a Theory of Language Planning*, Almqvist and Wiksells, Upsala.
WOERTERBUCH (undated *ca.* 1935), *Woerterbuch mit Redewendungen Pidgin-English-Deutsch*, possibly Alexishafen.
WURM, S.A. (1969), "English, Pidgin and what else?" *New Guinea*, 4/2, 30–42.

WURM, S.A. (1976), "Disintegration of Pidgin is causing problems in PNG", *ANU Reporter*, **7/1**, 1.
WURM, S.A. (1977), *Language Planning and New Guinea Pidgin*, Paper presented at the XII International Congress of Linguists, Vienna.
WURM, S.A. and MÜHLHÄUSER, P. (1979), "Attitudes towards New Guinea Pidgin and English", in S.A. Wurm (Ed.), *New Guinea and Neighboring Areas: A Sociolinguistic Laboratory*, pp. 243–262, Mouton, The Hague.
ZINKEL, L. (1977), "Pidgin schools in the New Guinea highlands", in Wurm, S.A. (Ed.), *New Guinea Area Languages and Language Study*, Vol. 3, pp. 691–701, Pacific Linguistics C-40, Canberra.

Subject Index

Acceptability of language 158
Accounting 127, 138
Action concepts 34
Action-process 22
Action, speech as a part of 137
Agrammatism 78
Anthropology 143
Aphasia
   intelligence in 64
   separability of language functions 74
Articulations of language 7
Artificial intelligence 69
Attentional vocatives 43, 47

Baby talk 37
Bodily classifications 146
Bush Pidgin 169

Case frame 25
Case grammar 22, 34
Ceremonies 130
Children, language acquisition 33
Circularity 117
Classification 143
Cognition and language 61
Cognitive codes, word meanings 88
Cognitive neuropsychology 61
Cognitive science and natural language understanding 70
Coherence theory of truth 95
Colour classification 143
Commands 102
Communicational efficiency, Tok Pisin 157
Communicative intentions 39
Competence 8
Constructional apraxia 67
Conversation 37
Correspondence theory of truth 95
Cultural relativism 144
Culture and language 144

Deep dyslexia 80
Double associations 73, 77

Embedded Figures Test 64
Evolution of speech 4
Excuses 139
Eye-to-eye contact 42

Feedback utterance 47
Force, sentence 100
Formal language, semantic theory for 108
Formats 40
Functional core model 35

General intelligence measures 64
Global aphasia 63
Graphemic jargon 62
Gricean cycle 39

Handshake 146
Horizontal stroke 106

Illocutionary force 50, 138
Indicating 50
Inflexion morphemes 34
Information-processing 69
   analyses 61
   components of the mind 72
Intelligence
   and natural language 61
   in aphasia 64
Intelligent artefacts 69
Intent to communicate 39
Intention-dominated formats 40
Intonation development 47
Intra-systemic meaning 136

Jargon aphasia 62
Joint attention 41, 42
Justification 139

Knowledge of a language 110

Subject Index

Label 47
Language acquisition
  device 32, 49
  social content 31
Language and cognition 61
Language and communicational efficiency 157
Language and linguistics 17
Language and social action 127
Language and speech 1
  executive distinction 6
  physiological distinction 3
  semiotic distinction 5
  sociological distinction 6
Language and truth 95
Language assistance system 49
Language evaluation 157
Language functions, separation 74
  lexicon 75, 79
  modality specific systems 78
  syntax 77, 78
Language planning 162, 166
Language, social anthropology 143
Language understanding systems 71
Langue 8, 21
Latin 19
Learning theories 32
Lexicon
  impairment in aphasia 75
  modality-independent 83
  modality-specific system 79
Line of regard 44
Linguistics 17, 128
Logology 17
Logos 1

Meaning
  concept of truth 97
  theory of 109, 136
Mental lexicon
  components 81
  two alternate models 84
Misleading words 174
Modality-independent lexicon? 83
Modality-specific systems
  lexicon 79
  syntax 78
Modes
  of being 20
  of significance 20
  of understanding 20
Modistae 18
Morphological naturalness, Tok Pisin 160
Mother–child interaction 39

Natural language understanding and cognitive science 70
Negotiable reference 52
Neuropsychological single-case method 73
Neuropsychology 61
Non-verbal intelligence 68
Non-verbal reasoning ability 64
Normalization 139

Object vocalization 43

Papua New Guinea, Tok Pisin 158
Parole 8
Performance force 138
Perlocutionary force 138
Phonetics 3
Phonologically constant form 46
Phonology 12
Physical symbol systems 69
Pidgins, Tok Pisin 157
  indigenous attitudes 168
Pluralization, Tok Pisin 159
Pointing by infants 45
Pragmatics 31, 35
Pre-lexical meanings 82, 89
Primacy of speech 13
Principle of reasonable ignorance 51

Query 47

Raven's Progressive Matrices 64
Reading ability, deep dyslexia 80
Reality, social anthropology and language 143
Reciprocal verbs 27
Reduplicated lexical stems 161
Reference 42, 51
Referential adequacy of language 158
Referential disability in aphasia 75
Referential learning 51
Relativism versus universals 143
Request
  format 55, 135
  nature and development of 53
Rules of society 134

Semantic boundaries 76
Semanticity Hypothesis 46
Semantics 24
Sense, notion of truth 100, 103
Sentences, meaning 98
Signification 19

Subject Index

Simultaneities 153
Social acceptability, Tok Pisin 161
Social action
  and language 127
  speech as a part of 137
Social anthropology, language and reality 143
Social force of a performance 133
Social syntax 132
Socially damaging words 173
Sound spectrogram 10
Source-model 131
Speech
  as an analogue of social action 128
  as part of social action 137
Speech act 36
  development 137
  theory 6
Speech – language 1
  executive distinction 6
  physiological distinction 3
  semiotic distinction 5
  sociological distinction 6
Stroke, language impairment 62
Surface linguistic detail 71
Syntax
  in aphasia patients 77
  modality-specific systems 78
Systemic adequacy of language 158

Theorizing 130
Theory
  of meaning 109, 136
  of speech acts 127
Tok Masta 169
Tok Pisin 157
Transformations 18
Truth and language 95
Truth-predicate 107
Truth-values 105

Undifferentiated deictics 43
Understanding 70
  a sentence 98
Utterances 34

Verbal practices 6
Vocal cords 3
Vowel differentiation 4

Without language 62
Word-deafness 82
Word-meaning deafness 83
Word-meanings 81, 83
Word-substitution errors of speech 89
Writing 13